"Work, give us work"

"Work, give us work"
Jacob Coxey and the Industrial Army Movement of 1894

Steven L. Piott

McFarland & Company, Inc., Publishers
Jefferson, North Carolina

ISBN (print) 978-1-4766-9703-1
ISBN (ebook) 978-1-4766-5483-6

LIBRARY OF CONGRESS CATALOGING DATA ARE AVAILABLE

© 2025 Steven L. Piott. All rights reserved

No part of this book may be reproduced or transmitted in any form or by any means, electronic or mechanical, including photocopying or recording, or by any information storage and retrieval system, without permission in writing from the publisher.

Front cover images: Jacob Coxey, circa 1894 (Library of Congress, Prints & Photographs Division). Montana Division of Coxey's Army commanded by William Hogan at railroad tracks in Forsyth, Montana, after being captured by the 22nd U.S. Infantry, April 26, 1894. Photograph shows Northern Pacific Railway box cars in the background. Some of the men hold American flags (L.A. Huffman, Creator, Collection # 981-801, Montana Historical Society Research Center Photograph Archives, Helena, MT).

Printed in the United States of America

McFarland & Company, Inc., Publishers
Box 611, Jefferson, North Carolina 28640
www.mcfarlandpub.com

To Cindy

Table of Contents

Preface   1

Introduction   5

1. The Inspiration: Coxey's Army   11
2. Fry's Los Angeles Army   33
3. Kelly's San Francisco Army (Part 1)   53
4. Kelly's San Francisco Army (Part 2)   70
5. Hogan's Montana Army   87
6. Scheffler's Portland Army   106
7. The Northwestern Industrial Armies of Cantwell and Jeffries   125
8. The Industrial Armies of Colorado and Utah   146

Conclusion   165

Chapter Notes   173

Bibliography   179

Index   183

Preface

In the midst of the first severe economic depression in this country, Jacob Coxey, a wealthy manufacturer and monetary theorist, and Carl Browne, a career agitator for "radical" causes and ardent theosophist, organized the first protest march from Massillon, Ohio, to the nation's capital. They hoped to have 100,000 sympathizers join them in Washington on May 1, 1894, but only 500 tired and ragged men marched up Pennsylvania Avenue that day. Coxey and Browne strove to achieve two greatly needed goals: first, to draw attention to the suffering felt by millions of unemployed workers during the depression, and second, to implore Congress to pass legislation (much like that which would later see passage during FDR's New Deal in the 1930s) that would create jobs for struggling American workers building roads across the United States. They called their march a "petition in boots," and it proved to have a rippling effect on society.

A protest march to Washington, D.C., today is fairly common and a tactic that has become entrenched in our political culture. But that was not always so. Those who read about the march of "Coxey's army" in the newspapers, or who observed it firsthand, did not know what to make of it. No single group had ever laid claim to the national capital as the stage for a public protest. To the more conservative members of the population, to President Grover Cleveland and Attorney General Richard Olney, and to the vast majority of editors and reporters for the nation's newspapers, the march was viewed as a threat to the national political order. Might it cause civil unrest or suggest the possibility of mob rule? Could it threaten private property? Would it set a bad precedent and inspire future organized protests? Whereas Coxey and Browne hoped to use the march as a catalyst for congressional action, most members of Congress refused to grant it legitimacy. Instead, they saw it as a violation—a mob trying to dominate Congress by the physical presence of its numbers. To them, the capital was the symbol of representative government, not the place to publicly challenge those elected to make policy or respond to crisis. They viewed the protest march as an unacceptable form of direct democracy, much like their reaction in a few years to the idea of direct legislation or what we know today as the initiative and referendum. Such tactics were regarded—by lawmakers and many in the general public—as a means to coopt the prerogative of legislators to make law and to be responsive to the needs of the people.

Those living in the late 19th century had certainly seen their share of protest parades. Workers would often parade through the streets during strikes to underscore the issues in dispute between workers and their employers. Sometimes those protests won wage increases for the workers. Political partisans often designed political parades as public spectacles to win support for their party, and sometimes their candidates won. But these "protests" tended to be local in nature and underscored the sense that local and state issues dominated political discourse for most voters. But things were changing. As the country continued to industrialize, and as hard times and periods of unemployment seemed to occur with haunting regularity, experience had convinced many workers that jobs were not determined locally but, instead, by impersonal market forces. As a result, national action was warranted. And it was believed that a formal expression of concern through direct action could persuade Congress to take action.

The marches of the various "industrial armies," as they were called in 1894, were important on several levels. In drawing attention to their plight, these workers inevitably challenged existing attitudes toward unemployment and poverty in general. Was the inability to earn a living wage or to provide for one's family the result of personal failure—laziness, defects in character, personal misfortune—or was it the result of systemic problems in the economy? If the latter, what was the proper role of the federal government? What became known as Coxeyism suggested that it was time for the government to abandon its emphasis on self-help and its laissez-faire system of limited government, and to assume a larger role in supervising the welfare of its citizens and providing them with opportunities. A resolution adopted at an American Federation of Labor meeting in December 1893 had already emphatically stated that such change in thinking was necessary. It argued that "the right to work is the right to life, that to deny the one is to destroy the other. That when the private employer cannot or will not give work the municipality, State or nation must."[1] Thorstein Veblen, a prominent economist, noted at the time that there was "a class, shown by the Army of the Commonweal to be larger than was previously apprehended, which is, or has been, drifting away from" [the classic phrase] "life, liberty, and the pursuit of happiness." Instead, Veblen observed, "what is to be insured to every ... American citizen under the new dispensation is 'life, liberty, and the *means* of happiness.'"[2]

The protest marches of the unemployed in 1894 also helped to create the idea of what historian Lucy Barber termed a "national public space" located in Washington, D.C. As she noted, "For groups whose rights or status as citizens are slighted, the nation's capital has become the preeminent spot to reject such affronts and to claim full membership in the polity."[3] Washington has become a place where groups of citizens can project their own visions of national policy, make their demands heard by national policymakers, and build support for their causes.

The marches of the various Coxey "armies" during the depression of the 1890s also had a long-range impact on the labor movement. When the national protest for jobs caused such alarm in the spring of 1894, especially as marchers temporarily seized railroad property, it triggered a reaction in the way that the federal government dealt with domestic disorders. If railroad property was threatened, or if workers in their actions disrupted the transportation of the mail, then the attorney general could request that a federal judge issue an injunction to curtail such activity. If workers ignored the court's order, they could be held in contempt and arrested. If federal marshals proved incapable of making such arrests, then military intervention would follow. It was this repeated use of the injunction and military intervention that brought the industrial army protests of 1894 to a close. The actions on the part of the federal government set a precedent and would be used again against workers in the Pullman strike that began several weeks later. These actions opened the door for greater court involvement in limiting the effectiveness of strikes in general for decades.

The following account provides an overview of the activities of the various industrial armies in the western United States in the spring of 1894. Chapter 1 provides a brief account of Coxey's original march from Massillon, Ohio, to Washington, D.C. The chapter provides some

Preface

historical context to the era and aims to show that Coxey was perhaps most important as an inspiration for other dissatisfied workers at the time. Set in a backdrop of economic despair, Chapters 2 through 8 deal with each of the major western armies that followed in Coxey's footsteps and are considered more or less in chronological order. The efforts of the few industrial armies from the east (such as J.H. Randall's 450-man army from Chicago and Christopher Columbus Jones' group of 100 from Philadelphia) are not included.

Introduction

Most people today probably remember something of the great civil rights March on Washington in 1963 and Martin Luther King's famous "I Have a Dream" speech. For a few, that march might have evoked memories of similar protests at the nation's capital by some 45,000 World War I veterans known as Bonus Marchers in the summer of 1932 or the massive protest parade of 8,000 suffragettes down Pennsylvania Avenue the day before President Woodrow Wilson's inauguration in March of 1913. Fewer still, however, have any memory of the first march on Washington, D.C., made by a band of some 500 protestors who walked from Massillon, Ohio, to the national capital in the spring of 1894 as a "petition in boots." The marchers hoped to demonstrate the extent of economic suffering during the current depression and demand that the federal government create jobs for the unemployed. Newspapers across the country carried the story and sent reporters to provide day-by-day accounts of the march. The procession became known as "Coxey's Army."

Today, textbooks give the crusade only passing mention and fail even to note the numerous other and much larger "industrial armies" that formed in California, the Pacific Northwest, and in the Rocky Mountain states that sought to add their voices to Coxey's. I have a childhood memory of visits to my grandparents' house. As my sister and I would bound up the porch steps to knock on the screen door, my grandmother would invariably say "My God! It looks like Coxey's army." Drawing from her own historical memory, I guess she thought we looked enough like that stereotypical band of rag-tag, potentially mischievous ne'er-do-wells who, in the popular culture, tramped the country looking for work back in 1894. But the larger Coxey movement was much more than that. It was, as historian Carlos Schwantes noted, "a chapter in the history of American reform, particularly the history

Introduction

of the Populist revolt and of the formative years of organized labor."[1] And in the West, where most of the protests originated, this movement seemed to confirm an observation made only a few months earlier by historian Frederick Jackson Turner that the advancing frontier, and the individual opportunity that it signified, had now passed.

The Coxey movement was good melodrama. It had outrageous characters like buckskin-attired Carl Browne and a mysterious stranger known as the "Great Unknown," and colorful leaders like William Hogan, John Sherman Sanders, and Frank "Jumbo" Cantwell. It included locomotive chases, gun battles, sheriff's posses, troop deployments, and arrests that served as the essence of the best western dime novels. When the railroads refused to carry the men for anything other than full fare, the various industrial armies refused to be deterred. Sometimes they commandeered trains. As historian Donald McMurry commented: "They were self-reliant ... and they adapted available means to their ends without being much embarrassed by consideration for the fine points of law. When ... trains were available and they thought that the railroads ought to carry them ... they took the trains and used them when they could. Even when this was done without the consent of the owners, the trains might be considered borrowed rather than stolen."[2] In Montana, Iowa, and Colorado they built boats to continue their journey on one of the major rivers. In the process, much in the fashion of Mark Twain's *Huckleberry Finn*, they created their own adventure stories. Even Jack London's tales of struggles for survival might owe something to the Coxey movement as London himself followed Kelly's army halfway across the country and then marched and sailed with it across Iowa.

Behind the melodrama, however, was a story of the genuine economic ills that plagued the country. The nation, in the midst of a transition from an agrarian to an industrial economy, was often beset with severe contractions in the business cycle. Hard times in the 1870s had caused widespread unemployment, urban disturbances, and crippling railway strikes. A less severe economic slump in the mid–1880s caused anti–Chinese rioting along the West Coast, while the Panic of 1893 quickly turned into a four-year depression, the worst the nation had experienced up to that time. Farm income dried up, railroads fell into receivership, banks closed, and employers laid off workers. As Douglas W. Steeples and David O. Whitten noted, "Distress was evident in knots of idle men clustered murmuring around plant or

Introduction

store entrances, whiling away time at home, or tramping the countryside."[3] Although accurate statistics were unavailable, most economists placed the number of unemployed in 1893 at around 20 percent. Perhaps as many as 200,000 were out of work in New York City, 100,000 in Chicago, and 62,500 in Philadelphia. Those lucky enough to hold on to their jobs saw their wages drastically reduced. Public assistance was limited, and private charities could do only so much. Appeals to the federal government fell on deaf ears. The common thinking was that economic laws dictated circumstances, unemployment was a natural phenomenon beyond human control, and that government tinkering with the economy would only make things worse. "Laissez-faire" summed up the government's philosophy for inaction.

What was an unemployed worker, many of whom had a marketable skill, to do? Patiently endure his suffering? When personal resources were exhausted, the only options seemed to be asking for help from private charities or from local relief agencies. Those private charities generously contributed loaves of bread and articles of clothing, while some relief agencies ran soup kitchens. Some cities funded short-term public works projects and offered temporary employment digging ditches for sewer lines at bare subsistence wages. Portland's mayor proposed that unemployed men could be put to work breaking rock for a downtown street repair project and that, in return, the city would provide vouchers for two meals and one lodging. In other places, groups organized community gardens in an effort to supplement general food insufficiency. Cincinnati offered work to heads of families at $1 day, while single men were offered work in exchange for meals and lodging only. In Chicago, where more than 100,000 were reportedly out of work during the winter of 1893–94, city officials hired 20,000 snow shovelers for a few hours to clear its streets. In San Francisco, the city hired some of the unemployed to sweep streets for two half-days each week at a wage of $1.40, enough to live on for a week at the Salvation Army "Life Boat."[4] But, as one contemporary observer noted in the early summer of 1894, "such relief has been ... transient and desultory.... After a brief period, the provisions were exhausted, the means of charitable institutions were overstrained, work ceased upon the public highways, and the hordes of downcast toilers were again turned loose to meet what fate might overtake them."[5]

Denver was one place where the problem proved to be especially acute. When the unemployed, many from outside the state, continued

Introduction

to pour into the city, a sympathetic governor had the state militia loan them tents and cooking utensils while rescue missions supplied food. It was not long before a giant tent city had sprung up along the banks of the South Platte River in an area known as River Front Park. As the population at the encampment grew to more than 1,500, local relief agencies could no longer keep up. Anger over the influx of non-residents caused donations to drop off and the quantity and quality of the free meals declined. Soon, those living in the tent city were reduced to a diet that amounted to little more than bread and coffee. With the rail yards heavily guarded, there seemed to be no way for a hungry man to even catch a freight car out of the city. Local relief efforts, however well-intentioned, were simply unable to confront the problem of widespread unemployment in any fundamental way.

As historian Donald McMurry noted, the men who enrolled themselves in the various industrial armies did so because "they were denied what they regarded as their fair share of this world's goods." Many who had lost all hope of a remedy through their own efforts alone "were ready to follow any leader who proposed a plausible remedy and tried to organize a following, thereby converting an inarticulate clamor into a 'movement.'"[6] Jacob Coxey was one individual who had a plan. He proposed that Congress initiate a massive public works project, building and repairing roads across the nation, and hiring the unemployed to accomplish this much-needed task. Abandoning laissez-faire thinking, Coxey wanted the federal government to finance the grandiose venture by issuing $500 million in paper money. To Coxey, the benefits were plentiful. His plan would alleviate unemployment, improve the nation's infrastructure, and expand the currency, all of which would help alleviate some of the glaring inequities in the economic order.

Westerners, inspired by Coxey's bold thinking and a simmering discontent, created their own industrial armies and penned their own regional agendas for Congress to consider: employing idle workers on various internal improvement projects, such as irrigating arid lands in the West, and then allowing individuals to establish homesteads on the reclaimed lands; restricting the number of immigrants who were seen as competitors for jobs; or calling for the resumption of the coinage of silver (seen as a way to revitalize the mining industry, put men back to work, and inflate the money supply). One group from the Pacific Northwest even suggested that the federal government could

Introduction

dig a canal across Central America, an idea that held out the promise of increased shipping and economic benefit to the region.

The depression of the 1890s exposed the vulnerability of wage workers when the economic system collapsed. There simply was no safety net. But in dramatizing the failures of industrialism and underscoring the maldistribution of wealth in society, the depression caused Americans to reconsider the proper role of government in times of extreme economic privation. Ray Stannard Baker, who marched with Coxey's army as a young reporter for the *Chicago Record*, had, like most members of the middle class, initially dismissed the Coxeyites as a laughable group of fanatics. But Baker came to change his thinking and take the industrial army phenomenon more seriously. "I soon made up my mind that there could have been no such demonstration in a civilized country unless there was a profound and deep-seated distress, disorganization, unrest, unhappiness behind it—and that the public would not be cheering the army and feeding it voluntarily without a recognition, however vague, that the conditions in the country warranted some such explosion."[7] Sensing something very similar, the *Cleveland Plain Dealer* editorialized, there is "something wrong when such a large number of people are thrown up like driftwood on the shore, out of place, out of use."[8] Those who joined or supported Coxey's army—or the numerous other Coxey armies of the West—hoped they could change that.

1

THE INSPIRATION: COXEY'S ARMY

On May 1, 1893, newly inaugurated President Grover Cleveland officially opened the World's Columbian Exposition in Chicago as a celebration of American progress and the promise of an even brighter future. Four days later, on "Industrial Black Friday," the stock market crashed. After Wall Street reported that stock in the National Cordage Company had collapsed, traders had responded with a frenzied sell-off. The collapse on Wall Street, known as the Panic of 1893, accelerated the recession that was evident earlier in the year into a major contraction that rapidly spread throughout the economy. The hard times that farmers had been experiencing for years had finally hit the industrial East. Banks began calling in loans and refused to make new ones. By year's end, more than 600 banks had failed along with more than 15,000 businesses.

This downward spiral continued into the new year. As Douglas Steeples and David Whitten noted, "Savage unemployment and demoralizing wage reductions reflected the corrosive impact of the depression at the 1894 trough and after." Describing the winter of 1893–94 as a time of "exceptional distress," they estimated that the "cumulative picture depicted an economy operating perhaps 20 to 25 percent below capacity through 1894."[1] By June of that year nearly 200 railroads had declared bankruptcy and fallen into receivership, a legal device that had the effect of making them wards of the court in order to prevent their dismemberment by creditors. Although the railroads, including the Union Pacific and Northern Pacific, continued to operate with their own managers, they were under the immediate supervision of the federal courts. The general assessment was that the railroad system was over built, over capitalized, and plagued by mismanagement. Growing public antagonism toward the railroads, provoked by the railroads' immense size and power and by the general feeling that they discriminated against small shippers, had caused the industry to become less attractive to investors. The Panic had triggered a full-blown business and industrial depression. Hundreds of thousands of workers lost their jobs as mills, factories, and mines closed, and railroads, cutting back on construction and maintenance, laid off workers. Nationwide, industrial unemployment hovered at 20 percent (between two and three million workers) while farm prices dropped more than 20 percent. It was the beginning of the worst depression in the nation's history, and it would last for four years.

The industrial development that fueled American economic growth in the last half of the 19th century occurred in a society that emphasized the value of unrestricted individualism, the importance of an unregulated market economy, and a laissez-faire system of limited government. Social Darwinism had gained currency as a social philosophy and its proponents talked with conviction about natural evolutionary laws and "survival of the fittest." They underscored the widely held belief that the automatic functioning of society was the best path for continued evolutionary progress. Government intervention to ameliorate hardships, they claimed, would undermine self-reliance, instill insecurity, and open the door for mayhem.

In 1887, during his first term in office and in the midst of a serious drought in Texas, President Cleveland vetoed a farm bill that would have supplied $10,000 worth of seeds to hard hit farmers in that state. In doing so, he declared: "I do not believe that the power and duty of the General Government ought to be extended to the relief of individual suffering which is in no manner properly related to the public service or benefit.... The lesson should be constantly enforced that, though the people support the Government, the Government should not support the people."[2] It was an opinion that he continued to hold during his second term in office and one that was held by many others. New York Governor Roswell P. Flower was in complete agreement. "In America the people support the government; it is not the province of the government to support the people. Once recognize that the government must supply public work for the unemployed, and there will be no end of official paternalism."[3] Governor Flower was certain that the "security of Democratic government is its purity and simplicity. Break down those safe-guards, and you invite corruption, socialism, and anarchy."[4]

1. The Inspiration: Coxey's Army

Hard times triggered a heightened sense of unease. As legions of jobless workers began to traipse across the country looking for work, many began to fear a "tramp menace." Riding the rails, clustering in public parks or in rail yards at the edge of towns, begging for food or work at the back door, the tramp became the national bogeyman, an object of both scorn and fear. In reality, the risk that tramps posed was exaggerated, but public paranoia expressed itself in the widespread enforcement of local vagrancy laws. No one wanted tramps to pass through their community, and no one wanted them to stay. Some towns provided food and shelter to the unemployed, but did so on the condition that they would move on. Others simply turned a cold shoulder.

Perhaps the root cause of the unease was not so much the threat of lawlessness but the reality that there were such large numbers of tramps in the first place, and that the numbers appeared to be growing. The initial reaction for many was to argue that the tramp wanted something that he had not earned. When numbers of unemployed citizens began to collect in dozens of towns, cities, and mining and lumber camps, and began to be referred to in the press as incipient "industrial armies" prepared to march on Washington to demand work, the problem became even more vexing.

The term "industrial army" actually had origins that were quite different. French philosopher Charles Fourier had envisioned a utopian society in the early 19th century that would need huge industrial armies. Instead of being destructive, however, these vast mobile armies of peaceful workers would be constructive, the ancestors of the New Deal's CCC and WPA. They would traverse the countryside engaging in community public works projects like reforestation, bridge building, and land reclamation. In the late 19th century, a growing number of writers were at least beginning to entertain the notion that demands for relief or work did not stem from laziness or personal failure, but rather from larger, systemic problems in the economy—factors that were beyond any one individual's control. Writer Edward Bellamy had wrestled with this problem before writing his best-selling utopian novel *Looking Backward* (1888). In thinking about the book he wanted to write, a fictional account that would offer a solution to the human crisis confronting industrial capitalism in America, Bellamy realized that he needed to reshape his thinking and shift the focus from a "mere fairy tale of social perfection" to that of a "definite scheme of industrial reorganization."⁵ In doing so, he popularized the term "industrial army" in an attempt to show how workers could be humanely organized in order to produce the goods society needed and receive an adequate income for their labor.

The economic downturn that began in 1893 was not the first time the country had experienced hard times. Similar, although less severe, depressions had struck in 1873 and again in 1883. In each instance, critics questioned the proper role of government in economic life and what measures could and should be taken to alleviate privation during the crisis. One recurring theme involved the nation's currency and how much money should be in circulation. One idea that gained some political traction in the 1870s and 1880s was called greenbackism. Drawing on monetary ideas advanced earlier by Edward Kellogg, the Greenback Party argued that bankers had manipulated the money supply to keep metal currency (gold) scarce and interest rates high. As a result, many Americans had become overburdened, and inequality expanded unfairly. The prescribed remedy was to have the government, rather than the banks, control the availability of credit and the amount of money in circulation. One way to do this was to inflate the money supply by issuing paper currency (greenbacks or "fiat money") or by coining silver dollars in addition to gold (bimetallism). More money in circulation was seen as a way to put more money into the pockets of farmers and laborers and to provide relief from oppressive debt obligations.

As the current depression deepened, and the burdens and stresses of the crisis fell most heavily on the unemployed in all sections of the country, some began to advance the idea of government-funded public works projects to help those who could not find work. The concept was not a new one. Unemployed laborers had demanded such action, at least on the local level, during the Panic of 1873. In December of that year, 4,000 individuals filled the Cooper Institute in New York City while thousands more spilled onto the streets outside to demand action. Beneath a banner that read "THE UNEMPLOYED DEMAND WORK," speakers called for New York's municipal government to provide jobs for the unemployed on projects to improve the city's streets, parks, and piers, and to utilize a 100-acre tract of land that had been set aside as a military parade ground to build small, affordable housing for workers. Similar rallies were held in Boston, Chicago, and Cincinnati.

1. The Inspiration: Coxey's Army

Labor leader Samuel Gompers expanded on the idea of government assistance under similar circumstances 20 years later. In an address to 80 or 90 delegates representing 30 different labor organizations at a convention in New York City on August 20, 1893, Gompers placed blame for the distress of unemployed workers on "the wealth possessors of this country" and called upon governments at all levels to initiate public works projects. He suggested that New York City could "build its rapid transit road, improve its streets, sewerage, wharfage and docks," that the state of New York could "improve its roadways and deepen the Erie Canal," and that the national government could "dredge the Mississippi and make one navigable ship canal from it to the Peninsula of Michigan."[6]

Another with similar ideas was writer Edward Bellamy, who in 1894 submitted to the Massachusetts Board on the Unemployed a proposal for a system of state-run workshops for the unemployed. As Bellamy envisioned the plan, the state would provide support for the unemployed "out of their own product, which should not go on the market for sale, but be wholly consumed within the circle of producers."[7] The state would issue scrip in place of wages and guarantee to the unemployed a decent minimum, without the stigma of charity or any threat to outside prices or wages.

The individual with the most imaginative program, however, was Jacob Sechler Coxey. Born in 1854 in Selinsgrove, Pennsylvania, where his father was a sawmill engineer, the family moved to Danville, Pennsylvania, when Coxey was five or six. Quitting school at the age of 15, Coxey worked in the rolling mills for 10 years. He left the Danville mill in 1878 to become a partner with his uncle in a scrap-iron business near Harrisburg. In 1881, his business brought him to Massillon, Ohio, where he took advantage of an opportunity to purchase an idled silica sandstone quarry about four and a half miles outside of the northeastern Ohio town. Restoring the operation of the quarry, Coxey added his own crushing mill and was able to take advantage of the Baltimore and Ohio Railroad that ran alongside his property to ship his high-grade silica sand to nearby steel companies in Ohio and Pennsylvania. He was soon able to employ 50 workers.

A prospering business soon enabled Coxey to indulge his passion and purchase a 160-acre farm for breeding thoroughbred racehorses. Slight of build and unassuming in appearance, Coxey had the outward look of someone who was studious and respectable—usually

"Work, give us work"

photographed wearing gold-rimmed spectacles and attired in a staid business suit with a winged collar. A Greenbacker and a Populist in politics, Coxey felt that an expanded money supply would do much to relieve economic distress and renew opportunity in America. He was also an ardent believer in the need for improved roads and felt that the country could not grow and prosper without them.

When the depression struck, Coxey's advocacy of the good-roads idea grew stronger as he now saw it as a way to put thousands of unemployed men back to work. What he proposed was that the federal government create a giant public works project (as was done later during the New Deal) to be funded by issuing $500 million in legal-tender notes (paper money). The money would be spent on the construction of good roads throughout the United States. Employment would be offered to the unemployed at the rate of $1.50 for an eight-hour work day. The plan would give employment to all, and it would put more money in circulation. The plan was also seen as a way promote the eight-hour idea then being advocated by labor groups as it would put pressure on employers who paid less or demanded longer hours to match the federal standard.

Since good roads would primarily benefit rural areas, Coxey soon supplemented this plan with a non–interest-bearing bond scheme. Local governments would be permitted to issue non-interest-bearing bonds worth up to one-half the value of the assessed property within their jurisdiction. These bonds would be deposited with the U.S. Treasury as security for a federal loan (issued in legal-tender notes) which could only be used for public improvements—the construction of schools, courthouses, libraries, museums, and other public buildings in addition to city streets and roads. The principal of the loan would be repaid in 25 annual installments (four percent of the loan each year) through local taxes. Coxey just needed a way to spread the word and convince the public to support his good-roads panacea.

Thirty-nine-year-old Jacob Coxey first met forty-four-year-old Carl Browne at the American Bimetallic League convention in Chicago in August of 1893. The assembled delegates hoped to mount an effort to stop Congress from taking action to repeal the Sherman Silver Purchase Act of 1890. The act, a concession to western mining interests, had authorized the federal government to make large-scale purchases of silver as a basis for the issuance of paper currency redeemable in either gold or silver. Bimetallists favored an

1. The Inspiration: Coxey's Army

elastic currency (not a rigid gold standard) as the key for economic recovery. Coxey, a steadfast Greenbacker, wanted to see the circulation of paper money (legal tender) divorced from metal and backed by the government. If he could not get that, he at least wanted the government to preserve the current bimetallic currency backed by silver as well as gold.

During breaks in the formal sessions of the convention, Coxey would sometimes wander down to Chicago's Lake Front Park to listen to open public debates along the lines of London's famous Hyde Park. Browne, usually attired in an outfit that resembled that of Buffalo Bill Cody, was one of the frequent speakers. Referred to by reporters as the "flower of American demagoguism," and the "Calistoga Cowboy," the flamboyant Browne soon caught Coxey's attention and the two began to discuss the merits of Coxey's good-roads plan.

Browne was an eccentric character. During his life he had been a printer, journalist, editor, painter, cartoonist, cattle rancher, farmer, politician, patent medicine salesman, and carnival barker. He was also an agitator for numerous "radical" causes, and claimed to have been arrested a number of times for his efforts on behalf of the working class. Inspired by reading about the West, he migrated there, eventually settling in northern California in 1872. It was the Great Railway Strike of 1877, however, that drew Browne into working-class protest in California and transformed him into an active agitator. Becoming involved in street demonstrations in San Francisco organized by the Chinese Exclusion movement, he met Denis Kearney, soon to become

Jacob Coxey, ca. 1894. Coxey hoped to use a protest march from Massillon, Ohio, to Washington, D.C., to persuade Congress to authorize an expansive public works program (building roads) that would provide jobs for the unemployed during the depression of the 1890s. The program would be funded by inflating the money supply by $500 million in legal-tender notes (paper money). Library of Congress, Prints & Photographs Division.

"Work, give us work"

the key figure in California's nativistic Workingmen's Party, and became Kearney's secretary. Browne began writing, illustrating, and publishing his own newspaper called the *Great Strike*. When authorities forced him to shut that down, he started an openly anti–Chinese newspaper called *Open Letter* and contributed to the anti–Chinese rioting that marred the city that summer.

The highlight of Browne's involvement with the issue of Chinese exclusion came in 1878 when he joined Kearney on a speaking tour of the eastern United States and even gave a speech against Chinese immigration on the Capitol steps. The police had threatened to arrest the men for violating a local ordinance but declined to do so when the event attracted only a few spectators. The occasion, barely covered in most newspapers, may have instilled in Browne the idea that the best way to attract attention and challenge the established political system was to stage a dramatic public protest in the nation's capital.

By the early 1890s, Browne had become a career agitator and had spent the last couple of years traveling the country promoting the coinage of silver in addition to gold. He also began to cultivate his maverick persona by outfitting himself in a showy western getup comprised of a buckskin coat with fringes, buttons made of Mexican silver half-dollars, high leather boots, a beaded necklace, and a sombrero that he stylishly tilted over one eye. If the weather got chilly, he donned a fur cloak. Tall, heavy-set, and bearded in the manner of a Wild West buffalo hunter, he possessed a hearty bass voice and particular talent as a stump speaker.

Carl Browne, organizer of Coxey's Army, between 1911 and 1920. An agitator for numerous "radical" causes and a showman of the first order, Browne caught Coxey's attention as someone whose colorful personality and proven experience as a stump speaker could help him popularize his good roads program. Library of Congress, Prints & Photographs Division.

1. The Inspiration: Coxey's Army

Carl Browne was also a theosophist who claimed to have mystical insight into divine nature. He embraced the idea of reincarnation and believed that at death the human soul entered a reservoir ("like a huge cauldron") that contained a mixture of all the souls that had gone before. Each individual at birth gained a small portion of this larger pool and became a fractional reincarnation of the souls who had previously departed. As the reservoir also included the soul of Christ, Browne came to the conviction that he and Coxey (one of Browne's recent converts) possessed an especially large quantity of Christ's soul. It explained how the two had come together behind a grand plan to help humanity. Browne referred to Coxey as the "Cerebrum of Christ" and modestly bestowed upon himself the title "Cerebellum of Christ." He further argued that the same force that had brought he and Coxey together would draw others to their quest. No one but Browne and Coxey seemed to take this theory seriously. Whether they shared these views or not, recruits would travel under the banner of the "Commonweal of Christ" (some banners actually pictured a likeness of Jesus Christ and carried the slogan "Peace on Earth Good Will to Men, He Hath Risen, but Death to Interest on Bonds"). Ignoring the religious overtones, newspapers simply referred to the demonstrators as Coxey's army.

Coxey, who was actually soft-spoken and somewhat dignified in his manner, perceived that Browne might be the colorful personality that could help him popularize his relief program. He hired Browne to campaign for his good-roads idea during the late summer and fall of 1893. As their friendship developed, Coxey invited Browne to stay at his Massillon home that winter. During their conversations, Browne mentioned that he remembered marches of the unemployed demanding relief when he lived in California. That triggered the thought of duplicating the protest as a march on Washington. The idea also fit well with Browne's cosmology. With the arrival of the Commonwealers in Washington, so great a part of Christ's soul would be gathered together and brought to bear upon Congress that Coxey's ideas would be irresistible. Congress would have to enact Coxey's good roads bill. Some were beginning to believe that Browne had cast some magical spell over Coxey. Reporter Ray Stannard Baker, who would follow the army all the way to Washington, stated that his editor had instructed him, "Don't put Browne too much in evidence as the hero of the plot is Coxey, though he seems to be rather a puppet in Brown's [sic] hands."[8]

"Work, give us work"

The idea of a march, later claimed by both individuals, was envisioned as a "petition in boots" "in order to demonstrate both the need and the available manpower for his program of federal jobs."[9] It seemed like a brilliant idea, demanding legislation in numbers that Congress could not ignore. Journalist W.T. Stead commented at the time that Coxey mastered the art of "converting the Press into a sounding board." "Everyone in America knew of the existence of the unemployed. Every newspaper reader had grown weary of the discussion as to what should be done with tramps and out-of-works. It seemed almost impossible to contrive any device by which this grim and worn-out topic could be served up in good saleable newspaper articles. But Coxey did the trick."[10]

Coxey's march brought the unemployment problem to everyone's attention. The idea of a great mass of jobless workers descending upon the national capital caused a great deal of consternation among conservatives and proponents of law and order, but it also served as a plan for direct action on the part of the unemployed. They could now do something about their situation and express their dissatisfaction at the same time. After all, did not citizens have the right to petition the government for a redress of their grievances?

Plans for the upcoming 400-mile march to the nation's capital were announced in late January 1894. Coxey would provide most of the money for the march and take care of the details of mapping out a route. He oversaw the plotting of each day's march (based on the assumption that the men would be able to travel 12 to 15 miles a day depending on the terrain), and pre-selected the site for each night's campsite. He also smartly realized that he would need an advance party to travel a day ahead of the army to prepare the next campsite, solicit donations of food, and advertise the nightly Coxey-Browne lectures (entrance fee required). For his part, Browne would assume the roles of organizer, day-to-day general manager, and press agent. Robert Skinner, reporter/editor for the *Massillon Independent*, saw the potential for a colorful, human-interest story and ran it. Wire services soon picked up on the story and it appeared in newspapers across the country.

As the anticipated march gathered notoriety (one writer said that it had "an innate sense of spectacle"), newspapers decided to send their own reporters to cover it.[11] The army of the unemployed (writer W.T. Stead referred to them as the "peripatetic advertisers of social misery")

1. The Inspiration: Coxey's Army

was to leave from Coxey's farm in Massillon on March 25 (Easter Sunday), gather more recruits along the route, and arrive in Washington on May 1.[12] On March 19, Representative Thomas Geary from Browne's home district in California and Populist Senator William Peffer of Kansas introduced Coxey's two bills (good roads and non–interest-bearing bonds) in Congress. As March 25 approached, the organizers hurried to make last-minute preparations. There were three commissary wagons to carry the food, a band wagon, and a panorama wagon that would become Carl Browne's on-going illustrated lecture platform. Although the march might begin with a small number of marchers, Coxey confidently predicted that by the time the "army" reached Washington, it would have grown to 100,000.

When Coxey's army began its march into a biting wind on a raw and chilly Easter Sunday, it included 122 marchers. A few of those were undercover agents sent by the chief of police of Pittsburgh, a city on the planned route, as well as a number of federal Secret Service agents. In addition, there were approximately 44 press correspondents (only a dozen or so would remain with the march over the 35 days from Massillon to Washington, D.C.) and 4 Western Union telegraphers. In noting the exceptionally large number of correspondents in attendance, writer W.T. Stead commented: "Never in the annals of insurrection has so small a company of soldiers been accompanied by such a phalanx of recording angels."[13]

A crowd estimated at 10,000 lined the streets of Massillon to catch a glimpse of the quixotic crusade. Jasper Johnson, an African American man from West Virginia led the march as standard bearer accompanied by a bulldog named Bunker Hill. Behind him followed the seven-piece "Commonweal of Christ Brass Band," Carl Browne (mounted on one of Coxey's prized stallions), Jesse Coxey (the General's 16-year-old son attired in a blue and gray outfit to signify the union of opposing Civil War forces), the "General" himself (Coxey objected to the title and preferred to be referred to as the president of the Good Roads Association) riding in a fancy carriage called a phaeton, and a wagon carrying Mrs. Coxey and their infant son (appropriately named Legal Tender) who only rode with the army to the outskirts of town.

Trailing the whole procession were four covered wagons carrying camping gear, baled straw, and several quarters of beef. Following the carriages and wagons, mounted on one of Coxey's steeds with a bright red saddle and barking orders to the marchers was the compelling

"Work, give us work"

figure known as the "Great Unknown." Tall, slim and erect in his bearing and looking very much like a former military officer, the mystery man carried the demeanor of the company's disciplinarian.

Rather than focusing on the root causes of the protest or the general feeling of distress, or hypothesizing about the larger meaning of opportunity in America, reporters chose to focus on the comical side of the procession and the general circus-like atmosphere. As historian Carlos Schwantes noted, what Coxey and Browne did was to "create an unemployment adventure story" packed with perilous encounters and colorful players that readers would find irresistible.[14] One of the leading characters was J.M. "Cyclone" Kirkland from Pittsburgh who claimed to be the reincarnation of an Indian chief and served as an amateur physician for the troupe. He was also a self-proclaimed astrologer who claimed he could foretell the success of the march from the stars (they told him that it was the greatest movement in the history of the world). He was also said to be working on an epic poem along the lines of Homer's *Odyssey*. "Oklahoma Sam" Pfrimmer was a tall, real-life cowboy from one of Coxey's horse ranches who performed trick-riding skills for the children who came to watch.

Another popular character was William Iler, a veteran of the U.S. Army and a former steamboat man who volunteered to act as the army's commissary officer. Instead, Browne assigned him the task of driving the panorama wagon. The latter conveyance, which resembled a junk dealer's wagon, carried dozens of Browne's colorful Commonweal banners and an oversized depiction of Christ, which bore a rather close resemblance to Browne himself. To the eager followers of the march in the press, Iler became known as "Weary Bill" because he always looked tired.

Far more mysterious was the tall, handsome man sporting a neatly trimmed moustache who was introduced to a large crowd in Massillon's city square on the night of March 19. About 35 years old and well-dressed, he walked with a cane and a noticeable limp which some assumed must be the result of a battlefield injury. When he arrived in camp just prior to the start of the march, he refused to disclose his name, saying "I am the Great Unknown and the Great Unknown I must remain."[15] He quickly showed himself to be a born leader of men and was promptly designated assistant marshal of the Commonweal in charge of imposing a degree of military discipline amongst the recruits. Coxey provided him with a magnificent stallion to ride at the head of his men so that he might make a striking appearance.

1. The Inspiration: Coxey's Army

This intriguing persona was actually the creation of Carl Browne. Browne needed someone who could assume much of the day-to-day duties of the march and smartly understood that this new mystery man would be a great advertising ploy. The Great Unknown charmed everyone accept Browne, whose ego soon caused him to brood about the figure he had created. Although reporters would eventually find out that the Great Unknown was actually A.P.B. Bozarro, one-time patent-medicine man (he hawked his own blood purifier which he claimed could cure almost any ailment), occultist, and former associate of Carl Browne's from Chicago, they deliberately teased their readers by concealing his real origins. Adding even more mystery to the Great Unknown was the arrival, not long into the march, of the "veiled lady." Attractive, said to be about 30 years old, and shrouded in a black crepe veil, reporters suspected that she was actually the wife of the Great Unknown. Afraid that the appearance of a woman in the army would cause the press to generate negative comments and raise the suggestion of immorality in the ranks, Browne ordered the veiled lady to travel well ahead of the army.

The army marched nine miles to Canton, Ohio, on its first day, fighting wind, sleet, and snow that turned the trek into a slog. At Canton, local townspeople donated 200 boiled hams, 200 loaves of bread, and 5 bushels of potatoes. Donations of food would be common in the days ahead and usually more plentiful in areas where trade unions were strong or where Populists resided in numbers. It was the hope of Coxey and Browne that those who chose to "enlist" under their banner would be representative workingmen, the respectable unemployed, not tramps and freeloaders. That seemed to be the case. The Central Labor Council of Richmond, Indiana, distributed copies of a song entitled "Marching with Coxey," written by an AFL member. One line of the song spoke to the general composition of the marchers: "We are not tramps nor vagabonds that's shirking honest toil, / But miners, clerks, skilled artisans, and tillers of the soil."[16]

It did not take long for bad weather, muddy roads, and uncertain food rations to quickly weed out any professional "hoboes." To provide the army with some protection from the elements, Coxey and Browne procured a 60-foot circus tent in which the marchers slept on straw. A blanket was to be had only if a marcher brought one with him. Most were ill-prepared for cold weather, and few had gloves or coats. In addition to the circus tent there was a headquarters tent in

"Work, give us work"

which officers, teamsters, and a select group of others slept. Coxey and Browne lodged in hotels as did the reporters.

When the army entered a town, its arrival was much like a circus parade. Everyone had heard of Coxey's army and were interested to see what it was all about. Some towns met the marchers with a brass band, others sent out their bicycle club to hail Coxey as the champion of good roads. Spectators usually followed the marchers to their campsite where a nightly meeting, open to the public, was held. Ceremonies began with the singing of hymns to emphasize the religious nature of the movement. Coxey then mounted the panorama wagon to explain his bills and how their passage would end unemployment, bring about the eight-hour day for wage-earners, and usher in general prosperity as the money supply expanded. Browne usually followed Coxey on the platform with a recitation of a different type. He told parables to teach moral lessons, quoted scripture, and drew cartoons to explain

Coxey's Army on the march, April 1894. Missing from this particular photograph are the members of the local bicycle club who would often join Coxey's marchers as they entered a town. To the bicyclists, "good roads" meant smooth roads. Library of Congress, Prints & Photographs Division.

1. The Inspiration: Coxey's Army

his financial theories. He advocated for an inflated currency and condemned plutocrats, national banks, and interest-bearing bonds. W.T. Stead described his entertaining talks as "a strange mixture of prophecy and politics, of theology and finance."[17] At the end of each meeting, a collection was taken up.

As the army entered Pennsylvania, the weather improved, the pace quickened, and enthusiasm returned. When the army approached Beaver Falls, people ran out of their houses to cheer the marchers as they passed by and it seemed like all 30,000 inhabitants of the industrial valley (a region heavily populated with union men who worked in the nearby steel mils) lined the route to cheer the marchers as they passed. It was at Beaver Falls that the army collected over five tons of food and other provisions, most of which were shipped ahead to Uniontown where the army would have to begin its ascent over the Allegheny Mountains. At a public meeting held that night in the local opera house, the lower floor of which had been used as a skating rink and had no seating, people stood for nearly three hours crowded together "as thick as willows in a swamp," while the galleries were packed to capacity.[18] People in all the little towns along the line of march in western Pennsylvania gave the marchers a warm reception. At Rochester, all the factory girls in the glassworks came out to cheer, while workingmen from Aliquippa greeted the army at Conway and "marched" a few miles with it to show their support. In noting the outpouring of support for the Commonwealers, a *Pittsburgh Press* reporter remarked: "There is existing between workingmen an affinity that on such occasions as this makes them all of a kin."[19]

When the marchers neared Allegheny City on April 3, spectators and bicyclists lined the road. But instead of hundreds, there were now thousands, with many onlookers wearing red, white, and blue Coxey badges. As correspondent Ray Stannard Baker recalled the day in his column for the *Chicago Record*:

> The newsboys on the street corners have been calling "Coxey! Coxey! Coxey!" all day long. The crowds packed forty deep on the dusty pavements stood for hours and shouted "Coxey! Coxey!" until they were horse. Shop girls whispered "Coxey," to one another in the half-deserted stores. The children in the public schools were dismissed because Coxey was coming to town, and they danced merrily away with eyes as round as saucers to catch a glimpse of Coxey and hear him speak.[20]

The army was soon joined by 200 workmen with their own fife and drum corps, 100 members of the Iron Molders' Union, and 500 bakers, boilermakers, and patternmakers. However, the size of the spontaneous parade and the enthusiasm of the crowds alarmed the local police who decided to reroute the marchers to their campsite via back streets. When the Commonwealers arrived at Exposition Park, they were informed that they would be confined to the park until they left the city. The police were under orders to arrest any of Coxey's men found outside the encampment. That night, tired of sleeping on the cold ground in a steady drizzle, about 30 Coxeyites escaped the park looking for warmer quarters only to be apprehended by the police and charged with vagrancy. When the Commonwealers were ready to leave the camp in Allegheny on the morning of April 5, a squad of 50 policemen met them at the gates to the park and escorted them to the city limits.

As the army marched into Pittsburgh, the reception was just as enthusiastic as it had been two days earlier. Working-class crowds estimated to be near 100,000 again lined the streets in an impressive show of labor support. Sympathetic merchants contributed generously to the army's commissary. Kaufman's department store donated 300 pairs of shoes, while another merchant contributed 500 pairs of socks. The whistles of locomotives and steamboats cheered the marchers as they wound their way along the Monongahela River. At Homestead, the population came out in force to salute the marchers, while a welcoming banner read, "Homestead Believes in Coxey's Good Roads Bill." It was there, at the home of the Carnegie Steel Company, that a large number of new recruits increased the army's numbers to between five and six hundred.

The festive atmosphere in the Steel City did, however, take on a foreboding character suggestive of future difficulties the army would encounter when it finally reached Washington. Apprehensive local authorities were not too keen on seeing a large number of unemployed men marching together and potentially stirring up trouble. Memories of the bitter Homestead steel strike of two years before had not been forgotten, while persistent labor violence was currently disrupting coke production in districts south of the city. Although the Commonweal was allowed to pass through, and onlookers cheered it wildly, it was kept under tight surveillance by a full complement of the police.

From Pittsburgh the Commonweal marched to Uniontown, the point at which the army would have to cross the mountains. Complicating matters, the weather turned worse. A spring snowstorm turned

1. The Inspiration: Coxey's Army

the road to slush and the army had to march through ankle-deep mud. Some of the marchers tied strips of burlap around their shoes in a futile attempt to keep warm. Before the army had made it halfway on its six-mile climb to the summit, the snow was several inches deep, and the driving wind cut visibility to about 50 yards. At this point, desertions reduced the army's numbers to about 250 men on foot, with an additional 30 or so riding mounts or serving as teamsters. When the horses struggled with their loads, the marchers had to push the commissary wagons up the slippery slopes. At the summit of the Alleghenies only 140 men remained in the ranks.

In addition to confronting bad weather and the difficult climb, the army had to deal with a dispute between Carl Browne and the Great Unknown, two born leaders with clashing egos. Friction had been developing between the marshal and his assistant for some time. Rumors had been circulating that Browne's officious manner and domineering attitude was about to provoke a mutiny among some in the Commonweal. The opportunity presented itself when Coxey was away from the march on a short business trip. On the morning of April 14, Browne gave the command to the Commonwealers to halt so that he could address a group of onlookers about his monetary theories, a recurring practice that most of the marchers found irritating.

At that point, the Great Unknown countered Browne's command and ordered the men to resume their march. Asked if they would rather follow him or Browne, everyone in the army, including Jesse Coxey, chose the former. Humiliated, Browne hopped into Coxey's phaeton and raced to Frostburg, Maryland, where he wired news of the mutiny to Coxey. When Coxey hastily returned after an all-night carriage ride from Cumberland, he held a quick conference with Browne and the Great Unknown. He then stepped onto a soapbox in the center of a big room in the Frostburg Opera House where the army had spent the night. Commanding the attention of everyone in the room, Coxey called on those who supported the Great Unknown to rise. As the men rose together as a group, with only four of their number still seated, the Great Unknown sensed triumph. But Coxey, loyal to the man who had helped create the movement, surprised everyone by announcing that he cast 154 votes for Browne. He then ordered the Great Unknown to leave the army.

Not wishing to challenge Coxey's authority, or his pivotal role as financial backer of the crusade, the army acquiesced. In a parting shot directed at Browne, the Great Unknown shouted, "I have been deposed by a patent-medicine shark; a greasy-coated hypocrite; a seeker for personal advancement."[21] Taking a small breakaway contingent with him, he vowed revenge. The Great Unknown continued to be an irritant, running ahead of the army and falsely representing himself and his followers as the collectors of donations for it.

When the tired and footsore ranks reached Cumberland, Maryland, after their five-day trek over the mountains, Coxey decided to hire two canal boats to haul his recruits 85 miles down the Chesapeake and Ohio Canal to Williamsport. Two hundred men, eighteen horses, five wagons, a buggy, and supplies were loaded onto two scows that the Commonweal christened *"Coxey"* and *"Good Roads."* Six mules pulled each boat along the tow paths. The hiring company charged Coxey 52 cents per ton or about $85, half of which was paid for by admission fees charged to the curious who wanted to visit the army's camp at Cumberland.

During the trip thousands of onlookers lined the canal banks, bridges, and locks to cheer. As trains rolled by on nearby tracks, engineers sounded their whistles while passengers lowered their windows and waved hats and handkerchiefs at the intrepid sailors. Following the flotilla was a third barge of correspondents who dubbed their craft the *Flying Demon.* Earlier in the march Browne had lost his temper after reading satirical reports of the journey and struck back at reporters calling them "the forty argus-eyed demons of hell."[22] The name stuck, reporters embraced it and began using it in a fraternal sense.

When the army finally resumed its march, it numbered about 300 men. When the marchers arrived at Rockville, Maryland (about 20 miles from Washington), they were joined by 50 marchers from Philadelphia under the leadership of Christopher Columbus Jones. Jones, another colorful character, wore a silk top hat, sported a long gray beard, and liked to quote poetry. A true sympathizer, he also believed in reincarnation and supported Coxey's bills. As the new recruits blended with Coxey's contingent, 10,000 spectators turned out to see the army march to its camp on the outskirts of the nation's capital.

As Coxey readied his following to enter the capital district, local resistance to that idea began to manifest itself. Newspapers heightened fears with accounts like the one that appeared in the *Washington News*: "Coxey's Army is no longer a joke. The growth and progress of this horde of dangerous characters are most serious matters for

1. The Inspiration: Coxey's Army

Coxey's Army on the Chesapeake and Ohio Canal. After a difficult five-day trek over the Allegheny Mountains, Coxey hired two coal boats to haul his recruits eighty-five miles from Cumberland, Maryland, to Williamsport, April 1894. Library of Congress, Prints & Photographs Division.

Washington to contemplate. It is time for Washingtonians to consider what can be done to avert the threatened invasion of the district by this swarm of human locusts."[23] Some were concerned that Coxey's army might even try to loot the U.S. Treasury.

Coxey had been informed that the metropolitan police intended to enforce an 1882 "Act to Regulate the Use of the Capitol Grounds" against him. The law prohibited making any formal oration on the grounds or to "parade, stand, or move in processions or assemblages, or display any flag, banner, or device designed or adapted to bring into public notice any party, organization, or movement." The chief of police noted that if anyone attempted to assemble on U.S. Capitol grounds, they would be arrested. Joining the official police position were the district's three commissioners who issued a formal statement condemning the movement and stating that the "constitutional right of petition does not justify methods dangerous to peace and good order."[24]

To ensure preparedness, Washington mobilized on several fronts. The metropolitan police underwent special training drills, 1,600 district militia troops made ready, and all soldiers and marines based anywhere near the capital remained on full alert. Despite all the restrictions placed on the U.S. Capitol grounds, parading through the streets of the district was allowed. As a result, Coxey went ahead and acquired a parade permit. Despite warnings from the authorities, Coxey was convinced that the U.S. Constitution protected his rights of free speech and assembly. He fully intended to challenge the authorities and complete his mission.

On May 1, the Army of the Commonweal began its march up Pennsylvania Avenue. Members of the local Public Comfort Committee led the procession, followed by the Commonweal band playing "Marching through Georgia." Next in line was the Goddess of Peace—in reality, Mamie Coxey, the 17-year-old daughter of the general—upon a prancing white stallion. Dressed all in white with a blue liberty cap and a small parasol to shade her face, she immediately won over the crowd who responded with cheers. Behind her rode Carl Browne, followed by Jesse Coxey, and then Mr. and Mrs. Coxey in an open carriage with their infant son Legal Tender. Next came the 500 soldiers of the Commonweal carrying banners that said, "Peace on Earth, good will toward men, but death to interest on bonds." Spectators lined the streets, and a crowd estimated to be between fifteen and twenty thousand massed at the base of Capitol Hill.

When the marchers reached the end of Pennsylvania Avenue, however, they found that a squadron of policemen had moved into position in front of the east entrance to the Capitol (30 additional officers had stationed themselves throughout the building). At that point the army made a turn and stopped just beyond the B Street entrance to the House of Representatives. After a hurried conference, Coxey, Browne, and Christopher Columbus Jones climbed over a low stone wall and made haste toward the Capitol steps. Jones was quickly apprehended and taken away to a patrol wagon. Browne, who had hoped to lead his pursuers away from Coxey, was finally tackled by a dozen officers who then beat him about the head, tore his shirt to the waist, and ripped off a necklace of beads that had been a gift from his deceased wife.[25] When police proceeded to usher Browne toward a patrol wagon, bystanders tried to come to his aid. At that point, things got out of control. Police charged into the crowd, indiscriminately assaulting everyone within reach with their billy clubs. Mounted policemen rode down men, women, and children.

While most of the attention was drawn to Browne and the riot around him, Coxey managed to reach the steps of the Capitol. As he

1. The Inspiration: Coxey's Army

began to ascend the steps, policemen blocked his way. He asked to be allowed to speak, but his request was denied. When he pulled papers from his pocket and began to unfold them as if to begin an address, the officers pushed him back down the steps. As they did so, Coxey tossed his speech to the press. An excerpt from that speech read:

> Up these steps the lobbyists of trusts and corporations have passed unchallenged on their way to the committee rooms, access to which we, the representatives of the toiling wealth producers, have been denied. We stand here today in behalf of millions of toilers whose petitions have been buried in committee rooms, whose prayers have been un-responded to, and whose opportunities for honest, remunerative labor have been taken away from them.[26]

All that was left was the legal aftermath. Although officers released Coxey after he had been led away from the capitol grounds, Browne and Jones were taken to jail and then, later, released on bail. The three leaders appeared in police court the following day to be formally charged. Coxey, Browne, and Jones were found guilty of carrying banners (Coxey's "banner" was actually a two-by-three-inch ribbon he had pinned to the lapel of his coat), and Coxey and Browne of walking on the grass in violation of the local ordinance. After hearing the verdict against him, Coxey returned to his camp to speak to his followers. Mounting a wagon, and with bitterness in his voice, he told them: "This country is like a big bunch of straw, and all that is necessary to start it into a roaring blaze is the torch. Do you dream that in court today the torch was applied?"[27] Called back to court three weeks later, Coxey, Browne, and Jones were sentenced to 20 days in jail and fined five dollars.

The police brutality and the arrest of the Commonweal's leaders sparked a storm of protest among trade unionists, Populists, and other sympathizers. Calling the excessive use of force demonstrated by the police "A Crime Against Freedom," the *American Federationist* denounced the attack as a shameless attempt "to crush out the constitutional and natural rights of free speech, free assemblage and freedom of petition."[28]

Coxey's comment about the torch being applied was not far off the mark. As he spoke, Coxeyism was gaining strength in the Far West as more than a dozen new armies of the unemployed spontaneously appeared in California, the Pacific Northwest, and the Rocky Mountain states. A few saw themselves as reinforcements demanding roads and jobs, while others carried agendas that were more attuned to their specific geographic regions. For several weeks after Coxey's "defeat" in the nation's capital, western armies, headstrong, fiercely independent, and with a tinge of that lawless western spirit, carried on Coxey's crusade. Too poor to buy the train tickets that would take them 3,000 miles to Washington, they stole rides on freight trains or, on occasion, stole trains themselves. When blocked from use of the rails, they built boats and plied the rivers, all in a determined effort to have their voices heard.

2

Fry's Los Angeles Army

As in other major cities on the Pacific coast, the impact of the depression of 1893 was severe in Los Angeles. In the summer of that year 500 unemployed men petitioned the Los Angeles City Council to start a public works program. Initially, the council delayed making a decision, but a worsening economic crisis only increased the pressure to act. Finally, in January 1894, it agreed to a public works program and appropriated $10,000 for a six-week trial project. However, at the end of the trial period there was not enough money to keep the program going. The failure of local relief efforts coincided with the news of Jacob Coxey's intended march on Washington.

One of those who took an interest in Coxey's plan, and who was in sympathy with Coxey's broader national public works program, was Lewis C. Fry.[1] Fry also happened to be a former California associate of Carl Browne. Around that time, Fry attended a meeting at the Church of the New Era in Los Angeles where the question under discussion was, "What is best to promote the welfare of the human family?" Given an opportunity to speak, and certainly aware of the inadequacy of recent relief efforts, Fry suggested that "the best thing for the great army of the unemployed of America is to organize and present itself to Congress at Washington."[2]

Interest piqued by that address led to a follow-up meeting of workers at the Central Labor Hall. As interest in Fry's idea grew, supporters decided to form an organizing committee. A series of meetings followed, and the committee assembled processions to march through the city under the banner, "On to Washington," to elicit recruits. By early March, organizers had enlisted 800 men and procured the Meyer warehouse which they converted into a barracks. Feeling like the "army" was nearly ready for departure, representatives approached the city council and asked for their assistance in persuading officials of

"Work, give us work"

either the Southern Pacific or Santa Fe Railroad to transport the Los Angeles industrial army to Washington. While railroad officials deliberated, those assembled elected Fry to command the upcoming expedition and approved an elaborate constitution. On a letterhead that featured a dove, an olive branch, and a gold bug, Fry's organization sent a call to the unemployed in 80 communities throughout the West, hoping to spark the creation of similar marching units.

Lewis Fry was a tall man in his late 40s with thinning hair and a mustache. When photographed, he could usually be seen wearing a slouch hat and an overcoat. Originally from the Midwest, Fry had moved to California at the age of seven. Apparently not well-educated, Fry once playfully responded to a reporter who raised the topic that he had acquired his education "with other kids in the street reading circus bills."[3] He had been in the regular army at some point, which probably explains why his organization had more of a military quality about it than other industrial "armies." His well-drilled companies often paraded the streets. Occasionally, these same companies would march into meeting halls to listen to the discussion of social questions. As one lecturer recounted the experience:

General Lewis C. Fry, chief organizer of "Fry's Army." When Coxey was arrested in Washington, D.C., and forced to serve a twenty-day jail sentence, he offered Fry a special commission as temporary commander of the Commonweal. Digitally edited photo plate from Henry Vincent, *The Story of the Commonweal: Narrative of the Origin and Growth of the Movement*, 1894. Digital editing by Tim Davenport ("Carrite") for Wikipedia.

Among the multitude of people who came to listen to a discussion of social and religious problems, I observed to my amazement several companies of the recently organized "Industrial Army." ... [A]s they filed into the hall and quietly took their seats they were greeted with thunderous applause. I noticed that my most attentive and appreciative listeners were these same sallow-faced and sad-hearted unemployed.[4]

Unlike Coxey or Browne, Fry was a workman and trade unionist rather than a businessman or showman. As a mechanic, he had been employed at various times by the Southern Pacific Railroad in its shops in El Paso, Tucson, Los Angeles and elsewhere. When he took the side of fellow workers against the company in a labor dispute, he lost his job and was blacklisted. His pro-labor sympathies and socialist political beliefs led him to become something of an itinerant labor reformer. He met Carl Browne in the late 1880s or early 1890s when the California labor agitator had suggested leading a march of the unemployed to the state's capital in Sacramento.

The group's constitution emphasized the growing maldistribution of wealth in the country, claiming that 3 percent of the population owned 76 percent of the nation's wealth. In a forceful yet rather nativistic preamble to the constitution, Fry elaborated on that theme and asserted that "the evils of murderous competition; the supplanting of manual labor by machinery; the excessive Mongolian and pauper immigration; the curse of alien landlordism; the exploitation by rent, profit, and interest, of the products of the toiler—has centralized the wealth of the nation into the hands of the few, and placed the masses in a state of hopeless destitution."[5] Accordingly, Fry's organization demanded redress from the government in the form of: employment for all citizens; a 10-year moratorium on all foreign immigration; and a ban on alien ownership of property. When later asked to elaborate on the first point, Fry failed to mention Coxey's good-roads plan, but stated that he wanted the government to employ all idle citizens on various internal improvement projects such as the irrigation of arid lands, a common theme among a number of western armies.

As in the case of Jacob Coxey, reporters sensed a good story and quickly pressed Fry for details of his planned march. Fry told them that, with the help of the railroads, he thought the trip could be made in 20 days. He would travel ahead of the army to organize meetings in all the large towns on the route to encourage municipalities to feed and provision his army. He would also use those opportunities to seek new recruits. Fry imagined that he might have a million marchers by the time his army reached the nation's capital. When asked what he might do if the government should interpose and prevent his progress,

"Work, give us work"

Fry responded, "Lay down as prisoners of war and demand that the government provide for us."[6]

For all the unemployed industrial armies organized in the western states, transportation by rail was key. And in no state was the power of the railroad more omnipresent than in California. To inhabitants of the Golden State, the Southern Pacific Railroad was a monopoly, the "Octopus," a corporate entity powerful enough to dominate the economy and control the political system of the state. It was the state's largest landowner and its largest employer of labor. With the completion of the Santa Fe Railroad in 1886, however, the Southern Pacific had a competitor. That competition drove down freight rates, while lower passenger rates encouraged thousands of settlers to migrate to the West Coast. The population of Los Angeles quickly grew from 12,000 in 1880 to more than 50,000 ten years later and that rapid growth meant new employment opportunities. But the Panic of 1893 changed all that and now earlier optimists were looking to return to the East or to find jobs elsewhere. With passenger rates no longer a bargain, many of those newly unemployed simply hopped aboard outbound freights. But the number of new transients was creating a problem for the railroads. When asked what could be done with the problem of "deadheads," one Southern Pacific official stated: "What can we do? We are powerless to do anything but protest. Law is impotent."[7] When representatives of various industrial armies asked for free transportation for 500 or 1,000 men, railroad officials were already primed to regard such requests as an insult.

Fry's optimistic prediction of reaching Washington in 20 days was compromised when the railroads refused to provide a train. Afraid that Fry's men might attempt to steal one, the Santa Fe Railroad assigned its chief detective, J. Frank Burns, to closely monitor the army's movements. When Fry's army grew to 850 men, local authorities began to become alarmed and looked for ways to diminish the perceived threat. At one point they arrested a dozen of Fry's men for vagrancy and for begging on the street. When hauled into court, the judge gave them 24 hours to leave town. When rumors began to circulate that a police raid on their encampment was imminent, Fry decided it was time for the men to march.

On the morning of March 16 (ten days before Coxey and Browne set out from Massillon) Fry's army of 600 members (about 200 men remained behind in the barracks as an "industrial reserve"), led by

2. Fry's Los Angeles Army

a fife and drum corps, set out on foot from Los Angeles. While Fry traveled ahead to Tucson to make arrangements for the army's arrival there, J.L. Gould commanded the troops on the first day's march to Monrovia, where they camped for the night. The next day, already desperately short of food, the army took the liberty of expropriating some oranges from the groves along the roadway near Pomona. At Colton, a junction for the railroad across the desert about 60 miles east of Los Angeles, they were met by the San Bernardino County sheriff who provided the tired marchers with hardtack biscuits, salt meat, and beans with the understanding that the army would keep moving. Forced to take immediate action, and cognizant that the only way to cross the desert was by train, the army proceeded to "capture" an eastbound freight of the Southern Pacific (the train's crew protested but did not seek to deny them transit). The train carried the men across the desert to Yuma and then on to Tucson in Arizona Territory.

The army arrived in Tucson, a town with a population of about 5,000, at daybreak. Despite the early hour a large crowd was there to greet the train, its car tops covered with the forms of dusty, poorly clad, and hungry men. As their advance man, "General" Fry had done well as the residents of the town gave the men a warm reception and treated them to a special meal, appreciated by all as they had not eaten in 38 hours. The army spent the day in the old town of one-story, adobe buildings. At their makeshift camp, bakers baked bread, some of the men washed their clothes, while others passed the time reading or playing cards. At five o'clock that evening the well-behaved army boarded another freight train for the 300-mile journey to El Paso, Texas.

As the army crossed Arizona and New Mexico misinformation preceded them, and the 10,000 residents of El Paso thought they were about to be invaded. As planned, Fry had gone ahead of the army to make arrangements. Upon his arrival, the mayor of the Texas border town called him a tramp and had him arrested for vagrancy as soon as he stepped off the train. The mayor then further heightened tensions by issuing a proclamation calling on "all able-bodied men to arm themselves, meet at the Courthouse, and organize [as a local militia], with a view to protecting their homes and families against the invasion of the horde of thieves and tramps, who plundered and robbed the various towns through which they passed."[8] Complicating fears was the wire received from the Southern Pacific office in Tucson

"Work, give us work"

that stated that the town was being burned and looted by an army of tramps because they had been refused food. In a state of panic, the mayor wired Texas Governor James Stephen Hogg in Austin requesting that he contact the War Department to have troops from Fort Bliss placed on alert. Governor Hogg informed the overwrought mayor that Texas could handle the matter without federal assistance. Then, just as the hysteria peaked, the mayor of Tucson sent word that the previous rumors were false and that the passing army had been "well-behaved" and, in fact, "the most orderly that had ever passed through the city."[9] Doing an about-face, the citizens of El Paso put down their weapons and began a subscription to purchase food for the approaching visitors.

When the 10-boxcar train carrying Fry's army finally arrived at the depot the next evening, more than 1,000 people were there to greet it. General Fry was there as well, the local court having overturned his bogus arrest for vagrancy. Given a chance to address the crowd, Fry took the opportunity to explain his mission. Nature, he said, was not to blame for the current conditions that prevailed in the country. Instead, they had been brought about "by vicious and ignorant legislation in the interest of the plutocrats." What his men wanted, he said, was for the government to issue a billion dollars in legal-tender money to employ all unemployed citizens "on internal improvements, such as irrigating canals to reclaim the desert waste; also to improve harbors and navigable rivers."[10] Once the army had detrained, it marched in companies to city hall where a meal of beans, bacon, bread, and coffee had been prepared. Afterward, the army was allowed to camp on the city hall grounds where local residents had kindly provided wood for campfires that night. That, however, was the extent of the hospitality as officials informed General Fry that his troops would have to move on.

The following morning, Fry, acting as advance agent, purchased a coach ticket to take him southeast to San Antonio, expecting that his army would soon follow. In the meantime, the men marched back to the Southern Pacific rail yards to await the next freight. But no freight train came through the yards, not that day or the next. Then, on Easter Sunday, March 25, the same day Coxey's army was to set out from Massillon, someone spotted an east-bound Southern Pacific freight coming through the yards. As the men hurriedly climbed aboard, they had no idea that they had just fallen into a trap set by the railroad.

2. Fry's Los Angeles Army

Officials of the Southern Pacific had decided that it was time to send a message to all "vagabonds" who thought they could freely ride the rails at company expense. If Governor Hogg, who had made a political career out of haranguing the dominant corporation in his state, would not act on the railroad's behalf, the company would have to take action on its own.

The train carrying Fry's army rolled on across the arid expanse of west Texas until it reached the small hamlet of Finlay (consisting of a telegraph office and the homes of half a dozen Mexican families), about 70 miles east of El Paso and more than 500 miles west of San Antonio. At that point, the engineer switched the train onto a siding where crewmen uncoupled the cars from the locomotive and left the men stranded. The Southern Pacific would have been hard-pressed to find a more desolate spot to dump the men. The company then stopped running east-bound freight trains through Finlay and ordered crews not to haul the stranded men out. In the meantime, Southern Pacific officials persuaded a judge at Marfa, Texas, to issue an injunction forbidding the men to tamper with the contents of the cars on the siding (which contained mostly citrus fruit being shipped from California) and to order a company of Texas Rangers to proceed to the site to enforce his order. If the men did nothing, they would starve. If they opened the cars and stole fruit, they would be arrested.

Texas newspapers and the wire services quickly picked up the story of the abandoned men stranded in the desert and how they were forced to go for days without food while the cold-hearted railroad officials seemed callous to their suffering. As one outraged newspaper reported: "They have been camped on a desert of sand and cacti for three days without food, and some of the men are so weak they cannot stand. Many of them are mere boys."[11] In fact, Fry's men were able to survive on a diet of flour and cactus roots which they boiled in a battered coal-oil can, but their situation was dire.

Texans were outraged, while Governor Hogg threatened the Southern Pacific with reprisals if it continued to do nothing. The Governor's position was that the railroad had brought the men into the state, and it was the company's responsibility to move them on their way. When Governor Hogg learned that Texas Rangers armed with Winchester rifles were guarding railroad property at Finlay, he sent an angry message to John Hughes, the unit's commander: "By what authority are you in the service of the Southern Pacific company, guarding their trains at Finlay and preventing the removal of the starving men at this point? You are hereby commanded to remove your force from Finlay and to interfere in no manner whatever unless either side resorts to arms."[12] Sufficiently chastised, Hughes, who meekly claimed that he and his men had been summoned to Finlay under false pretenses, immediately withdrew his men to Sierra Blanca, a small town about 20 miles to the east. Fry's men were forced to trudge along behind on foot, garnering some assistance from train crews who defied company orders and transported some of the more desperate stragglers by handcar.

What followed in the interim was a war of words between Governor Hogg and Julius Kruttschnitt, the general manager for the Southern Pacific rail system in southwest Texas. Hogg had framed his career as a champion of the people against rapacious corporations. "Food, not fines," he promised, "will be the treatment of the law-loving, law-abiding element in this state when men commit no greater crime than traveling as tramps for lack of work." Responding to the verbal blasts from the governor, Kruttschnitt attempted to defend his actions and told reporters: "We are beset by a mob of nearly a thousand men. They boarded our train and compelled the crews to take them to El Paso." When asked if the railroad had acted improperly, Kruttschnitt responded: "It is a mystery to me how in the world some people persist in calling these men 'confederates' and express sympathy for them as an army of unemployed men. The great majority of these men are professional tramps." When asked by reporters if the Southern Pacific would haul the men out of Sierra Blanca if the governor ordered it to do so, Kruttschnitt replied: "Well, I hardly think that there is any law to compel us to transport people who refuse to pay their fare. Of course, if there is, we will obey its mandate."[13]

Angered by the general manager's contemptuous attitude, the governor fired off a telegram to the *Dallas Times Herald* which stated: "When a railroad company hauls tramps or unemployed penniless men into this state, it cannot dump them into a barren desert and murder them by torture and starvation without atoning for it, if there be any virtue in our machinery of justice. Nor will I permit them to be shot down on Texas soil by any armed force whatever, no matter how much the Southern Pacific or other enemies of the state may howl about the Commune."[14] When Kruttschnitt, in response, suggested that Governor Hogg had been misinformed, that the railroad had not

2. Fry's Los Angeles Army

willingly carried the men into the state, and that they only had themselves to blame for being stranded in the desert without food or water, the governor lost all patience. "Let me tell you, if the Southern Pacific had taken out and left a lot of cattle or hogs in that barren place, where they would have starved to death, I would hold the road responsible. It seems very strange to me that these men would have sidetracked themselves in a place where they could get nothing to eat, and yet it is charged that they misplaced a switch in order to commit this suicidal act."[15]

Sensing that further verbal grappling with governor would only be counterproductive, Kruttschnitt, without acknowledging fault, offered to have the railroad carry the men back to El Paso. But the citizens in El Paso were not eager to have the problem referred back to them. To ward off a return of the army, the people of El Paso quickly collected $200 worth of provisions, which they sent ahead by express, and then paid for a special passenger train with seven coaches and three baggage cars to take Fry's army southeast to San Antonio. When the rescue train finally steamed into Sierra Blanca, the 500 men were elated. They had been trapped for more than five days in the desert, forced to walk 20 miles in the heat, and been fed only the beef from two scrawny cows and 500 pounds of flour.

Unfortunately for the army, the residents of San Antonio were no more eager to receive them than those in El Paso. The men expected

Texas Governor James Stephen Hogg, ca. 1905. When the Southern Pacific Railroad sidetracked one of its trains and stranded Fry's Army at a remote west Texas location without food or water, Governor Hogg intervened in their behalf. Image courtesy of the Texas State Library and Archives Commission, Wikimedia Commons.

that they would be allowed to remain in the town for a few days to recuperate from their ordeal. But when the special train arrived at the station at almost midnight, dispatchers immediately switched it to the line of the International and Great Northern and sent it north. A few hours later, the train paused for a 30-minute stop in Austin so the men could stretch their legs. After that, the army, numbering about 600 men packed into 14 boxcars, continued north to Longview. At that stop, sympathizers fed the men before they were transferred to a Texas Pacific train that would take them to Texarkana on the Arkansas border and then northeast toward St. Louis on the Iron Mountain line.

As the army prepared to leave the state of Texas behind, General Fry told a group of onlookers at Texarkana that he owed a debt of gratitude to Governor Hogg: "Say, you fellows have a great governor in Texas. He believes starving workingmen have got some rights." The governor, however, did not really sympathize with the movement as Fry assumed, stating: "I acted as I did for humanity's sake alone and the sober second thought of the people will approve my action." Governor Hogg provided an even more honest assessment of his feelings in an open letter to Texas Coxeyites in general: "Of all the chimerical schemes, unpatriotic steps or foolish freaks into which American citizens have ever been allured, this 'National Tramp' is the most pitiable and inexcusable."[16] Unfortunately for the army, that rather jaundiced view of their mission was one shared by most politicians encountered on their route.

On April 2, just about the time that Fry's beleaguered army was leaving Texas, the reserves of that army who had remained behind in their Los Angeles barracks, set out to join Fry. This second regiment of 167 men included 67 skilled mechanics of whom 27 were married and was under the command of Arthur Vinette. Vinette was a native of Colorado and a carpenter by trade. The original plan of this second group was to ask the Santa Fe Railroad to transport them to Kansas City. They offered to pay their way in work for the railroad. When railroad officials rejected that proposal, the army set out on foot with a lone wagon to carry blankets and other supplies. Their reception along the way was mixed. At Whittier, a Quaker community about 10 miles east of Los Angeles, residents greeted the army warmly and added 90 dozen eggs, 275 loaves of bread, 24 pounds of butter, 100 pounds of beef, 50 pounds of pork, 50 pies, and 2 cases of canned fruit to their commissary. At Orange and Santa Ana, however, the reception was quite different. Met by the sheriff of Santa Ana, the army was warned not to stop since the local residents "did not approve of such organized bands of men tramping over the country and would not encourage the same by feeding or harboring them."[17] Things improved when the footsore marchers reached Riverside, where townspeople donated bread, beans, bacon, coffee, flour, oranges, and a small amount of money.

Vinette's men encountered their first formidable opposition when they reached San Bernardino, a city located at the edge of the fertile coastal plain and the harsh, arid desert that they would soon have to cross. After Commander Vinette's offer of $150 for four freight cars to carry the men to Deming, New Mexico, was rejected by the railroad, the army and local sympathizers called a mass meeting to put pressure on the railroad. Several hundred citizens attended, but when Commander Vinette asserted that if the railroad refused to transport the men, the city of San Bernardino might be called upon to pay their fares, support began to dwindle. As days passed with no resolution to the impasse in sight, local residents began to tire of the demands being placed on their larders.

On April 13, after a group of men unsuccessfully tried to board one of the trains, the city formed a committee of public safety and deputized citizens who began carrying rifles and shotguns. Residents were urged to boycott the army by refusing to sell or give it any food. As mass hysteria intensified, Commander Vinette and several others were arrested and released only after they agreed to move the army, whose ranks now numbered 250, out of town. Seeking friendlier environs, the army marched to nearby Colton and set up Camp Determination. But the men had grown too impatient to loiter any longer and again tried to board a train. Responding to the alarm in San Bernardino, the sheriff there quickly organized a posse of 60 armed men and headed to Colton. In the meantime, the Colton city marshal ordered the city fire hose turned on the men who had swarmed onto the train. Some local residents tried to come to their aid by turning off the hydrant and slashing the hose with knives and axes. Although the men heartily cheered their rescuers, their jubilation was short-lived. When the posse arrived with guns at the ready, the army had no choice but to climb down from the train and surrender to the authorities.

After the incident, Commander Vinette and seven other leaders were arrested. While their leaders sat in jail, the army waited, sustained primarily by the generosity of the local Farmers' Alliance which sent them several wagonloads of provisions.[18] When Vinette gained his release from jail (he was fined $20) a week later, he announced that the army would immediately continue its march on foot. But before the entire army was ready to move, 50 unemployed industrials again boarded an eastbound freight in the Colton yards. This time no attempt was made to stop them, and the train rolled over the Beaumont-Banning divide toward the desert. At Indio, however, the train was sidetracked. Fearing possible arrest, the men abandoned the cars, and the train proceeded. After walking another 12 miles in the desert, the group finally gave up and disbanded.

In the meantime, Vinette and seven other leaders of the army were rearrested in Colton and charged with non-payment of railroad fares (a charge that was later dropped) and inciting to riot. The men pleaded not guilty, demanded a trial by jury, and then tried to subpoena all the members of the army as witnesses. The rather ingenious idea was to manipulate the proceedings so that the men might earn a *per diem* throughout the trials of the eight leaders. While under arrest, Vinette sent orders to the rest of the army at Colton to start their march toward Yuma, Arizona, with the hope that they might catch a ride on a freight along the way. Following orders, 167 men left Colton and marched to Beaumont, although a number of men dropped out along the way. The army was down to only 66 men when it left Beaumont for Banning, where locals refused to offer food and authorities ordered the men to move on. As the remnants of the army marched eastward in the direction of Palm Springs, it was the last that was seen of them as an organized group.

Commander Vinette, who had been in and out of jail in San Bernardino for almost a month, was finally brought before the Los Angeles Superior Court in mid–May where the charges against him were dismissed. About a week later, Vinette, undaunted, asked the Southern Pacific Railroad for a special freight car rate to carry 50 men east, but the company refused. At that point, Vinette apparently decided to divide his contingent into squads and have them hop trains toward Topeka, Kansas, where they would reassemble. On June 19, the day after Sanders and his Colorado industrials were given 30-day jail terms by a Kansas judge for stealing a Missouri Pacific train, the *Topeka State Journal* reported that Commander Vinette and 34 Commonwealers had arrived in town and that 25 others were in Emporia and would soon join them.

2. Fry's Los Angeles Army

"We work as we go along," said Vinette. "About thirty of the boys got work a couple of weeks ago at Bowie, Arizona, on a railroad and will stay there as long as the job holds out. I myself got work [as a carpenter] on a house at Albuquerque and worked several days." The next evening, after a meeting of Vinette's men and Populist sympathizers at party headquarters, those in attendance marched as a body to the county jail and gave three cheers for Sanders and his men locked up inside. "Ye have friends on the outside, boys," yelled one of the Californians, while another added, "Yes, millions of 'em."[19] Vinette and the lead group of his followers finally reached Washington on July 25, 1894, just about the time local authorities were starting to evict the remnants of the various industrial armies from the District.

While the initial progression of Vinette's army had been thwarted by authorities in Southern California, Fry's army continued to advance. Leaving Texarkana, the army continued its rail journey via Little Rock, Arkansas, and Poplar Bluff, Missouri, to St. Louis. Citizens at each stop greeted the marchers warmly and generously provided provisions. However, when local newspapers in St. Louis reported that General Fry had refused an offer of $1.50 per day from the East St. Louis Water Board to have his men work at digging ditches and laying pipe, the kind folks who had been donating food stopped doing so. When asked to comment on Fry's decision, Jacob Coxey remarked: "Why should they accept work and let themselves be sacrificed for the main issue by temporary relief."[20] Eventually, St. Louisans raised money by subscription to transport the army across the Mississippi.

The offer of "work" was a delicate issue for many industrial armies because rejection of an offer implied laziness and an unwillingness to work. A Portland army was offered work breaking rocks for a downtown street repair project. The offer was for six hours of labor in return for vouchers that would give the men two meals and one night's lodging. Captain Charles E. Kain turned it down saying that he wanted work at honest wages, wages on which a man could support a family. Members of the Seattle-Tacoma industrial army declined an offer of work in the hop fields near Yakima, Washington, for 75 cents a day, saying that they needed to continue their protest march for all the unemployed. General John Barker, who led a led a short-lived march of the unemployed down the Central Valley of California before food shortages and a blinding sandstorm in the Mojave Desert led to train stealing and arrest at Barstow, California, refused to "scab" on striking

No. 1.

INDUSTRIAL ARMY MARCH.

BY P. FELTON, LOS ANGELES, CAL.

(TUNE: "Marching Along.")

From ocean to ocean hear ye the cry;
Like thunder the voice of the people rolls by.
It sweeps o'er the length and the breadth of the land;
"Justice" the voice of the people demand.

CHORUS.

Onward to Washington; bring forth the lights;
Rouse ye the people; strike for your rights.
Break off the shackles and rise from the past;
The toilers unite for their freedom at last.

We war not with rifle, or cannon, or sword,
But the voice of the people, the help of the Lord.
The power of the tyrants shall crumble and fall,
And blessings of God shall be blessings for all. *Chorus.*

Then fall into line, boys; oh, why do you pause?
'T is noble to fight in humanity's cause.
There are millions of hearts that are crushed down with care;
Gird on the armor, and never despair. *Chorus.*

No. 2.

AWAKE, AMERICA.

My country, 't is of thee,
Land of lost liberty,
 Of thee we sing.
Land which the millionaires
Who govern our affairs
Own for themselves and heirs,
 Hail to thy king.

workers or to accept jobs that could be done by local laborers. Henry Bennett rejected an offer of free rail transportation and work at $1.40 a day for his entire Denver regiment at building a railroad line in northern Wyoming because he found the contract terms unacceptable. And Henry Carter rejected a never-formalized offer of $1.50 a day for his Salt Lake City army to work at railroad construction in Montana because he thought it was a veiled attempt to break up his march to Washington.

The act of refusing offers of work suggested a complex psychology within the various industrial armies. For many, the determination to traverse over thousands of miles to their ultimate destination was fueled by a larger sense of purpose. As historian Donald McMurry stated: "They were crusaders bent on a mission suggested by their leaders in response to their needs."[21] As a result, there simply was no time to stop for temporary work. But because the various "industrial" armies were comprised mostly of skilled workers, trade unionists, and professionals, there were other principled grounds for rejecting the various forms of temporary work offered. Some of the men undoubtedly objected to working at occupations outside their own trades as skilled workers. Union men might well have objected to working for less than union wages, while others might have balked at wages that were deemed degrading to them as American workman.

At East St. Louis, Fry's army encountered resistance of another sort as the railroads refused to furnish transportation. Local authorities compounded problems by informing Fry that there was a limit to their hospitality and that the army would not be allowed to loiter. After two days of failed negotiations with the railroads, police ordered the army to move out. Having no other option, Fry ordered his men (now numbering about 800) to set out on foot in the direction of Indianapolis. The march soon became an ordeal as the raw, wet weather quickly turned the roads into muddy quagmires. As the advance slowed to only five miles a day, the dropout rate accelerated. Finally,

Opposite: Industrial Army March from "Industrial Army Songs as Sung by 'The Mohawks' of Second California Regiment, U.S. Industrial Army, 1894." The Second California Regiment was a reserve body of Fry's army led by Arthur Vinette, organized at Los Angeles and reorganized at Topeka, Kansas. These People's party songs were aimed at galvanizing the organizational efforts to unionize the farm community. Kansasmemory.org, Kansas State Historical Society.

bickering broke out and, at Vandalia, Illinois, about half of the men (overall numbers now reduced to about 300) refused to march further. Demanding an opportunity to get back on a train, the breakaway group rallied behind the command of Colonel Thomas Galvin. Galvin was a Populist who favored government ownership of the railroads as well as public works jobs on irrigation projects in the West. This group eventually made it to the line of the Baltimore & Ohio Railroad (B & O) and took that road across Indiana to Cincinnati, Ohio.

After reaching Cincinnati, Galvin had his men proceeded toward Columbus. Somewhere near Washington Courthouse, Ohio, on the night of April 27, Galvin and his 200-man regiment boarded a B & O freight train to ride to Columbus. But officials of the B & O ordered the train sidetracked at Mount Sterling. At that point a standoff ensued. Galvin's men refused to descend from the tops of the rail cars, while the local sheriff refused to act unless he had warrants issued against the men as vagrants. At that point, both the sheriff and railroad officials requested Governor William McKinley to dispatch the Ohio National Guard. The governor quickly responded sending four companies of infantry and two Gatling guns to Mount Sterling. When the trainload of troops arrived at the scene, they set up their Gatling guns and aimed them at the industrials on the top of the cars. When the men again refused to climb down, a company of militia climbed to the top of the train at one end and forced the men to jump down as they moved along the tops of the cars. Having vindicated their authority, the troops allowed Galvin's men to move on to the state's capital after the people of Mount Sterling raised the required $45 fare demanded by the railroad. The no-nonsense response of Governor McKinley allowed him to maintain the respect of the state's businessmen and newspapers across the country applauded his action.

At Columbus, the army, now newsworthy and the subject of local sightseers, picked up 30 new recruits (more than half of whom were trade unionists), enjoyed the hospitality of sympathizers, and gratefully accepted the assistance of local trade unions that raised enough money to charter rail coaches to take them as far as Wheeling, West Virginia. At that point, which was reached on the day that Coxey was arrested for walking on the grass in Washington, local labor organizations again came to the aid of the marchers and contracted with the B & O railroad to send the army on to Pittsburgh. Upon arrival, the army was met by a large contingent of policemen who promptly marched the

2. Fry's Los Angeles Army

men through the city to Homestead where residents received them as they had Coxey's army a month earlier. When asked by a local reporter why he had been so successful thus far, Galvin stated that his division consisted of a body of specially selected men, most of whom carried union cards.

After the army had a chance to rest, the order was given to set out again on foot. Galvin's men initially followed Coxey's old route up the Monongahela River but decided to turn eastward towards Johnstown. Galvin, however, soon found that towns along the way were not as hospitable as Pittsburgh. After a failed attempt to board a freight train at Blairsville, the decision was made to break up into small groups and for the men to ride the rails as best they could. After that it was reported that every eastbound freight carried a quota of Galvinites.

Back in Illinois, Fry's men continued to make slow progress. At Terre Haute, Indiana, where the men were subjected to vaccination by the county board of health, Fry chartered a freight car into which the men loaded wagons, horses, and other baggage. Fry claimed that he had also paid for the men to ride on the train as well, but when the freight car was loaded, the train started without the men. Forced to camp in the train yard that night, the army captured a Vandalia train headed for Brazil, Indiana, the next morning claiming that they were owed a ride by the railroad. At Brazil, where large crowds lined the streets and gave the army a warm welcome, Fry chartered a boxcar to Indianapolis. This time, when Fry's army of 300 men climbed aboard, the conductor let them ride.

General Fry had planned for a prolonged stay at Indianapolis and, as enlistments outpaced desertions, the army increased its ranks to 500 men. The army paraded through the streets, while members turned into book agents and sold copies of Henry Vincent's recently published *The Story of the Commonweal* (40,000 copies of the book had been consigned to Indianapolis alone) to raise money to continue their journey. Sympathizers were generous in providing the army with provisions, but the large number of unemployed men camped out in the city began to worry local labor leaders who regarded them as potential competitors for jobs. Responding to their concerns, the mayor requested that Fry and his followers move along. But transportation was once again a problem as the railroads refused to accept anything less than regular fares.

Stymied, as they had been in East St. Louis, the army divided into

"Work, give us work"

Encampment of Fry's Army, near Terre Haute, Indiana, April 1894. After making camp, Fry's men were subjected to vaccination by the county board of health. Digitally edited photo plate from Henry Vincent, *The Story of the Commonweal: Narrative of the Origin and Growth of the Movement.* Digital editing by Tim Davenport ("Carrite") for Wikipedia.

two groups—a smaller group of 50 men (at times referred to as the "Hoosier" detachment) followed an Indiana Populist named Allen Jennings and proceeded south toward Kentucky. On May 20, it was reported that Jennings and his men had arrived on a steamboat at Frankfort, Kentucky. They reported that they were going to Washington by way of Virginia. The larger body of men under Fry's command set out along the old National Road. Fry's army, now carrying an old circus tent that the men had converted into a dual-purpose lecture hall and sleeping quarters, reached Cincinnati on May 18. At Cincinnati, Fry received a special commission from Coxey appointing him temporary commander of the Commonweal while he served his 20-day jail sentence. Union labor in the city then purchased a railway ticket to transport the new leader to Washington.

Arriving at Cincinnati not long after Galvin's detachment, Fry's army received a lukewarm reception from everyone except organized labor. Having already paid for Fry's ticket to Washington, trade

2. Fry's Los Angeles Army

unionists raised $400 in donations to hire a towboat and barge to take 276 men up the Ohio River to Parkersburg, West Virginia. At that point the army once again divided—one group deciding to follow the national pike to Washington, another to stay close to the B & O tracks so that they might steal a ride on a freight train, while a third group decided to remain in Parkersburg. A majority of the men reassembled 10 days later in Cumberland, Maryland, where they boated down the Chesapeake and Ohio Canal. General Fry rejoined about 125 of his troops outside Washington on June 23, three months and seven days after setting out from Los Angeles.

Galvin and about 150 of his tired and hungry soldiers finally arrived in Washington on May 30, well ahead of Fry's men, and were warmly welcomed by the remaining Coxeyites (sometimes called "industrials" or "wealers") at their camp. But it only took a few days before the newcomers rebelled against the imposed discipline. It seems they disliked having to wear a ridiculous badge decorated with Carl Browne's reincarnation designs and resented having to take orders from the youthful Jesse Coxey. As a result, the Galvinites soon left the camp and set up one of their own. When Fry and his men arrived in Washington in late June, they also proceeded to the Coxey camp. Upon arrival, however, Carl Browne informed Fry that his men did not display enough of the Commonweal spirit and that they were not welcome. It seemed that regional prejudices had bubbled to the surface, augmented by a scarce food supply. Rebuffed by

F.J. O'Connell barge carrying Fry's Army up the Ohio River, May 1894. Trade unionists in Cincinnati raised $400 in donations to hire a towboat and barge to take 276 men up the Ohio River to Parkersburg, West Virginia. From the Collection of Cincinnati & Hamilton County Public Library.

Browne, Fry and his men then joined the Galvinites at their camp. But being in close proximity to Coxey's men exacerbated the larger problem as it placed the two camps in competition for food donations that were becoming increasingly hard to come by. On the last day of June, the Galvin-Fry group left the District and established a new camp in a field in Rosslyn, Virginia, just west of the Aqueduct Bridge.

As the number of men at the original Coxey camp dwindled throughout July, the numbers at the camp in Rosslyn, which had now become the stopping place for other arriving contingents, increased dramatically. There were 600 men in camp in mid–July and over 1,000 by the end of the month. This time conflict developed between Galvin's and Fry's men. Galvin's followers accused Fry of playing fast and loose with the treasury and demanded an accounting, while an indignant Fry denied the Galvinites access to the food of the commissary. But by the end of the month, it did not really matter. The camp had simply run out of money and food to fight over. Desperate, some of the men picked blackberries, others tried fishing, but hunger eventually forced the men to go begging door-to-door. What had started out as an idealistic quest for justice had become a basic struggle just to survive.

During the second week of August, authorities convinced large numbers of men from Galvin's and Kelly's armies to accept transportation back west. The men that remained were largely from Fry's Los Angeles army and "Jumbo" Cantwell's Tacoma army. They were joined by Edward Jeffries and 40 of his men from Seattle who arrived on August 6. When Jeffries announced that several hundred more protestors would be arriving soon, officials became alarmed. In the early morning of August 11, as the men encamped at Rosslyn were having breakfast, they were greeted by a detachment of the Virginia militia under the command of Adjutant General Charles J. Anderson who ordered the men to move out. The soldiers then burned the camp. The ejected Commonwealers were then marched to the Aqueduct Bridge connecting Virginia and the District of Columbia and left there in limbo with the bridge gates locked at both ends. Sympathetic locals brought food to the men, but it was only after William McAdoo, the Assistant Secretary of the Navy, allowed them to camp on the grounds of the Naval Observatory for several days that the Washington side of the bridge was opened for the men to pass. As they had done earlier, authorities finally arranged to have the remaining Commonwealers transported back to one of the major cities in the Midwest.

3

Kelly's San Francisco Army (Part 1)

The largest of the industrial "armies," and one whose exploits were closely followed in the press, was a "regiment" organized in San Francisco in the spring of 1894 by George Baker. Baker, a thin, wiry little man, with bushy black hair and a dark moustache, was a 36-year-old common laborer who claimed no specific trade. He assumed the title of colonel, decorated his jacket with epaulets, and envisioned leading a citizens' army of the unemployed along the lines of William C. Fry's disciplined Los Angeles organization. Promoters of the idea of marching to Washington had staged rallies at the Furniture Workers' Hall and even published their own Coxeyite newsletter called the *Appeal*. By the end of March, Baker had 1,500 men, some of whom had been out of work for eight months, on his roll of enlistments.

On March 27, a delegation from Baker's organization called upon San Francisco Mayor L.R. Ellert to ask for his assistance in carrying out their plan to travel to Washington to join Coxey. Specifically, they requested barge transportation to Sacramento (where they hoped to then proceed east by rail), a couple of wagon loads of provisions, and a few hundred dollars. But the mayor was suspicious. Thinking their proposal might be nothing more than a scheme concocted by a group of swindlers for private gain, he turned them down. Hoping to change his mind, the leaders of the organization decided to increase public pressure on the mayor and arranged for the army to parade through the streets of the city. The demonstration appeared to have its desired effect as Mayor Ellert agreed to pay the one-way ferry passage for 600 men across the bay to Oakland. On April 3, those 600 men, carrying a large American flag and a banner that read "We Are Hungry and Discouraged," marched along Market Street to the ferry.

The arrival of the army in Oakland quickly got the attention of

"Work, give us work"

Mayor George Pardee, who certainly must have thought that his city had enough unemployed to deal with already. After sending a tart letter to Mayor Ellert protesting the imposition, the mayor instructed local authorities to feed the men, and he allowed them to stay in the spacious Mills Tabernacle. On the third day of their stay in Oakland, Mayor Pardee, looking to get the army out of his city, brokered an agreement with the Southern Pacific Railroad to transport the men to Sacramento for a few hundred dollars.

While these arrangements were being made, and under circumstances that are not entirely clear, Colonel Baker decided to step aside and allow 32-year-old Charles T. Kelly[1] to replace him as commander. Newspapers described Kelly as "a small, slight young man, with mild blue eyes, a soft, winning voice, and a breadth of forehead that indicates more than average intelligence" who, it was said, looked "more like a divinity student or the secretary of a Y.M.C.A. organization" than the commander of an army.[2] As Kelly later revealed in an interview, he had been born in Connecticut and educated in the common schools, but he had left home early. Eventually making his way to Chicago, Kelly sold newspapers on the street for more than a year while living in the Newsboys' Home. After that he moved to St. Louis where he learned the printing trade. He subsequently worked on a number of newspapers in various cities before arriving in San Francisco. Along the way he married a Salvation Army girl and joined that organization for a time with her.

Unemployed at the time of the march, Kelly was a staunch union man and had learned something about organizing workers. He was also a member of the Socialist Labor Party. Historian Donald McMurry stated that he was known among his acquaintances as a "first-class workman, but a crank on the labor question. The Industrial Army affair carried him away completely." He was leaving home, he said, because "[i]n a matter like this a man must be a man or a serf. He must do his duty, and his family must be a second consideration." Kelly seemed to have about him that unique quality of personal magnetism. As McMurry noted, "The extraordinary way in which he impressed himself immediately upon the army and held it together through a series of difficult situations, marked him as something more than an ordinary printer."[3]

After three days in town, everyone, especially the mayor, was eager to see the army on its way. As the men waited at the train depot

3. Kelly's San Francisco Army (Part 1)

for the special train to arrive, they were expecting to make the trip south in passenger cars. Instead, what arrived was a freight train pulling six boxcars. Commander Kelly immediately protested that the boxcars were not fit for hogs and demanded that the railroad furnish passenger cars as promised. After putting the question to a vote, the men chose to follow Kelly and headed back to the tabernacle. At this point, Mayor Pardee lost all patience. After wiring Governor Henry Markham to request militiamen, the mayor mobilized his entire police force and swore in 200 special deputies. Then, at two o'clock in the morning, with the army asleep in the tabernacle, police sounded the general fire alarm and 1,200 men armed with pistols, Winchester rifles, and clubs surrounded the building.

The sheriff presented the men with an ultimatum, they would have to leave the city within two hours. The police then hauled Kelly off to jail. When the men refused to leave as long as Kelly was in police custody, authorities relented and released him an hour later. Upon his return, the men hailed him as a hero. At that point, Kelly made a speech to his followers where he counseled moderation, reminded them that they were on a mission of peace, and asked them to comply with the demands of local authorities. Escorted by 200 armed police and citizens, the army, numbering between six and seven hundred men, marched back to the depot where, at four o'clock in the morning, they were herded into Southern Pacific freight cars (a seventh car had been added as some sort of compromise) for the trip to Sacramento.

Kelly had arranged for Colonel Baker to accompany the troops east, while he promised to catch up with the train en route after attempting to organize additional companies in the Bay area. When the army arrived in Sacramento around noon, officials allowed the men to set up camp in the Agricultural Park while sympathizers fed them lunch. While in the state capital, the army picked up enough provisions for the next five days. It also added an additional 350 recruits to its ranks. Some of the new men were laborers who had been at work on the city's streets and decided to quit their subsistence-wage jobs to join a larger cause. As arranged, the Southern Pacific agreed to carry the men, now numbering more than 1,000, over the Sierra Nevada mountains and across the Nevada desert to the terminus of its line at Ogden in Utah Territory. The fare to haul 1,000 men in 17 boxcars appears to have been paid by the mayor of Sacramento and the governor of California.

"Work, give us work"

Near the bustling small town of Reno, Nevada, the army added a few more recruits while the railroad added 10 more boxcars. City officials, however, refused to allow the special train filled with unemployed workers to stop in town. As a result, several hundred additional recruits who had planned to join the army in Reno were left behind (they would soon regroup and continue as the Reno Detachment of the Industrial Army). One of those who did catch the special train was William "Big Bill" Haywood, future officer in the Western Federation of Miners and, afterwards, leader of the Industrial Workers of the World (IWW). The tall, husky, 25-year-old had been living in Winnemucca, Nevada. Finding himself without a job and without prospects, he left his wife and daughter in the care of his in-laws and beat his way west chasing a rumor of mine work in Auburn, California. Arriving there, he discovered that the rumors were false. It seemed that everywhere he went he found men traveling east and west in search of employment and the railroad yards crowded with desperate men like himself chasing nonexistent jobs.

After joining Kelly's army near Reno, Haywood traveled with it through the snow-covered Truckee River valley in an unheated boxcar. As he later recalled the experience, "It was so cold that the frost hung in festoons inside the car from the top and sides. We had to keep walking up and down the car to keep from freezing to death." At the small town of Wadsworth, about 30 miles down the track, he met a former acquaintance, a railroad man, who invited him home to dinner. Warmed and fed, Haywood promptly deserted the army to go fishing with his friend. Haywood did get a job on a freight train bound for Chicago with a load of cattle. The steers were packed so tightly in the cars that any animal that lay down was in danger of being trampled. Haywood's job was to poke the drowsy steers with a stick to keep them standing. Through one long, freezing night he stood in the car doing his job. Then, when the train reached Winnemucca, he quit. "I dropped off in Winnemucca," he stated, "and went home more depressed than I had ever been in my life."

As Haywood later recalled his thinking at the time, "I could not understand the problem of unemployment, nor could I find the reason for thousands of men crossing the continent to go to Washington.... These panics in which the workers were the chief sufferers were the outgrowths of the capitalist system. But the cure or preventive did not then occur to me. I struggled along in mental darkness." When

3. Kelly's San Francisco Army (Part 1)

Haywood published his *Autobiography* in 1929, he remembered the industrial armies of 1894 as "one of the greatest unemployed demonstrations that ever took place in the United States."[4]

After a chilly overnight journey in unheated boxcars across the arid expanse of northern Nevada, the special train carrying Kelly's army entered Utah Territory north of the Great Salt Lake. At Corinne, where the train was sidetracked to allow two westbound passenger trains to pass, the army suffered its first tragedy. Looking to take advantage of the unscheduled stop, Gus Holmquist, an unemployed waiter, crossed the tracks to wash his face in a nearby pond. Hearing the first passenger train pass behind him while still wiping the water from his face, he turned and started back across the tracks oblivious to the second locomotive that was bearing down on him. Others yelled out to warn him, but it was too late. The incident was a stark reminder that many perils awaited the men on the road.

Approaching its final destination on April 8, the train stopped about seven miles outside of Ogden while arrangements were made for the army's entrance into the city. At that juncture, problems arose on several fronts. First, officials of the Southern Pacific, with memories of the recent confrontations connected to the march of Fry's army across Texas fresh in mind, had apparently decided that it was easier to transport the industrials for even a reduced fare than to fight them. Other railroads, however, thought differently. The Union Pacific, one of the connecting lines out of Ogden, flatly refused to carry the men for less than full fare. The Denver & Rio Grande, the other rail line east from Ogden, posted the same terms or roughly $40,000 to take the men as far as Denver, Colorado.

While the railroads stubbornly refused to cooperate, the territory's federally appointed governor, Caleb West, created a second problem. Hoping to sidetrack the train in Nevada before it ever reached Utah, West had declared that the Southern Pacific had no right to bring indigents into the territory in violation of Utah law. He had apparently given orders to prevent the entry of the train even "if the tracks have to be torn up."[5] When he discovered that the train had already left Nevada and had moved to within a few miles of Ogden, he tried to prevent the Southern Pacific from bringing the men into the city and demanded that the company take the industrials back to California. Supporting the governor editorially, the *Salt Lake Tribune* commented: "If Utah was an independent power and California was another, there would be ample cause for Utah to declare war upon California for conspiring with the Southern Pacific to send their hoard of destitute men in upon this soil."[6]

Governor West had tried to stop the Southern Pacific by obtaining a court injunction to prevent the railroad from bringing "indigents" into Utah. But Southern Pacific officials ignored the law and the governor's threats and ordered the train to move into the Ogden yards. At that point, the Southern Pacific claimed that its decision was "a humane act that had to be performed, regardless of the law."[7] It further informed the governor that it would not take the men back to California for anything less than full fare, which, at $35 per person, was approximately $40,000 to $45,000. With the governor and the railroad deadlocked, the court tried to push things forward by reaffirming the injunction it had issued the day before. In response, the Southern Pacific brazenly ordered the Kellyites to vacate its rail cars or pay a daily rental fee of $3 per person. The charge was to be paid by the parties who had chosen to confine the men in the first place—namely the city, the county, and the territory. The move alarmed taxpayers who now began to look upon the governor's demand for an injunction and the subsequent stalemate as an action that could end up costing them more each day.

In the meantime, Governor West asserted his authority by activating the territorial militia (recently commissioned as the Utah National Guard) and sent two companies of infantry from Salt Lake City, along with a special police unit of 30 deputies under the command of police chief Arthur

Caleb West, governor of the territory of Utah from 1886–1888 and from 1893–1896. It was West who tried to prevent Kelly's Army from entering the territory and then fought just as strongly to have it sent back to California. Date unknown. Wikimedia Commons.

Pratt, to Ogden. When the tired, cold, and hungry Kellyites climbed down from the cars they found themselves surrounded by hundreds of armed militiamen whose orders from the governor were to keep the men confined to the rail yard. An accompanying battery of artillery men carried a Gatling gun which they conspicuously placed on City Hall square.

Gazing upon the scene from the tops of parked freight cars were thousands of onlookers who had gathered to watch the live melodrama. Although many Utahans who were more distanced from the scene approved of Governor West's tough rhetoric and show of force, most of Ogden's residents adopted a much more sympathetic stance. The town was something of an industrial hub populated by a large number of railroad workers, and thousands of them gazed upon the spectacle at the rail yards in disbelief. Sending out an armed militia with a machine gun to subdue a defenseless group of vagabonds just made no sense at all. One *Salt Lake Tribune* reporter described the scene: "Men, pale, cold, without covering or blankets, and wan, with hollow, sunken eyes, hunger and destitution pictured in their faces, looked out of the sides of the common cattle cars." In concluding his observation, the reporter noted, "Many a tear-dimmed eye gazed on the misery and utterly hopeless, downcast and despondent occupants of that train."[8]

The people of Ogden were actually displeased with both the governor and the railroad. They regarded the governor's treatment of unemployed men, who asked for nothing more than to be moved forward on their journey, as heavy-handed, and they were angry at him for foisting the Salt Lake militia and police on them. As local sympathy shifted to the weary industrials, the local press accused Governor West, a Grover Cleveland appointee, of being "an agent of the 'Washington Junta.'"[9] But the railroads were also blameworthy. As giant corporations, they wielded enormous power in many parts of the West. As corporate giants, "they had been given huge quantities of public land and subsidies out of the public treasury, and then charged what they pleased for transporting freight and passengers and paid what they pleased to their employees."[10] As historian Carlos Schwantes noted, "not only were their passenger, freight, and express services often the sole links to the outside world, but their ratemaking authority gave them the ability to prosper some of the region's newly established communities and blight others. In short, railroads dominated the lives of townspeople in the West … and many citizens resented it." As Schwantes concluded, "the railroads were simply reaping the harvest of their past and present acts of arrogance and occasional folly, acts that were plainly visible in an age that had yet to discover the magical arts of public relations."[11]

On the fourth day of the impasse, Commander Kelly caught up with the army at the Ogden rail yards and was hailed by the men as their savior. Governor West quickly paid the popular leader a visit and informed him that he and his men would have to return to California. Kelly then polled his followers who voted that they preferred to go to Washington, by rail if possible, but on foot if necessary. The outlook for progress darkened, however, when Federal District Court Judge James A. Miner amended his earlier injunction and granted territorial officers the authority to use force to evict the Kellyites from the rail yard. Governor West saw this as a tremendous victory and talked of running the train back to the Nevada state line under military control if the railroad failed to comply.

At that point, the citizens of Ogden preempted the governor and adopted a resolution that condemned his use of the militia and staged a parade to show their support for the beleaguered men. Among the banners carried in the parade was one that read "Spike Your Gatling Guns" and another that proclaimed, "Men Are Not Cattle." These events precipitated a meeting between Ogden Mayor Charles M. Brough and Governor West. Then, after 15 minutes of unproductive arguing, the mayor called in his staff and declared that he was going to march the industrial army out of town and stated: "We have stood this damned monkey business long enough. Salt Lake has run this thing up to date. Now Ogden will take a hand."[12] A few minutes later the mayor entered the army's camp and told Kelly and his men that he would escort them to the edge of town where they could begin their march east to the Wyoming line. He also informed the men that the people of Ogden had taken up a subscription to buy food, clothing, and blankets and that those supplies would follow the army in wagons.

In less than 45 minutes the army was ready to march. With the mayor and city officials in the lead and the army of more than 1,400 men, including 60 new recruits, falling in behind, the column proceeded down the main street of Ogden with flags and banners flying. Several thousand people quietly watched the procession pass by. As if to have the last word in their battle with the governor, the men carried

3. Kelly's San Francisco Army (Part 1)

one banner that read, "Favors for corporations, but none for Hungry Men—C.W. West." As promised, nine wagon loads of provisions including blankets, hats and shoes caught up with the army at Uintah, a siding on the Union Pacific line about eight miles east of Ogden. A few hours later, a Union Pacific freight train rolled onto the siding carrying 27 empty boxcars. On board was the railroad's assistant superintendent, Garret O'Neil. Surprisingly, crewmen offered no resistance as the men loaded themselves and their supplies into the cars. Once on board, O'Neil ordered the conductor to formally request fares from the men. When they refused to pay, the conductor pretended to order them to get off the train. At that point, he closed the doors and superintendent O'Neil signaled for the train to move ahead. He then wired headquarters in Omaha to report that Kelly's army had commandeered the train. The entire bizarre affair seems to have been staged to allow the Union Pacific to avoid the charge that it had brought indigents into Wyoming in violation of the law.[13]

Informed about the advancing train carrying Kelly's industrial army, Wyoming Governor John E. Osborne promised to take no action as long as the men were peaceful. When the train reached Evanston, the first scheduled stop in Wyoming, the citizens turned out in large numbers and gave the army five dressed beeves and other provisions which were thought to be sufficient for two days. A similar crowd greeted the train at Rawlins where the army picked up 30 new recruits, while at Laramie an immense crowd gathered at the depot to greet the east-bound crusaders only to be surprised when the train sped by without stopping. In seems that local authorities had arranged to have the train stop instead at a point just east of town as a precautionary measure. It was there that the industrials set up camp, cooked a quick meal, and picked up 10 new recruits. In Cheyenne a crowd estimated at 12,000 gathered to meet the train at the station. As the special train approached, the industrials waved flags and banners while the cheering residents waved hats and handkerchiefs, but, to everyone's surprise, the train once again did not stop. Local authorities had apparently decided to avoid contact with the crowd. The train did, however, stop briefly just beyond the east edge of town to pick up a ton of beef that had by donated by the citizens of Cheyenne.

Similar throngs of country dwellers and townspeople turned out all along the Union Pacific main line running through Nebraska to greet the train. A large crowd gathered at the station in North Platte to hail Kelly's men. Buffalo Bill Cody sent the army three head of cattle from his Scout's Rest ranch, but the train departed before the cattle arrived. At Lexington, a crowd estimated at more than 1,000 cheered the industrials as they passed. As the 27-car train approached Kearney, spectators could see men on the tops of cars, standing in the boxcar doorways, and hanging from the ladders. One soldier waved a big flag from the front of the engine already covered in bunting. Banners with hard-hitting slogans could be seen everywhere: "Government employment for the unemployed"; "Gold at a premium, humanity at a discount"; "Wealth produced only by Labor." More than 3,000 people enjoyed the carnival-like atmosphere. Responding to a special request, Kearney donated two 100-pound bags of sugar, while local sympathizers collected a large sum of money. Although the army was in Kearney for only 20 or 30 minutes while they waited for a passenger train to go by, citizens had a chance to chat with some of the men whom one reporter described as a "motley lookin array, dust-begrimed, bewhiskered, travel-stained and dirty, but withal smiling and good-natured."[14] At Grand Island, residents went all-out and donated 1,000 loaves of bread, 50 dozen boiled eggs, 100 pounds of bologna, 200 pounds of cheese, bacon, 50 pounds of coffee, 10 cases of crackers, 6 cases of canned pork and beans, and 100 pounds of ham. Kelly gave an impromptu speech thanking the citizens for their generosity.

As the train approached the eastern terminus of the Union Pacific line at Omaha, the people of the town—closely following news reports as had the citizens of El Paso in anticipation of Fry's arriving army—expected trouble. According to the *Omaha Bee*, "the people of Omaha expected to find a body of tramps, if not desperados."[15] But when residents learned that the reported "capture" of the Union Pacific train in Utah had been conducted with the knowledge and consent of the managers of the road, and that the army comprised law-abiding workingmen out of work, their mood quickly changed. Commander Kelly had wired ahead to the mayor and the city council asking for their assistance with food and shelter. Mayor George Bemis, a popular pro-labor politician, had replied favorably to the request, but asked that the men remain on the train. As would become the pattern as the army crossed the country, Mayor Bemis hoped to have the train move quickly out of his jurisdiction to the Union Pacific transfer station at Council Bluffs, Iowa. Following his plan, the mayor had the train stopped on a sidetrack just inside the Omaha city limits where it was met by the chief of police, a platoon of officers, and two or three thousand citizens. Sympathizers helped the army load 2,500 loaves of bread, 2,000 pounds of cooked beef, and 1,000 pies (the latter donated by a local merchant) into two box cars which were added to the train. Loaded with provisions, the train proceeded across the Missouri River bridge to Council Bluffs.

When the train finally came to a halt at the Union Pacific station around 9:30 in the morning, 8,000 citizens were there to greet it. As the men climbed down from their boxcars which were decorated with red, white and blue bunting, American flags, and a large banner that read: "Government Employment for the Unemployed," spectators gave them a loud cheer. Tired and dirty from their long days on the road, the men washed up before receiving a hearty breakfast. After that, the Kellyites set up makeshift barber chairs and enjoyed the luxury of a shave and a haircut. Through it all, the center of attention was none other than Charles T. Kelly. Dressed in a uniform consisting of a short overcoat and a middy cap, he looked more like a Salvation Army captain than the pugnacious, cigar-chomping "general" that most expected. Realizing that a spectacle had arrived in town, the crowd in the railway yards soon grew to forty or fifty thousand. Spectators came by foot, carriage, and streetcar, and at least 20,000 came over the bridge from Omaha. Sympathizers donated carloads of bread and other food items, bedding, and $1,000 in cash.

Kelly and his men quickly won over the local residents with their good behavior and their practice of holding Sunday prayer meetings (conducted by Chaplain William Parsonage) at which the men sang Methodist gospel hymns. The *Omaha Bee* noted: "The inoffensive conduct of the men, the courtesy and forbearance of commander Kelly under the most trying circumstances, have won for them sympathy and aid."[16] They also learned that the men in the army took their mission seriously and were willing to obey orders. Each member carried his own enlistment papers and wore a small American flag pinned to his lapel. At the time of enlistment, each recruit signed a pledge to uphold the law, recorded his name and occupation, and received a serial number as if he had joined the regular army. The army itself was well organized into two divisions with 14 different companies, each headed by a contingent of colonels, captains, and sergeants. Kelly's army also maintained a camp hospital, while a central commissary collected all food donations and distributed them to each company which, in turn, prepared its own meals.

"Work, give us work"

Although the Union Pacific was anxious to pass the trainload of men on to the four railroads that operated connecting links running east from Council Bluffs (the Chicago, Milwaukee and St. Paul; the Chicago, Rock Island and Pacific; the Chicago and Northwestern; and the Chicago, Burlington and Quincy) those roads were just as anxious not to receive it. On the day before Kelly's special arrived in Omaha, Judge Nat M. Hubbard, attorney for the Chicago and Northwestern Railroad, asked Iowa Governor Frank Jackson to protect the road's property and offered to transport troops if they were needed. Realizing the seriousness of the request, Governor Jackson hurried to Council Bluffs on a special train provided by the Chicago and Northwestern where he huddled with Hubbard, the state's attorney general, agents of the railroads, the mayor, and Sheriff John T. Hazen of Pottawattamie County. As a precaution, he ordered seven companies of the state militia (about 400 men) to proceed to Council Bluffs. When Kelly's men made their initial camp at the Union Pacific rail yards, they discovered that they were being guarded by 300 militiamen encamped only a few hundred yards away.

After a night camped at the Union Pacific rail yards, Kelly's men, numbering about 1,400 and stretched out in a column about a half-mile long, marched to their new camp site at the Chautauqua fairgrounds several miles east of the city. The army had several wagonloads of donated provisions and were able to find wood for fires at the site. Following the army to the grounds were two militia companies. When the rest of the militia joined the force at the Chautauqua grounds later that night, they moved into the pavilion, the only building on the site. This large facility had a seating capacity of 6,000, but the industrials were left out in the open air. On Tuesday, April 17, a storm blew in bringing a cold wind, sheets of rain, and pelting hail. Their fires extinguished and the camp left in darkness, the men found themselves totally exposed to the elements. When the industrials appealed to the militia to allow them to share the shelter of the pavilion, they were turned away with bayonets. Prevented from sharing the cavernous building by the troops, Kelly's men were forced to stand wet and shivering in the mud of their camp as a cold rain soaked them to the bone. A number of the men suffered badly.

When word got out regarding the military's treatment of the industrials, an outraged local citizens' committee demanded that the governor withdraw the troops. Governor Jackson tried to pass the blame for the inhumane treatment of the men on to Sheriff Hazen, who he said was in charge of the militia at that location, but he eventually assumed responsibility and relieved them from duty. It seemed, however, that popular anger with the governor, who came across as the puppet of the railroads, was actually directed more at the railroads who were blamed for demanding special protection from the military in the first place. Judge Hubbard was especially vilified as the personification of a heartless corporation. His steady stream of inflammatory comments seemed to offend almost everyone. In a newspaper interview the outspoken attorney stated:

> If these tramps and bums try to capture one of our trains there will be trouble. Should they succeed in getting possession of a train we would ditch it regardless of consequences. We will not carry these vagabonds for love or money, or be forced to by their capturing of our rolling stock. In the eyes of the law they are a band of beggars, who are organized for an unlawful purpose and to prey on the people, who are compelled to feed them and move them on to the next station. Why, if we would carry this crowd over the Iowa railways, we would be compelled to carry ten thousand more idlers just like them.[17]

On another occasion he actually suggested that if the army were to hijack a train, the Chicago and Northwestern Railroad would be willing to see Kelly's men killed in order to defend the prerogatives of management. In describing a possible scenario, Hubbard stated in a threatening manner: "We will steam up a wild engine, open the throttle and send it down to meet the captured train, and let the wreck solve the problem of whether we are obliged to carry these men without remuneration." As one of Kelly's officers remarked: "Judge Hubbard must be two or three kinds of an ass."[18]

After the callous treatment of the men at the Chautauqua grounds, organized labor groups in Omaha invited Kelly to come and speak. When the crowd grew too large for the Knights of Labor Hall, it adjourned to nearby Jefferson Square. There, before a throng of 10,000, Kelly, as the keynote speaker, recounted the journey of his men and told those assembled that the aim of his men "was to impress the Government at Washington by their presence as mere petitions would not, and that the Government might understand and appreciate the condition of multitudes of laborers and devise some measures of relief."[19] It was Kelly's hope that if Congress would put the jobless to work for three years digging irrigation ditches in the arid West, the people could get back on their feet again. As he later elaborated,

> My idea is that by the time those arid wastes have been wrested from the sage brush and jack rabbit, and have begun to bloom, the men who have worked there will have saved enough money to carry them through the first year of farming. They can settle on the lands they have reclaimed, and, within a short period, will have developed from homeless wanderers into sturdy farmers and property owners.[20]

In Kelly's mind, there was just no reason why, in the richest country in the world, anyone should have to beg for food. Other speakers were not as temperate as Kelly and seized the occasion to criticize Governor Jackson, the railroad officials, the Wall Street crowd, and the Congress of the United States. Following the speeches, the meeting adopted a resolution which pledged all in attendance to boycott any merchants who patronized any railroad refusing to haul the industrials. At the close of the meeting, those in attendance donated several hundred dollars for the men.

While the Kelly's men remained at the Chautauqua camp, Governor Jackson and the mayors of Omaha and Council Bluffs continued to negotiate with the railroads to obtain transportation for the army either to the Mississippi River or on to Chicago, even offering to pay for the cost. But the railroads remained adamant, stating that they were unwilling to set a precedent that would encourage other bodies of men to move eastward, and that they had no legal right to carry the men into the neighboring state of Illinois without any means of support. Refusing to budge, Northwestern officials declared that they would not carry Kelly's unemployed army under any circumstances, not even for payment of full fare. As Kelly would later discover, the heads of the various railroads had apparently established a pooling agreement where they would share the costs of refusing to carry Kelly's army. The railroad nearest to the line of march would simply stop operating its trains or reroute them over another line, while the companies, as agreed, would share the resulting losses.

After allowing the army to linger on the outskirts of Council Bluffs for four days, county authorities abruptly informed Kelly that the army needed to move on. As the railroads adamantly refused to cooperate, that meant the men would have to proceed on foot. Given the order, it did not take long for the army, which now numbered more than 1,400 men and included a battalion of 200 new recruits from Denver who had traveled to Council Bluffs on the Union Pacific Railroad under the command of General Gorman, to get ready. With flags

3. Kelly's San Francisco Army (Part 1)

and banners flying, and with more than a dozen wagons carrying provisions, supplies, and those too sick to walk, the army headed toward Des Moines. That night the men camped near the village of Weston on the Rock Island and Milwaukee line, about nine miles from Council Bluffs. Mr. Fields, the Weston postmaster, offered the use of the village hall as sleeping quarters, but it only accommodated about one-fifth of the men. Coming to the rescue were local farmers who offered the use of their barns for "accommodations." The rest of the men took shelter in neighboring sheds and corncribs.

While Kelly's men camped at Weston, popular anger over the railroads' intransigence continued to boil in Omaha and Council Bluffs. On several prior occasions, Union Pacific shop men had staged solidarity marches from Omaha to Council Bluffs bringing food and money to Kelly's men. In one instance, perhaps looking to intimidate railroad officials, they actually marched with loaves of bread stuck on pikes. Finally, on the morning following Kelly's march to Weston, 1,000 sympathizers crowded into the Knights of Labor Hall in Omaha and agreed to march in protest. As a signal for workingmen and women to join in a massive march to Council Bluffs, sympathizers agreed to blow whistles in the Union Pacific shops and local factories and ring bells in the churches. Upon arrival, they would demand that the railroads transport the unemployed industrials. Motivations for the march were undoubtedly mixed. Many were certainly in sympathy with the stranded men and their mission. Others were probably just as concerned about the economic impact on the larger community if the army of 1400–1500 unemployed, homeless, and hungry men were suddenly forced to disband along the urban boundary between Nebraska and Iowa.

Responding to the prearranged signal, 500 Union Pacific shop men and their families along with hundreds of others, including a large number of burly packinghouse workers from south Omaha, marched across the bridge to Council Bluffs. Upon arrival, they joined a crowd already gathered before the Grand Hotel. By the time the crowd finally confronted the governor and representatives from the railroads, its numbers had swelled to more than 8,000. Astonished by the size of the protest, a reporter for the *Council Bluffs Nonpareil* commented, "Such a scene as that upon the streets of Council Bluffs will probably never be seen but once in a lifetime." After delivering their demand, the crowd of protesters then moved to a city park to await a response from the railroad officials. At about four o'clock in the afternoon, word came down that the railroad bosses had refused to carry the Kellyites. As the crowd booed and hissed the news, a cry could be heard from the crowd, "We won't wait any longer. Let's get a train."[21]

At that point, the women, who had been front and center in the day's activities, took control and led 1,000 people to the Milwaukee and Rock Island yards. When they arrived, however, they found the gates locked and the engines and cars gone, the railroads having moved their rolling stock to a safer place. Just then, a three-car Union Pacific passenger train rolled across the bridge from Omaha, and the crowd clambered aboard. One of the crowd's leaders, a young engineer and member of the Omaha Knights of Labor, jumped into the cab and came face to face with his father. "Pop," he said, "you are our prisoner."[22] Angry, but unwilling to confront the crowd, the older man surrendered his perch and climbed down. When he did so, a dozen women crowded into the cab and decorated the engine with American flags.

The young engineer then stated that although he was willing to run the engine, he did not want to be the one to start it (apparently looking to avoid any legal responsibility for his action). At that point, Edna Harper, one of the women who had filled the cab, pulled open the throttle. After others attached additional freight cars from the yards, the special, with its bell ringing and whistle blowing, steamed down the Rock Island tracks the short distance to Weston. The army, caught in the middle of its evening religious service, cheered the arrival of the train thinking it was their salvation. Giving a short speech, Kelly thanked his female sympathizers. When he asked Annie Hooten, one of the female insurgents, to address the men, she acknowledged the foolhardiness of her action but stated that she only wanted to lend assistance to the cause. Delighted with their heroism, the men presented each of the women with the badge of the army.

The incident, however, left Commander Kelly with a dilemma. Knowing that there was no way to march through the sparsely populated Iowa countryside and still find the means to feed the nearly 1,500 men in his army, he desperately needed transportation. But to accept a stolen train would ruin the goodwill he had earned by his policy of peaceful transit and respect for property and the law. Hijacking could only turn the public and the government against him and curtail his mission. Noting that the 11-car train was too small to accommodate

3. Kelly's San Francisco Army (Part 1)

all his men anyway, Kelly requested that his sympathizers return it to Council Bluffs along with 20 of his men who were in need of medical attention. Although sympathizers in Omaha and Council Bluffs continued to supply provisions for the army, Kelly was in a spot. He had to figure out a way across Iowa, and he had to decide what to do with two of the women—Edna Harper and Annie Hooten—who were afraid to return to Council Bluffs for fear of being arrested as train hijackers.

The issue of whether or not to allow women to participate in the various industrial armies was problematic. Jacob Coxey had considered the question when he was planning his march on Washington but concluded that the rigors of life on the road precluded the inclusion of women. Coxey did, however, acknowledge a role for women in the crusade as organizers of various home guard units and women's auxiliaries. Every western city that sent an industrial army east had one, and they provided crucial assistance in caring for wives and children left at home and in forwarding clothing and food to the men on the road. When another industrial army in Montana hit a difficult patch while stranded in Bismarck, North Dakota, the home guard back in Butte actually forwarded money to buy food. Charles Kelly had established a policy of not accepting women in the ranks. When a number of women asked to join the army after the stolen train incident, Kelly refused, joking that he had his hands full just managing men. As a religious man, Kelly also worried about perceptions and what outsiders might think on moral grounds about allowing women to join the army. An open-door policy could cost the movement vital popular support. But Kelly made an exception for Hooten and Harper, arguing that his concern for humanity caused him to allow the women to remain temporarily with the army. He also stated that he was fearful of losing the support of organized labor if he forced them to return to Council Bluffs and face arrest. Although tongues did wag at his decision (even among some of his own men), Kelly did take steps to maintain an aura of propriety—providing the women with their own special tent and taking steps to lodge them in a hotel whenever possible. He also allowed them to ride in a carriage with the army's official photographer.

4

KELLY'S SAN FRANCISCO ARMY (PART 2)

A group of 80 to 85 new recruits christened the "Reno Detachment of the Industrial Army," joined Kelly and his men while they camped at the Chautauqua grounds. Included in this body was a 19-year-old, self-proclaimed "hobo" by the name of Jack London, whose fame as a writer still lay in the future. London had intended to join Kelly's army back in Oakland, California, but missed the connection when authorities in that city forced the army to make a hasty, early morning departure. He had just quit his job in a jute mill after discovering that he was doing the work of two prior employees but only being paid for one. Seeking release from the exploitation of factory work, London was ready for a new adventure and the freedom of traveling on the road. As historian Donald McMurry commented, "He was out on a lark ... seeing new sights and gaining new experiences of a kind well calculated to give him an insight into the characteristics of some of the lower strata of society."[1] Fortunately, he kept a diary

Portrait photograph of Jack London, between 1906 and 1916. London chased after Kelly's Army from California, finally catching up with it at Council Bluffs, Iowa. He then marched with the army to Des Moines and then sailed with it down the Des Moines River to Keokuk. He also kept a diary of his experience. Library of Congress, Prints & Photographs Division.

4. Kelly's San Francisco Army (Part 2)

of his overland adventure as well as his account of traveling with Kelly's army in Iowa.

London again failed to connect with the Kelly's army at Sacramento but decided to chase after the train carrying the men and, hopefully, join it in transit. To do that, however, he would have to hop freight trains—riding in boxcars, in the ice box of a refrigerator car, on the roofs of coaches, or on the "bumpers" while hoping not to be "ditched," "side-tracked," or clubbed by an angry brakeman. His diary records that he found the days "burning hot" and the nights "freezing cold." "I thought my face was sea tanned," he said, "but it is nothing to this. The sun has peeled the skin off my face till I look as though I had fell into a fire." He also noted that all along the line from Oakland on, he "met hundreds chasing the first detachment of the industrial army."[2]

In a passage from his diary, written in the language of someone familiar with the road, London described a typical day in the life of a veteran hobo riding the rails:

> I took the Overland out ... riding the blind with two other fellows.... We made a 45 mile run to Elko & a 23 mile run to Peko where they tried to ditch us.... We waited until the train had almost run by when two of us jumped the palace cars & decked them while the third went underneath on the rods.... I waited & when the train stopped I climbed down and ran ahead to the blind. The brakeman again rode her out but I took the next one behind him, & when he jumped off to catch me I ran ahead & took the platform he had vacated. The fellow on the roof with me got ditched, but I made her into Wells, the end of the division....[3]

Finally, just east of Laramie, Wyoming, "riding the blind baggage [an open box car behind the tender] through a blizzard with snow so thick that 'one could not see over a rod ahead,' he overtook the 'Reno Detachment of the Industrial Army,' consisting of 'eighty-four husky hoboes' lying in a dense mass on the straw-strewn floor of an empty refrigerator car attached to a through freight, and he climbed in to join them."[4] This Reno contingent had missed Kelly's long train when it passed through, but it was finally able to join up with Kelly and his men at Council Bluffs. It had taken Jack London, their newest recruit, 11 days to catch Kelly.

With the addition of new recruits like the Reno detachment, and enlistments from among the local unemployed, enrollment exceeded 1,500 by the time the army reached Weston. It was soon obvious to Kelly that the army would have to walk to Des Moines where he

"Work, give us work"

hoped one of the connecting railroads might agree to transport his men. When the army finally broke camp and set out for the next little town (Neola) on their route, it was led by 20 bicyclists from Omaha, 60 farmers on horseback, and 4 female sympathizers who marched at the head of the column. At the little village of Underwood, residents greeted the men with a warm welcome, several barrels of coffee, and piles of sandwiches for lunch. Hundreds of people wanted to shake hands with Kelly, and as the commander held his middy cap, the townspeople poured coins into it. As the army resumed its march toward Neola, it was encouraged by the local band playing John Phillip Sousa's "Cadet March," a fireworks display, and the cheers of hundreds of local residents. Once again it was evident that farmers, fellow workingmen, and common Americans supported these unemployed and under-employed citizen protesters.

Over the next week, the army covered nearly 130 miles on the road to Des Moines. Passing through the small towns of Neola, Avoca, Atlantic, Adair, Stuart, and Van Meter, it was greeted warmly at every point of the march. Wagon loads of provisions contributed by the Iowa farmers' movement awaited the army at almost every stop. Farmers came from as far as 25 miles away in their wagons to see the passing spectacle. Others welcomed the advancing procession with brass bands or provided the men with hot lunches along the route. As Jack London recounted: "the good citizens turned out by hundreds, locked arms, and marched with us down their main streets. It was circus day when we came to town, and every day was circus day for us, for there were many towns."[5] At one point a Catholic priest arranged for farmers to provide 150 teams and wagons to assist the army to the next town.

Along with all the spontaneous enthusiasm was a great deal of careful planning. The secretary of the Central Labor Union of Council Bluffs and the president of the Nebraska Federation of Labor acted as advance agents for the army, keeping one town ahead and making necessary arrangements for food, wagons, and an evening campsite. Joining them were the members of the Sovereign Grand Consul of the Woodmen of the World who had lodges in most of the towns along the line of march and provided teams and wagons to carry provisions and the sick.

The march, however, was not without incident. Commander Kelly temporarily expelled Colonel Baker, who had originally organized the

4. Kelly's San Francisco Army (Part 2)

men in San Francisco and then deferred to Kelly's leadership, when it appeared that he had been observed drunk and consorting with a prostitute. The appearance of impropriety was something that Kelly constantly worried about. Having successfully cultivated a reputation for morality and proper conduct, he could not risk losing public sympathy and the popular support so necessary to the forward momentum of the army. Baker vehemently denied the charges against him, arguing that he was not inebriated and that he was merely walking his companion back to her hotel.

Then there was a dust-up between the Sacramento men (led by Colonel George Speed) and the San Francisco men (led by Kelly) reminiscent of the quarrel between Carl Browne and the Great Unknown in the middle of an arduous march in bad weather over the Allegheny Mountains during Coxey's march. The Sacramento men claimed that the San Francisco men had been receiving preferential treatment when everyone was supposed to be taking turns riding in the limited number of wagons furnished by local farmers. Complicating matters, Colonel Speed appeared to disobey orders by allowing men to leave camp in violation of the rules. Speed, an impetuous man whose socialist principles were far more radical than Kelly's, had long resented Kelly's unwillingness to take bold action. After a heated exchange between the two men, in which Speed demanded that Kelly account for several thousand dollars that had been raised by supporters in Council Bluffs, Colonel Speed broke from the main body taking about 200 of his loyal Sacramento followers with him. The feeling of camaraderie broken, two separate groups of sullen men trudged along the dusty Iowa road from Walnut to Atlantic.

By the time the marchers reached the town of Atlantic, about halfway between Council Bluffs and Des Moines, tensions were so high that it appeared that a fight might break out between the two factions and endanger the entire crusade. Fortunately, local officials acting as intermediaries were able to affect some sort of reconciliation. In a scene that resembled a religious revival meeting, the three leaders—Kelly, Baker, and Speed—met on stage before an overflow crowd of local townspeople at the Atlantic Opera House, swore to forget past grievances, and then knelt in prayer as a sign of repentance. In hindsight, these rather petty disagreements seem to have been primarily the result of tired men, blistered feet, and clashing egos more than anything else.

"Work, give us work"

Just as it seemed that Kelly's army had resolved some of its internal differences, the telegraph brought news of another crisis in Montana. The Associated Press dispatch reported that an army of Montana Coxeyites under the command of General William Hogan had stolen a train and then had been captured by troops of the United States Army. During the ensuing train chase, at least one person had been killed during an altercation between deputies and industrials at Billings, Montana. Alarmed by the news, Kelly thought that it might harm his own peaceful march. "This is the worst blow we have had," he told his men. "We will now be regarded as lawless men, we who have broken no laws. But we will march to Washington through thousands of regulars and tens of thousands of the militia. Not by physical force, men, but by law and through favorable public opinion."[6]

More troublesome were the on-going confrontations with the railroads. When members of the army, usually stragglers weary from walking, tried to steal a ride on a passing freight, extra crewmen and Pinkerton detectives hired by the Rock Island Railroad to keep freeloaders off the trains used force to remove the trespassing Kellyites. On several occasions, those who had been "ditched" hurled rocks back at the guards. Worried that the army might try to copy the recent train hijacking in Montana, Rock Island officials distributed printed circulars warning the men of the legal consequences that would result from such an act. Kelly responded that the army would not board a train unless the train was either donated or paid for. The men in the army, however, saw the railroad's notice as a threat and immediately issued their own warning that if any Pinkertons were caught trying to infiltrate their ranks they would be dealt with harshly. Kelly took the view that these notices were intended to provoke and anger the men, incite them to violence and thereby provide the railroad with a pretext to request the U.S. government to send in federal troops as had occurred in the case of Hogan's army in Montana. Respect for Kelly restrained the men, but many, footsore and weary, were spoiling for a fight.

As the army tramped along through the small villages of rural Iowa, townspeople consistently donated food and offered wagon transportation for the weary. It was common practice for certain "captains" to proceed on horseback or in buggies in advance of the army and visit houses for about a mile on each side of the line of march, requesting farmers to send their teams to help transport the tired members of the army as far as the next town. When the army entered the small town of Anita, no fewer than 300 wagons from the surrounding countryside were waiting to carry the army ahead to its next destination. At Adair, residents donated 1,200 loaves of bread, beef, and 50 pounds of coffee, a fairly standard measure of local generosity.

On Saturday, April 28, the army reached Stuart, Iowa, a week's march from Council Bluffs but still 40 miles short of Des Moines. Looking toward a warm welcome in the state capital, an opportunity to replenish food and supplies, and maybe even a chance to rest up a bit, the men were upbeat. They had also heard an encouraging rumor that their supporters in Des Moines had secured a Chicago & Great Western train to take them east. With the possibility of an easier path ahead, Kelly made a fateful decision. He would ask his tired men to make the last 40-mile stretch in one long march.

The long march was a lot to ask of an army of exhausted men. After 11 miles, Jack London noted in his diary that his "feet are in such bad condition that I am not going on any further, unless I can ride. I will go to jail first."[7] Fortunately, London was able to elicit sympathy from some of the locals who paid for his rail ticket to the next town. When the rest of the army began to straggle into the town of Van Meter at dusk, they were still nearly 20 miles from Des Moines. The men rested until nine o'clock when Commander Kelly gave them the order to move on. Trudging into the darkness where it was difficult even to see the road ahead, the army's luck played out as nature unleashed its fury on them. It began as a severe windstorm of epic proportions. Men stumbled on the road in confusion, trying not to inhale blowing dust and sand that stung their faces and got into their eyes. Then, rain began to fall in torrents. Thunderbolts soon followed while lightning tore the limbs off trees. Many of the men, who had never before experienced such violent midwestern weather, were simply terrified. Some broke ranks and ran from the road, while others just lay prostrate on the wet ground. When the storm finally passed and the now-muddy march resumed, many of the men lost their bearings. In the darkness, men stumbled into potholes or into ditches filled with rainwater. In disgust, some of the men removed their waterlogged shoes and tried to protect their feet by wrapping them in their shirts. Muddy, drenched, dazed, and disoriented some of the men broke ranks and scattered, others, simply exhausted, just stopped where they were, deciding to wait until morning before resuming the trek to Des Moines.

"Work, give us work"

When dawn broke, Kelly found that he had temporarily lost his army. None of the wagons promised by his sympathizers in Des Moines arrived to rescue the men. In the capital, in contrast to their warm reception in Omaha, city officials proved to be antagonistic. Showing no compassion, the *Des Moines Leader* referred to the marchers as "an army of tramps and malcontents" and dismissed their misguided effort as akin to "hunting for snow to shovel in summer."[8] It took several hours for the army to finally reassemble on the city's west side where they would begin their final four-mile march through the city. But halfway through the march the rains returned, drenching the Kellyites and the numerous spectators who lined the main thoroughfare. By the time the army reached its new camp, an abandoned, three-story stove factory about a mile and a half east of the state capital, it was seven o'clock in the evening. It was their first chance to eat something in the last 24 hours.

The army's arrival in Des Moines proved to be problematic in yet another way. It seemed as if some of the sympathizers wanted to use the army for their own political purposes. One of those was General James B. Weaver, local leader of the Populist party and that party's presidential candidate two years before. Weaver had been instrumental in arranging a meeting of sympathizers, and had reached out to organized workers, women's groups, and clergymen for support. Together, they were supposed to collect enough food to feed the army, a cost estimated to be about $700 a day. But before this coalition really had a chance to get started, it split apart. Organized labor concluded that it was being used to promote a Populist agenda and drew back from cooperation. These divisions hampered food collection to the point where Des Moines Mayor Isaac Hillis had to get involved and issue an appeal to citizens to help the marchers. Luckily, local residents proved to be very generous—donating food and clothing to the hungry and tattered army. Good news was, however, again tempered by bad news. The rumor of the Chicago & Great Western train that sympathizers had promised turned out to be false.[9]

As the army had seemingly reached an impasse, Barton O. Aylesworth, sociologist and president of Drake University, took advantage of the delay and invited Kelly to campus as a guest lecturer. He also took the opportunity to learn more about the marchers and had his students conduct a statistical survey. The results showed that 549 of the 763 men questioned claimed to be American born. Students

4. Kelly's San Francisco Army (Part 2)

recorded 83 different trades and occupations, with mining being more numerous than any other. Politically, 240 professed to be Populists, while there were 218 Republicans, 196 Democrats, 11 independents, and 81 who said they were undecided. There were also 358 surveyed who claimed to be Protestant, 280 Catholic, and 114 who stated that they had no religion. The average time the men said they had been unemployed was six months.[10] Sounding somewhat surprised, Aylesworth noted that the men carried books and magazines and that one man could read Latin. The Board of Trustees of this Disciples of Christ–operated campus, however, regarded the entire Coxey movement as anarchistic and issued a repudiation of Aylesworth's misguided sociological study.

On another front, May 1 was to have been the day of Coxey's triumphal march in the nation's capital and the delivery of his living petition to Congress. Instead of the 100,000 marchers that had been predicted at the start, fewer than 500 made that fateful march up Pennsylvania Avenue. At the time Coxey was arrested, the press had reported that no fewer than 13 additional industrial armies were currently on their way to Washington with a combined total of 5,000 men. The largest of these was Kelly's army now seemingly marooned in Des Moines. When informed of Coxey's arrest, Kelly expressed his frustration by commenting that Coxey had forced a premature confrontation with authorities in Washington. Referring to Coxey's Ohio army as "only a little squad of Eastern men" and maligning Easterners for their indifferent support of Coxey, Kelly suggested that his army, generously supported by Westerners, was the "only hope" for the unemployed. "We go there with the influence of the laboring men of the great West behind us and will be supported by the Populist leaders in Congress from the West and also by other Western Congressmen."[11]

However, the immediate future of Kelly's army looked bleak. It still had half a continent to cross and absolutely no possibility of gaining rail transportation from Des Moines across the rest of the state. In fact, the railroads had removed their locomotives from the state capital to frustrate any hijack attempt. Tensions increased between the Kellyites and their supporters as well. Kelly was critical of General Weaver and thought that his intervention had politicized the march and kept many businessmen from assisting their cause. His sympathizers in Des Moines were becoming increasingly frustrated as well. After a few days, the novelty of feeding the marchers had worn thin;

local hospitality would obviously not last forever. On top of that, a growing number of men had reported sick. At one time two dozen men were hospitalized with 17 reported cases of pneumonia. As Jack London noted, "[w]e were bound for Washington, and Des Moines would have to float municipal bonds to pay all our railroad fares, even at special rates; and if we remained much longer, she'd have to float bonds anyway to feed us."[12] Members of organized labor, who had generously shared their food with the army, were concerned as well. There was a genuine fear that the army would disband and flood the local labor market with unemployed workers.

An epiphany changed the day. No one seems to remember who brokered the idea, but the ultimate solution to the army's dilemma was simple: turn it into a navy and have the men paddle out of town. With the assistance and tools of local carpenters, the army would construct its own shallow-bottomed boats and float down the Des Moines River to Keokuk on the Mississippi. From there, they would proceed downriver to St. Louis and then to Cairo, Illinois, where the army would head up the Ohio River to Wheeling, West Virginia. From that point they would be within 300 miles of Washington, D.C. Some of the locals thought the idea was impractical. Kelly's "sailors" would have to travel over 200 miles on a shallow river filled with hidden snags and troublesome sandbars and obstructed at several points by low dams. Complicating matters was the obvious problem of feeding the men when only a few small towns lined the river. But after a few of Kelly's sympathizers made a test run on the river and suggested that small boats could make the journey, Kelly agreed to give it a try.

On May 6, "Commodore" Kelly set up his navy yard at the confluence of the Des Moines and Raccoon Rivers as 15,000 spectators lined the banks to watch the shipbuilders at work. Also keeping a close eye on the preparations were officials from the Rock Island Railroad who were concerned about the safety of their rail lines that came very close to the river at several locations. Public-spirited citizens contributed money to purchase lumber and other materials (nails, tar, oakum and cotton, and 15,000 feet of rope), while Kelly contributed $500 from his treasury. The local carpenters' union helped with the construction. The boats were made of rough planks caulked with oakum and tar. Designed to fit the shallow river, the boats were 18 feet long, 6 feet wide, and 1 foot deep, with a 30-inch false bottom that ran the length of each craft. The boats had paddles but no sails, and each craft was

4. Kelly's San Francisco Army (Part 2)

decorated with American flags and bunting. Each boat drew only six inches of water when loaded to the limit with a crew of 13. During a practice run, however, crewmen had to do a bit of bailing to keep the shallow-bottomed craft afloat. When completed after just three days, the fleet numbered 134 boats (including one for the press) and carried more than 1,000 men who were brave enough to undertake the "voyage." Hoping to assist the men along the way, the Des Moines Citizen's Committee sent out a circular to towns along the river appealing to them to "not let them starve. Go and see them, and take with you bread, crackers, meat, sugar, coffee, potatoes, boiled eggs and anything they can eat. It requires 1,400 loaves of bread, 1,000 pounds of meat, and 50 pounds of coffee to make the men one day's food. Help them."[13]

Embarkation day was May 9, ten days after the army had first entered Des Moines. Businesses closed for the day and people lined the banks in a holiday mood. The weather was ideal, the normally shallow river ran full with rain that had fallen in the area in recent days, and the commissary boat had been stocked with provisions. Good fortune seemed to be with the fleet. But from the very outset, chaos reigned supreme. Given the word to go, the men hurried to their boats and quickly started racing each other, having too much fun to follow orders. Kelly had planned to have the boats rendezvous a short distance downstream and then proceed in an orderly fashion, but the men disregarded that idea and continued down the river at their own pace. Compounding the circus-like atmosphere surrounding the launch was the sight of maybe 500 women who boarded the boats for a brief ride. They were supposed to disembark after only a short joy ride, but about 50 apparently had no intention of returning. Onlookers soon noticed an excited Swede riding in haste on horseback along the riverbank out to reclaim his wife. Another wild-eyed man was seen going down the river in a skiff, carrying a shotgun and a stern look of determination. It seemed that his wife had run off with a Kellyite. The angry farmer declared that he would use one barrel of his gun on his runaway wife and the other on her "seafaring" lover. By nightfall, when the vanguard of the fleet stopped about a mile and a half above the town of Runnells and camped in a driving rain, the tail end of the convoy was still at least six miles behind. Commodore Kelly had lost control of his navy.

As some of the local newspapers had noted, it seemed as though Kelly's discipline had slipped even before the fleet left Des Moines.

He was accused of spending too much time escorting Edna Harper and Annie Hooten (the Council Bluffs train hijackers) around town and designating too much responsibility to others. When Kelly finally caught up with the rest of his navy at Runnells, he found that his men had picked up on that theme and complained about his lack of leadership during their first day on the river. They also accused him of spending too much of his time with "them women" whom members of the press were now calling "Kelly's angels." Although Kelly did assist law enforcement officers in capturing runaways from Des Moines and even broke up one company for refusing to oust a female stowaway, he refused to alter his policy toward Harper and Hooten. He continued to allow the ladies to sleep in a special tent guarded each night at a discreet distance by three of his men. No one was allowed to make inappropriate advances.

Kelly had other problems to deal with as well. One of those was the constant struggle to obtain enough food for his men. Although most of the townspeople along the Des Moines River were generous with their donations, the two small communities of Dunreath and Red Rock refused to sell the navy any food. Desperate, his men having gone two days without food, Kelly informed the local sheriff that if he could not purchase food, his men would simply take it. The warning worked as the sheriff convinced the local residents to change their minds, pointing out that there were too many industrials for either him or them to control.

Also troubling for Kelly were a number of men in the navy who possessed something of the "hobo" mentality that he had tried hard to guard against. Strongly individualistic and apolitical, they were driven by self-centered instincts that, given the opportunity, triumphed over the more politicized, collectivist ideal held by most members of the group. Young Jack London proved to be one of the individualists whose loyalty was primarily to himself. In an article written for *Cosmopolitan* magazine in 1907, London offered a more detailed account of the voyage down the Des Moines River with Kelly's army than he had recorded in his diary at the time. In describing the general disarray on the river, London left the following account:

> In any camp of men there will always be found a certain percentage of shirks, of helpless, of just ordinary, and of hustlers. There were ten men in my boat, and they were the cream of Company L. Every man was a hustler. For two reasons I was included in the ten. First, I was as good a hustler as

ever "threw his feet," and, next, I was "Sailor Jack." I understood boats and boating.... We were independent. We went down the river "on our own," hustling our "chewin's," beating every boat in the fleet, and, alas! that I must say it, sometimes taking possession of the stores the farmer folk had collected for the army.

My, but the ten of us did live on the fat of the land!....

This was hard on the army, I'll allow; but then, the ten of us were individualists. We had initiative and enterprise. We ardently believed that the grub was to the man who got there first, the pale Vienna [coffee made with cream] to the strong.[14]

It was left to Commodore Kelly to try to rein in these scofflaws. He first tried sending two rowers in a light, round-bottomed boat to overtake them and hold them as prisoners. But when the rowers did catch up, they found they were outnumbered by men who refused to be held. The two rowers then hurried ahead to the next town and appealed to the local authorities for assistance. Anticipating this move, the scofflaws merely waited until dark and then ran by the town undetected. As a second plan, Kelly sent riders on horseback down each bank to warn the farmers and townspeople against the food stealers. According to London, this worked. Local residents either refused to feed them, summoned the constables when they tried to tie up on the bank, or set the dogs on them. Forced to return to the main body of boats, the other members of the army scorned them as deserters and traitors. When Kelly tried to break up the recalcitrant gang of scofflaws (a group that seemed to comprise a number of the troublesome Sacramento men) and assign them to other boats, they threatened to leave as a body. In the end, they got off with a mere reprimand. Kelly did, however, create three police boats in an effort to restore some order to his command.

Each day of the 10-day journey down the river was a new adventure. After Runnells, the river turned rough for a time on account of snags and sand bars, and the navy made slow progress. During the night one boat capsized and the crew deserted and struck out for open country. When food became in short supply, the crews of some of the boats began begging at farmhouses along the river. On some days a strong wind slowed progress and made rowing a necessity. As the fleet of boats passed by, one onlooker commented: "In motion, the army might be described as a tatterdemalion *Carnival de Venice*."[15] Each boat was decked out with banners and flags. Some were decorated with wildflowers, and the sun-burned crews rowing them struck some as a flotilla of singing Italian gondoliers. As Kelly's navy plied the river, local newspapers continued to follow its progress and Iowans continued to line the riverbanks in large numbers to catch a glimpse of the procession. At Ottumwa, the largest town on their route, 10,000 people came into town to catch the spectacle. Local officials, however, remained apprehensive. Although they generously contributed provisions, they almost always requested that the navy dock at a safe distance from their town.

The 10-day journey down the Des Moines River might have passed without major incident except for the persistence of the Rock Island Railroad. Railroad officials had men shadow the navy all the way down the river and placed hundreds of armed employees (Jack London thought they were hired Pinkertons) at crucial spots. One very heavily guarded location was at Eldon, where the Rock Island tracks crossed the Des Moines River. At that point, nearly 100 special deputies waited with axe handles and other weapons to prevent the Kellyites from coming ashore. When one of the lead boats attempted to come ashore to collect provisions, Rock Island deputies refused to let it land. To emphasize that point, several of the deputies on shore actually threw stones at the mariners, breaking the ribs of one and knocking another unconscious.

The following morning, when one of the boats crossed to the opposite bank of the river, two dozen guards again refused to let them land. Spoiling for a fight, every other boat in the flotilla immediately crossed the river to come to the aid of their fellow mariners. Only intervention by Commander Kelly prevented bloodshed. Speaking for the angry residents of the town who resented the disturbance was the editor of the *Ottumwa Courier* who deemed the railroad's action "so senseless that it is little, if any, less than criminal."[16] It was only when the navy finally reached Keokuk on the Mississippi that the railroad finally ceased its harassment.

At Keokuk, Kelly decided to let the men rest up for a few days. As they did, nearly 10,000 visitors traveled by special train or excursion boat to catch a glimpse of the fleet. It had been a long five weeks since Council Bluffs, and the earlier sense of optimism had diminished considerably. Making matters worse, the men knew the trip would not get any easier. With a strong current and surface water that frequently swirled into giant whirlpools capable of swallowing a small boat, the Mississippi promised to be an entirely different kind of river and a formidable adversary. Anticipating trouble, Kelly's men lashed their boats

4. Kelly's San Francisco Army (Part 2)

together to form one large barge, while Kelly paid a steamship operator $100 to tow the barge downriver to Quincy, Illinois. At Quincy, Kelly's boyhood home for 10 years before he moved west, the commander was allowed to speak before 2,000 people in the city park for which he received half of the gate receipts.

It was at Quincy, noted Jack London, that "the raft idea was abandoned, the boats being joined together in groups of four and decked over."[17] At that point a number of Kelly's recruits began to "jump ship" and blend into the countryside. One of those was Jack London who managed to make it as far as Hannibal, Missouri. After a night of going without food, he noted in his diary: "We went supperless to bed. Am going to pull out in the morning. I can't stand starvation."[18] The next day he left for Chicago, hoboing his way by rail.

When Kelly and his men finally reached St. Louis in late May, they found that they still had a great deal of popular support. Viewing the crowd of 12,000 that greeted the army on the levee, a reporter for the *St. Louis Post-Dispatch* commented: "Barnum never drew a greater throng. The show isn't much in the way of a pageant. There are no roaring lions, no monster elephants, no hippopotamus, no dashing riders, no daring gymnasts. It hasn't a single novel feature, unless an army of worn out, tattered men may be considered novel."[19] But the fact that a volunteer army of 1,200 men had traveled almost 3,000 miles and was able to maintain itself from donations along the way was something remarkable to behold. The real support in St. Louis, as in most other northern cities, came from organized labor. Turning out to welcome the men and applaud their effort were the Trades and Labor Council, the Knights of Labor, and the German Arbeiter Verbund, who jointly sponsored a mass meeting in their honor.

But things were starting to unravel. The volatile Colonel Speed again clashed with Commander Kelly. As a result, Speed and about 60 men from his Sacramento unit deserted the main body in St. Louis and made their way east stealing rides on freight trains. Their hopes of reaching Washington before Kelly were dashed, however, when they stole a ride on a railroad that happened to be under the control of a federal court. They were arrested, charged with contempt, and sentenced to several weeks in an Illinois prison (Colonel Baker, the other troublemaker, would abandon the army in Cincinnati).

Also leaving the army in St. Louis was Edna Harper, one of "Kelly's angels" who had caused so much ado. She apparently departed to rejoin her husband, but not before touching off a minor scandal by suggesting to the press that there had been something improper going on between Commander Kelly and Annie Hooten (the other "angel"). The story, vaguely reported and then left for the reader's imagination, seemed odd, especially when Hooten married Thomas Sutcliffe, a carpenter from San Francisco, a short time after that.

Popular opinion also shifted as the men moved further down the Mississippi and then up the Ohio River Valley into territory that had previously shown a bias against northerners and trade unionists. As the number of onlookers began to dwindle at each landing, and press commentary grew more hostile, members of the army began to slip away in increasing numbers. At Cairo, Illinois, a manufacturing town with a population of about 10,000, the townspeople would not allow the men to land. This was problematic for the army as Kelly had abandoned the idea of continuing downriver to New Orleans, deciding to go up the Ohio River instead. When Kelly's men put ashore anyway, city officials quarantined them, patrolling their camp with 200 special guards armed with rifles and shotguns. Camped in a cornfield without tents or food, Kelly was forced to make an emergency appeal to sympathizers back in St. Louis: "Quarantined here and held without cause or provocation. Help us."[20] Organized labor promptly responded with a load of provisions. The stalemate was eventually broken when the Kellyites dismantled their boats and traded the lumber to local farmers in exchange for wagon transportation across the narrow neck of land to the Ohio River.

The ordeal at Cairo proved to be only the beginning of a long, difficult struggle. At Mound City, with some help from local residents who donated food and some money, Kelly arranged to have his men towed on two open barges (steamboat captains refused to haul the Kellyites out of fear that they might try to commandeer their vessels) up the river to the next large town. In this manner, with donations collected in one town being used to get the men to the next, the army moved up the Ohio Valley past Paducah, Evansville, and Owensboro. At Louisville, Mayor Henry Tyler balked at this policy, calling it a form of blackmail, and took steps to bar the army from the city. The Kellyites met similar resistance at New Albany and Jeffersonville on the Ohio side of the river where city officials again tried to use the quarantine tactic to keep the army out of the city, forcing Kelly and his men to camp well out of town.

4. Kelly's San Francisco Army (Part 2)

At Cincinnati, local labor organizations agreed to hold a benefit to raise funds for the army. But city officials, who had assisted the armies of Galvin and Fry earlier, now refused to give any aid to Kelly. In a spot, Cincinnati's labor groups again stepped in and hired a towboat and two barges to take the army 100 miles further up the river to Portsmouth, Ohio. But 12 miles short of their destination, the towboat captain dumped the men ashore claiming that his boat had only been chartered for 100 miles and he refused to haul his cargo any further. Tragically, Portsmouth's city officials did not want the Kellyites either and threatened to have the men sent back to Cincinnati. At that point, the army fell apart. Kelly reportedly became very ill and was confined to bed with what was apparently a case of typhoid fever. He ordered his men to try and reach Washington by any means possible. He would join them there later.

Kelly reappeared in Washington in mid–July and announced that he had 600 men on their way to join him. That was an overstatement. Just two days later, a detachment of about 275 members of Kelly's army were reported to have captured a north-bound freight train of the Ohio River Railway in West Virginia between Huntington and Parkersburg. Although 150 men got off the train at Parkersburg, the rest continued on north. At Wheeling, police met the train, now carrying only 25 men, and warned them not to enter the city. The remainder of the army appeared to be strung out along the rail line over a distance of 75 miles.

When a small remnant of Kelly's army did finally struggle into Washington, they joined the camp of other western marchers at Rosslyn, Virginia, across the Potomac River from the capital. They camped there until the governor of Virginia sent in militiamen to burn their camp and force them across the river into the District of Columbia. Authorities in the District, however, did not want the men on their hands either. Finally, in a decision loaded with irony, they decided to charter passenger coaches to provide the men with free railroad transportation to cities in the Midwest that were at least in the direction of where they had originated. On July 31, 1894, there were 66 Kellyites given second-class tickets to St. Louis, while another 80 or 90 were expected to leave the following day. By that time, Charles T. Kelly had returned home to his family in California.

Most journalists who covered the Coxey movement saw it simply as a misguided crusade on the part of tramps and malcontents

"Work, give us work"

that ended in failure. Historian Carlos Schwantes, however, has argued that it was a bit more complex than that: "[T]he transcontinental journey of Kelly's and other western contingents was ... the late nineteenth-century version of the overland trek by pioneers.... [T]he drama of people braving fantastic obstacles in the pursuit of some goal, or simply struggling to survive...."[21] On another level, the cross-country trek of Kelly and his men showed a tremendous commitment to their cause: honest work, a livable wage, and fairness for workingmen in the U.S.

5

Hogan's Montana Army

The Panic of 1893 hit the state of Montana hard. One would think that an economy dependent upon the mining of precious metals like gold, silver, and copper would be all but immune from severe economic downturns. But that was not the case. In the early 1890s the Treasure State ranked second in the production of silver. But when the depression struck the region in 1893, silver mining collapsed in spectacular fashion. As historian Thomas Clinch noted, "Heavy dependence on out-of-state investment, much of it Eastern and European, and a high degree of speculation in the mining industry laid the state open to the worst effects of economic dislocation."[1] The downturn signaled a death knell for dozens of small mining towns and extreme distress for thousands of miners and their families.

Unable to provide any sensible explanation for the general economic collapse, the business community and the Cleveland administration decided to place the blame on the Sherman Silver Purchase Act of 1890. This piece of legislation, a boon for the mining states of the West, provided for the large-scale purchases of silver as a basis for the issuance of paper currency redeemable in either gold or silver. Many in the West regarded the measure as a positive step toward expanding a badly deflated money supply. Others liked it because it provided a subsidy to western silver mining interests and held out the promise of plentiful, well-paying jobs for workers. But the legislation had a drawback. Under a bimetallic monetary system, gold would always have more intrinsic value than silver and offer more security in an uncertain economic environment. Consequently, holders of paper currency, both domestic and foreign, preferred to redeem those dollars in gold. After the onset of the depression, foreign investors, skeptical of the declining financial situation in the United States, increasingly sought to exchange their American securities for gold and gold reserves in the U.S. Treasury began to shrink to alarming levels. In October 1893, Congress acquiesced to the administration's wishes and voted to repeal the 1890 law.

Silver prices had been falling even before Congress took action and astute observers could see the industry starting to contract. Small silver mining towns quickly turned into ghost towns, while many of the biggest non–copper-yielding silver mines in Butte had no choice but to shut down and lay off workers. By the end of 1893, nearly one-third of Montana's workforce, something like 20,000 men, was unemployed. Idle men could be seen everywhere. Many were forced to live off free lunches provided by saloons. Some mining companies tried to alleviate unemployment by issuing credits to family men or by leasing veins and equipment to unemployed miners, while some municipalities offered relief in the form of public work paving roads or digging flumes. But these stopgap measures ultimately failed. Two years into the depression, 6,000 Montana workers were still without work. As conditions worsened, thousands of unemployed workers began to leave the state.

A mood of despair bordering on fear and panic quickly gripped the state. In a letter to a business associate, copper magnate Marcus Daly commented: "Butte is looking very savage. There are over 3,000 idle men on the streets. They are discontented and dissatisfied."[2] Butte, typical of the state's mining centers, was still in many ways a wide-open and only partially-tamed town (locals still called it a "camp") "where the intersection between an individualistic frontier heritage and the new industrial order was especially abrupt and violent."[3] As historian Benjamin Alexander noted, "A rough-and-tumble frontier culture, combined with a large, assertive labor union and extensive involvement in that state's Populist movement, had ensured that these men would not feel any shyness about making their demands."[4]

It was a place that was primed for a protest against unemployment. And once the realization of being without an income began to take hold, workers and their employers, sensing a common bond, began to construct their own explanation for the economic collapse. Easterners were at fault, not Montanans. "Goldbug" bankers, Wall Street speculators, and industrialists and their political backers were the ones to blame. As a result, rich mine owners and poor, hard-rock miners found common cause and rallied behind the call to restore the purchases of silver.

5. Hogan's Montana Army

In early April 1894, just a couple of weeks after Jacob Coxey began his highly publicized march from Massillon, Ohio, more than 200 unemployed members of the Butte Miners' Union, inspired by Coxey's message and example, gathered in front of the courthouse steps. They were there to listen to speakers looking to form a branch of a workingmen's organization to be called the Industrial Legion and seeking to advance the idea of a protest march, like Coxey's, to the nation's capital. The Industrial Legion was an idea of radical Populists, mainly miners, formed after the election of 1892 to promote the principles of the Omaha Platform. Presiding over that initial meeting was William Hogan, a 35-year-old, Shakespeare-quoting teamster recently laid off from William A. Clark's Moulton mine. The men elected Hogan as their leader and immediately began to make preparations for a march to Washington. Although the Hoganites sympathized with Jacob Coxey's general program of public works, their primary demand was for the government to restore the free coinage of silver. The "army" continued to hold mass meetings, drilled, and paraded carrying banners that read: "Gold at a Premium—Labor Pauperized" and "Free Coinage at 16 to 1." Meanwhile, as sympathizers donated supplies for the upcoming journey, two elected representatives from Hogan's army met with the Butte mayor and Silver Bow County commissioners to request train transportation east.

The rub in this endeavor, as in every other spontaneous march of an industrial army, was the railroad, in this case the Northern Pacific, and whether it would be willing to cooperate. As Butte's jobless army quickly discovered, the railroad refused to offer them any assistance. After several days of waiting for the company to reconsider, Hogan's impatient followers marched to the Northern Pacific freight yards, took over a number of empty boxcars and set up their camp. Fearing that the men might seek to hijack a train, Northern Pacific officials ordered that all freight trains be rerouted through Helena and demanded that local law enforcement move to clear the rail yards at Butte.

At this point, J.D. Finn, Northern Pacific's superintendent for the Montana division, decided to travel to Butte to assess the volatile situation. He also contacted Montana Governor John E. Rickards to ascertain what his position was regarding the occupied train yards. Rickards responded that his direct involvement was not necessary and reminded Finn that as his railroad was currently in receivership (seeking bankruptcy protection as a result of the depression) its property was currently under the protection of the federal courts. Seeing no other alternative, Finn turned to the courts and applied to Montana's federal judge Hiram Knowles for legal intervention. Knowles quickly granted an injunction and instructed U.S. Marshal William McDermott to serve the court's order and remove Hogan's men from Northern Pacific's property. Anyone found in noncompliance would be subject to arrest for contempt of court. Anticipating popular resistance in Butte, McDermott wired U.S. Attorney General Richard Olney asking for permission to hire extra deputies: "Public sympathy strongly in their favor.... Am I authorized to employ a great many deputies at large pay? Excitement runs high and I request some positive instructions by wire and will obey to the letter."[5] McDermott got his request for extra deputies, but for some unexplained reason neglected to have the injunction served in person. Hogan's attorneys would later argue that the failure to complete the injunctive process was tantamount to "implied non-interference"—a sign of tacit approval that should the Hoganites commandeer a train, the railroad would allow it to proceed without obstruction.

Meanwhile, a group of Butte's leading businessmen called on superintendent Finn and convinced him that the best thing to do to defuse the tense situation would be to offer free transportation to the unemployed men seeking to carry their protest to Washington. Finn's bosses in St. Paul, however, rejected the request. Another group headed by copper magnates Marcus Daly and William Clark and other major shippers then published an open letter asking the road what it would cost to ship 500 men as far as St. Paul. Northern Pacific officials again rejected the request. General Superintendent J.W. Kendrick of the Northern Pacific informed them that the issue was not one of revenue. The corporation simply did not want to be responsible for the safety of the men in transit and that to transport them would set a bad precedent—their logic being that to accept 500 riders from Butte would only encourage thousands more unemployed men from Seattle to demand the same thing.

As the town stood at the brink of a violent confrontation, leaders called another mass meeting at the courthouse to brainstorm a way out of the impasse. Three thousand people attended. Out of patience, one angry speaker suggested that the way to break the deadlock was to capture a train. After the meeting, as "General" Hogan and his men

5. Hogan's Montana Army

returned to the Northern Pacific freight yards, the thought of taking bold action continued to resonate. The army could not just sit and wait forever, it needed transportation, or it would never get to Washington.

Finally, on April 24 at 2:00 a.m. a group of 15 of Hogan's men broke into the Northern Pacific roundhouse in Butte. The men, experienced railroaders, rolled out engine 542 and quickly coupled together a train of six empty coal cars to carry the army and a boxcar to haul a week's supply of food. No one sounded any alarm. No marshal and his deputies tried to stop them. With nearly 300 Hoganites on board and a powerful locomotive to propel them, the commandeered train barreled down the track toward Bozeman at speeds approaching 60 miles an hour. The Butte dispatcher telegraphed that he had a "wild train" coming down the line—a warning that all other trains should clear the track. When superintendent Finn, who was in Livingston about

Coxey's Army group. View of group of men with lapel ribbons posed with soldiers before a Northern Pacific box car. Montana Division of Coxey's Army commanded by William Hogan, captured by the 22nd U.S. Infantry at Forsyth, Montana, 1894. L.A. Huffman, Creator, Photo # 981-1121, Montana Historical Society Research Center Photograph Archives, Helena, MT.

25 miles east of Bozeman, received word of the stolen train, he telegraphed the Northern Pacific attorneys in Helena and asked: "Where is the governor? Where is the United States marshal? Where is the Montana militia?" Then, with a note of exasperation, he added, "How in hell do you expect one Irishman to stand off the whole of Coxey's army?"[6]

After a short stop at Logan to connect to the Northern Pacific's mainline and to pick up 50 more recruits, the Hogan express reached Bozeman at 5:30 in the morning (about the time that deputies in Butte noticed that the army had left) where they were met by cheering crowds. Running at full throttle, the Hoganites had covered 95 miles over the Rockies in just under three hours. At that point, Hogan's men "borrowed" a fresh engine, refilled their coal supply, exchanged the six drafty coal cars for seven boxcars, and added on another boxcar full of provisions donated by the local residents. When the engineer who had brought the train from Butte declined to continue beyond that point, Hogan turned the throttle over to a young Irishman by the name of James B. Harmon.

As the train readied to leave Bozeman at shortly after 10 o'clock in the morning, the 400-man army received news that a cave-in blocked the tracks at the Bozeman Pass Tunnel, just a dozen miles ahead. Apparently heavy rains the day before had loosened the bank at that point and triggered a rockslide. Northern Pacific section crews had started to clear the track but were ordered to stop work as a way to halt the captured train. The Hoganites would have to do the work of clearing the debris if they wanted to continue their journey.

Back in Butte, the Northern Pacific readied a special train comprised of an engine and two cabooses to carry some 80 deputies (locals regarded them as nothing more than mercenaries) under the command of Deputy Marshal M.J. Haley[7] in pursuit of the train "hijackers." At the last minute, 15 of the hastily recruited deputies jumped off the train, deciding that a high-speed train pursuit might be a bit too dangerous. By the time the posse steamed out of Butte at about six in the evening, they were roughly 15 hours behind the train bandits. Meanwhile, Judge Knowles in Helena wired Attorney General Richard Olney to keep him apprised of the situation.

When Hogan's army reached the mile-long tunnel, they sent the locomotive and tender along with a group of about 20 men into the tunnel to investigate the extent of the slide. What they saw was that

5. Hogan's Montana Army

about 25 feet of track lay buried beneath 30 cubic yards of mud, rock, and fallen trees near the eastern portal of the tunnel. Complicating their situation, it looked like an overhanging bank was about to collapse as well. The army had neglected to bring tools with them, but after a search of the slide area discovered equipment (15 shovels and 2 axes) that had been hidden by the section gang. Working in alternating groups of 15 men, the army worked furiously to clear the track. But after nearly six hours of toil and new debris constantly inhibiting their progress, it began to look like the train carrying the posse might catch up with them after all. At that point, engineer Harmon took the initiative, backed the train away from the mud and debris, got up a head of steam, and blasted into the tunnel using the cowcatcher to break through the muddy impasse. When the drive wheels began to slip, Harmon pulled the lever that spilled sand onto the rails for traction. Successful, 300 cheering men climbed back on board and resumed their journey.

At five o'clock that afternoon, the Hogan special rolled into Livingstone, a town of 2,800 inhabitants, where it was again met by an enthusiastic crowd of sympathizers. At the train depot, William Cunningham, a Hogan "lieutenant" and former president of the Butte Miners' Union who was known for his oratorical prowess, climbed atop a boxcar to give the crowd a rousing speech. Local residents again responded with donations of food, clothing and blankets. Looking to make up for lost time, the army again exchanged engines, added four more boxcars and a tool car that they expropriated from the Northern Pacific shops, and continued east.

Any thought that Northern Pacific officials had tacitly agreed not to interfere with the wild train was put to rest when Hoganites, who had been following the news over the telegraph, learned that superintendent Finn had initiated his own delaying tactics. Staying ahead of the hijacked train, Finn ordered crews to dynamite a bluff above the tracks near Greycliff in an effort to spread more debris on the track and slow the train, and then to spike switches at Reed Point and Columbus to force the wild train onto a sidetrack and further delay its progress. This first ploy, however, proved to be only a minor hinderance as the men quickly cleared the rocks from the track. Before proceeding, they piled boulders back on the track hoping to slow the deputies who were rapidly gaining on them in the pursuit train. But Finn proved persistent, telegraphing ahead to Yellowstone County

"Work, give us work"

Sheriff James Ramsey asking him to stop Hogan's army at Billings. Because Finn had earlier lost an election to Ramsey, the deputy who received the wire thought it was a prank and ignored it.

For their part, the Hoganites tried to remain vigilant and posted a lookout atop the rear car to watch for any sign of Haley and his posse. But the lack of water for the engine was becoming a real problem. Between Greycliff and Columbus, the train had to slow to a crawl. Then, at about an hour after midnight on April 25, the Hogan special was forced to come to a full stop. It looked like it might not make it to the next water tank. Unhooking the boxcars, the engineer ran the engine and tender down the track looking for a water tank and luckily found one only a mile ahead. But, when they lowered the downspout to fill the tender, they found it to be empty. Finn's men had reached it first and drained it dry. Spying a pool of water nearby, the army formed a bucket brigade and were able to add a small amount of water to the boiler. Once recoupled to the boxcars, the wild train crawled along at a slow pace. Hogan's men knew that unless they found water, the game was up.

The army had hardly gotten underway when the rear lookout sighted a headlamp on the track about a mile back. Thinking quickly, Hogan spied a bridge ahead and ordered his engineer to stop the train in the middle of the span. If they had to stand and fight, the steep embankments leading up to the bridge would make it difficult for pursuers to capture them from the rear, while the fast-moving Yellowstone River made an approach from any other direction impossible. As the deputies cautiously approached the bridge with rifles drawn, Marshal Haley stepped forward and ordered Hogan to back the train off the bridge and surrender. If he refused, his men would open fire. At that point, a group of Hogan's men moved into the beam of light from the pursuing locomotive as it reflected off the rear boxcar, unfurled both the U.S. flag and the banner of the Butte Miners' Union, and dared the deputies to shoot. Having already been labeled Pinkertons and mercenaries for even pursuing the hijackers in the first place, the posse hesitated. Realizing that firing on unemployed miners holding the flag and representing the powerful miners' union would truly make them marked men in the state, the deputies retreated. Elated with their "victory," the Hoganites reboarded their train and proceeded. Uncertain what to do next, the pursuit train continued to follow but at a cautious distance.

5. Hogan's Montana Army

At Columbus, an announcement that the Butte contingent of Coxey's army with 648 men would arrive in the evening of April 28 created a great deal of excitement. But because the army had trouble finding enough water to fill their tank, the train did not arrive until the next morning. Many residents had waited up all night expecting the train to arrive at any hour. As the train pulled in to the station with flags flying, the entire population of the town gave them cheer after cheer. The train stopped at the water tank but had only been there a few minutes when the special train carrying the 65 deputies pulled in behind them.

At that point, William Cunningham again stepped forward to denounce the armed thugs who had been sent from Butte to arrest them and to restate their refusal to be taken in by a band of hired ruffians. He said that an offer had been made to the officials of the Northern Pacific to pay for their transportation to St. Paul, but the railroad had refused. He closed by saying that the Hoganites were honest workingmen on a peaceful mission on behalf of the unemployed in the country. Before he had finished, the deputies began running toward the engine with guns drawn hoping to stop the progress of the hijacked train. But in that moment before excitement turned to riot, the engineer opened the throttle and went speeding down the track having outwitted the deputies once again.

The wild train rolled into Billings around 11 o'clock. Once again town officials and a cheering crowd of nearly 500 turned out to greet the men with 400 pounds of beef, 250 loaves of bread, and 400 pounds of potatoes. Perhaps as many as 100 volunteered to join the industrials. As the Hoganites accepted the town's hospitality, no one noticed that about a dozen deputies from the pursuit train had quietly slipped into town and blended in with the gathering of well-wishers. Two of the deputies climbed onto the cab of the locomotive and pointed their guns at Hogan. They told him to surrender, or they would shoot. When Hogan reportedly told them to "shoot and be damned," pandemonium broke out.[8] At that frantic moment, a few of the unseasoned and ill-trained deputies panicked and started to discharge their weapons into the crowd. Several people were wounded in the melee while Charles Hardy, a local tinsmith who happened to be standing on the platform, was killed. Enraged townspeople then picked up rocks, bricks, pieces of iron or anything else within reach and began to pelt the deputies. Others in the crowd disarmed the deputies and smashed their rifles on the rails. Fearing for their lives, some of the deputies took refuge in the Northern Pacific roundhouse, while others fled back to their train. The local sheriff and his men arrested 10 of the deputies for the fatal shooting of Charles Hardy.

When news reached Butte later that day, a crowd of sympathizers held a mass protest meeting at the courthouse. Back in Billings, the *Weekly Gazette* commented that it came as a surprise that the town's inhabitants did not rise "*en masse* and crucify every slinking cur of a deputy implicated in the outrage." Speaking for many, the newspaper's editors went on to describe the federal deputies as "the scum of the great mining camp [Butte], mercenary ruffians who would assassinate their brothers if there was a dollar in it." In similar fashion, the *Butte Bystander*, a Populist weekly, editorialized: "Marshal McDermott has been severely criticized for selecting his deputy marshals ... from the lowest and most worthless class in the city ... composed almost entirely of pimps, prize fighters, rounders, ex-convicts, professional beats, and general all-around worthless characters."[9]

President Grover Cleveland, ca. 1896. After Coxey's 500-man march to the capitol grounds on May 1, 1894, and the fear that thousands more might try to join them, President Cleveland realized that he needed to take preventive action. Giving free rein to his chief law enforcement officer, Attorney General Richard Olney used the courts and the military to stop the Coxeyites. Library of Congress, Prints & Photographs Division.

With a renewed sense of urgency supporters coupled a fresh locomotive to the train and replenished the coal supply. When it was discovered that the water tanks had again been emptied at Billings, local firemen used their pumper and hose to refill the tender. As the hijackers sped east toward Miles City and the Dakota border (the trouble at Billings had given them a fresh head start), Finn's men continued to drain the railroad's water tanks along the line. This time, however, the Hoganites were better prepared, having procured a long hose which they could now use as a siphon to refill their tank from the creeks that flowed under the tracks. The contest would continue.

At this juncture, Governor Rickards wired President Grover Cleveland asking for assistance. The governor noted that the state's militiamen were openly in support of Hogan's army, and that it would be "impossible" "for the state militia to overtake" the hijacked train.[10] As a result, he asked the president to send federal troops to intercept, arrest, and detain the "Coxeyites" for violating previous orders of the federal court. After conferring with Attorney General Olney and General J.M. Schofield, commanding general of the U.S. Army, he had Schofield order Lieutenant Colonel John H. Page at Fort Keough (near Miles City) to halt the advance of Hogan's army.

When the regiment received its orders, rumors quickly circulated that the train hijackers were fully armed desperados, and that they had murdered and robbed peaceful citizens. Colonel Page, in cooperation with superintendent Finn, immediately loaded six companies of the 22nd infantry and a Gatling gun onto a special train that would take them to Forsyth. As historian Philip Dray summed up the moment, "such was the absurd character of the struggle for worker's rights in America—desperate men on a hijacked train determined to cross the country to petition Congress for relief, and heavily armed soldiers ... prepared to shoot and kill their fellow citizens, if need be."[11] Hogan, anticipating a possible confrontation with the military, telegraphed ahead that, if forced into a confrontation with federal troops, his men would offer no resistance.

Sometime after 10:00 in the evening of April 25, the Hoganites arrived at Forsyth in eastern Montana, about 45 miles west of Miles City, intending to remain there for most of the night. As expected, superintendent Finn's crews had spiked the switches open and removed the throttles from every engine in the roundhouse. Around midnight, however, the decision was made to continue, and the engineer was told to fire up a new engine from the roundhouse. As he did so about 50 of the men were able to intimidate the roundhouse foreman into finding them a replacement throttle. No one in camp realized that a long train of infantrymen was approaching at a high rate of speed. The arrival of the troops proceeded so quietly that Hogan and

"Work, give us work"

his men were taken completely by surprise. Although about 250 Hoganites managed to escape in the dark, the troops ultimately captured about 330 unarmed men who offered no resistance whatsoever. After 340 miles, Montana's great 48-hour locomotive chase was over.

The next problem facing federal authorities was what to do with 300 prisoners who had by this time become folk heroes in Montana. Judge Knowles wanted only to bring the ringleaders to trial and release the others, but railroad officials insisted that all the prisoners be tried. When railroad officials vetoed the idea of returning the prisoners to volatile Butte for their day in court, Judge Knowles acquiesced and had General Hogan and his men transported to Helena instead. It was obvious to most observers that few Montanans really desired to see the entire army imprisoned. As the *Anaconda Standard* commented: "It is admitted on all hands that it will be impossible to find a jury in Montana to convict these men whose only crime has been to help themselves to box cars."[12] Although there currently was no federal law that made train hijacking a crime, the participants could be tried for contempt of court. In such legal proceedings, no jury was required.

Due to their large number, the men were placed in a camp at the county fairgrounds where they were guarded by 110 soldiers. It took two weeks for the trial to get underway and Judge Knowles, as expected, found all the Hoganites guilty of violating the court's injunction. William Hogan, as ringleader, received a six-month sentence in the Lewis and Clark County jail, while his engineer and fireman and about 40 other "officers" earned 30-day terms. The remaining 275 men were allowed to go free after agreeing to respect Northern Pacific property in the future. Surprisingly, about 200 of the freed Hoganites chose to remain in Helena. They set up a new camp at the fairgrounds and the good people of Helena continued to supply them with food, clothing, and blankets. The men seemed to be determined to continue their protest march to Washington. Equally eager to see the men move on were Helena's city officials.

The idea finally concocted by Helena Mayor John C. Curtin and the local city council was to provide William Sprague, an experienced boat-builder, with a letter of credit that would be sent to Fort Benton, the terminus of former steamboat navigation on the Missouri River, to purchase building materials for the construction of boats. At that location, Sprague would direct the Hoganites, mostly metal miners, in the construction of flatboats on which they would float, row, and sail down the Missouri River. The plan was for the men to continue by

5. Hogan's Montana Army

Montana Division of Coxey's Army commanded by William Hogan at railroad tracks in Forsyth, Montana, after being captured by the 22nd U.S. Infantry, April 26, 1894. Photograph shows Northern Pacific Railway box cars in the background. Some of the men hold American flags. L.A. Huffman, Creator, Collection # 981-801, Montana Historical Society Research Center Photograph Archives, Helena, MT.

water transport to the mouth of the Ohio River, hire a steamer from there to Pittsburgh, and then seek rail transportation to Washington. The "Helena Relief Committee for Coxeyites" would purchase supplies for the trip and provide wagons to transport them to Fort Benton. The city also agreed to pay the men's rail fare to Fort Benton.

The idea of traveling down the river rekindled memories of an earlier time when first frontier explorers and then early entrepreneurs had travelled up the Missouri River to Fort Benton. The town was situated at the head of steamer navigation up-river and for 30 years or so operated as the supply and transportation hub for the northern plains and northern Rockies. But the coming of the railroad changed that dynamic and drained the upper river of its commerce. When the last steamboat arrived at Fort Benton in 1891, it signaled the end of an era. The arrival of the unemployed Hoganites must have also been a reminder of economic misfortune.

After about a week, the Hoganites had managed to construct a fleet of 10 homemade pine scows. Nine of the boats measured approximately 10 feet wide and 40 feet long. The fleet's flagship was 20 feet longer and also served as a cook boat complete with a brick oven for baking bread (bakers working in shifts normally made 300 to 600 loaves a day) and carried the army's provisions. Each craft had a rudder for steering and four oars (six for the flagship). In addition to the flagship *Montana*, the *Hogan*, and the *Free Silver*, the other boats carried the names of the seven Montana towns that had assisted the army on its journey. On the sides of one boat the crew painted symbols of silver dollars while the oars bore the free-silver call of 16 to 1. Banners carried the slogans "In Congress We Trusted," "We Come in Peace," and "Going to Meet Grover." Fort Benton residents donated American flags and red, white, and blue bunting for the crews to decorate their craft. After some basic training in river navigation, and a farewell parade through Fort Benton, roughly 340 inexperienced "sailors" set off on June 5, 1894, for what would be a two-month, 2,000-mile river journey.

The water journey proved difficult from the very beginning. Gale-force winds roiled the waters of the Missouri (swollen by the heavy spring runoff) on launch day and delayed the departure for hours. After waiting for the winds to diminish, the fleet finally shoved off in the late afternoon. But the river's powerful current frequently spun the boats around, demonstrating how difficult it would be to control them. Not many in the press gave the Hoganites much of a chance. As the *Butte Miner* pessimistically editorialized: "If the Coxey navy makes its trip on the treacherous Missouri without drowning half its men, it will be in luck. Navigation on the wicked old stream is none-too-safe even with the best of craft, but to attempt the journey in weak and hurriedly constructed boats is to invite disaster."[13] The comment from the *Butte Miner* came just two days after the news wire reported that a number of Colorado Coxeyites had drown attempting a similar boating expedition on the swirling, rain-swollen waters of the South Platte River near Denver. As the crews adjusted to the river, they were able to log 30 miles in just four hours. Traveling through one of the most isolated sections of the American West, the intrepid sailors would not see a town of any size again until they reached Williston, North Dakota, several days downriver.

Crews normally spent 16 hours on the river, usually starting around four o'clock in the morning and stopping at eight o'clock at

5. Hogan's Montana Army

night. Sailors manned the oars in four-hour shifts and alternated between half an hour on the oars and half an hour doing some other task. The expedition obviously demanded discipline, cooperation, and hard work. The men on board occasionally raised their square topsails in an attempt to increase speed, but the wind only rarely cooperated. In the evening the men tied up for the night, ate dinner, and then slept on the riverbank. Early in their journey the men elected an interim leader until Hogan could be released from jail to join them. Their choice was John Edwards, a 36-year-old unemployed metal miner who had come west 20 years earlier in search of gold and silver. Edwards had been with the army since Butte.

A week out of Fort Benton, after fighting headwinds and challenging rapids, the navy rowed into Williston. The sailors actually did not know what to expect in the way of a greeting from townspeople who were not Montanans. Rumors had spread that the sailors intended to leave the river at that point and commandeer another Northern Pacific train on the main track that paralleled the river. Worried that the rumors might be true, Northern Pacific officials hired Indian scouts to warn them of the navy's approach. The company then requested the commander at nearby Fort Buford to send three companies of troops to guard the railroad's property. When that request was denied, Northern Pacific officials persuaded the sheriff in Williston to swear in 50 extra deputies. But once the men had a chance to talk to the deputies and defuse any alarm, the townspeople welcomed them, contributing tobacco, pipes, and several new recruits.

The next stop on their journey was Bismarck, which the army reached on June 14. Again, the men worried about how they might be received and whether they would be able to replenish their dwindling food supply. But when they reached the North Dakota capital, the townspeople gave them a boisterous welcome. Crowds from Bismarck as well as from Mandan across the river lined both banks and cheered the new arrivals. Requests for provisions to the Bismarck City Council were rejected, however, as local officials claimed they were having difficulty supporting their own unemployed citizens. Local sympathizers did donate a considerable supply of provisions, but not nearly enough to carry the navy to Pierre, South Dakota, the next town of significant size on their route.

Just when it looked like all might be lost, an appeal to supporters back in Butte secured a check for $100, enough to purchase additional supplies to enable the navy to reach the South Dakota capital. The emergency relief had actually come from a local unit in Butte called a "home guard." Because something like two-thirds of the men in Hogan's army were married and many had children, they could not have joined the expedition to Washington without having local supporters back home helping to take care of their families. In tough spots, like the one that confronted the men in Bismarck, the home guard could be appealed to for financial assistance. All of the major, organized industrial armies of the unemployed in 1894 had a home guard system in place.

After spending three days in Bismarck, the navy, now down to 247 men, raised their flags, unfurled their banners, lifted their sails into a stiff breeze, and headed down river. For most of the men, the trip was not unlike a chapter out of a Mark Twain novel. Adopting the carefree manner of rivermen, some read books, others played cards, fished, or sang free-silver songs as they drifted along. In an attempt to find some relief from the constant exposure to sun, the men erected canopies from strips of tenting, blankets, and old clothes. Their primary worry, however, was always food. Fortunately, there were a number of small towns along the river in South Dakota that, for the most part, were very generous in their assistance. In Pierre, a town of 3,500 people, officials contributed beef, bacon, flour, coffee, rice, and salt. In the small village of Chamberlain, townsfolk donated 500 pounds of flour, 200 pounds of bacon, 200 pounds of beef, 100 pounds of beans, 50 pounds of coffee, 40 pounds of rice, and 2 pounds of hops which was needed for baking. That generous contribution was enough for a two-day supply of food for the men. When a storm badly damaged the fleet's oven, folks in Yankton donated 100 bricks, a stovepipe, and a barrel of mortar to repair it, along with a restocked commissary and a load of clothes and old shoes. They also added a bottle of liniment.

After a brief stop in Sioux City, Iowa, where police met them with two wagon loads of food but also with a brusque order to move on, the Hoganites finally neared Omaha. The city had a population of 140,000, which was larger than the entire state of Montana at the time. Eager to arrive in the city that had shown such generosity to Kelly's army earlier, the voyagers rowed hard and neared their destination at dusk, hours earlier than expected. But as the navy neared what they hoped was a landing, they failed to notice the East Omaha bridge in the darkness. Suddenly someone on the shore yelled, "turn to the

5. Hogan's Montana Army

right, or you'll upset." At that moment the current caught one of the boats broadside, slammed it against a bridge abutment, and capsized it. The accident tossed 17 men into the river. Six found handholds on the pier and safety, but the rest of the crew struggled for survival in the murky water. Although other crewmen and local police ultimately rescued all the men, it was a most unfortunate turn of events. Making matters worse, their early arrival had caught local supporters off guard (they expected the navy to arrive the following morning). As a result, the men were taken to an ill-chosen camping spot that was bordered by a railroad bridge, a garbage dump, and a municipal sewer.

Things did improve the following day, however, when Omaha's Central Labor Council held a public rally to show the city's support. The labor council collected provisions (potatoes, onions, eggs, sugar, coffee, and flour) from local businessmen, while county commissioners added $225 worth of supplies (including 100 bars of soap) and city commissioners donated $53 in cash. Local merchants also got in the spirit of things and provided new bunting to decorate the fleet for the Fourth of July. Each member of the army was also presented with a badge which bore the inscription: "Hogan's Industrial Army of Butte City, Montana."

Although Omaha's labor unions rallied to provide the men with some badly needed supplies, the Hoganites were learning that in towns where other industrial armies had preceded them the novelty of their quest had reached diminishing returns. And the need for foodstuffs was increasing. Four boatloads of Coxeyites joined Hogan's navy at Plattsmouth, Nebraska. These were remnants of an ill-fated Colorado army and included eight survivors of Scheffler's Portland army that had been arrested by soldiers in Wyoming. This change in attitude would certainly become evident in southern states like Missouri and others along the Ohio River Valley that had always regarded the armies of northern vagabonds with suspicion.

When the flotilla reached Leavenworth, Kansas, on July 11, the men got a good look at shifting popular attitudes for the first time. Although the town's Populist police force allowed Edwards and other leaders to speak in the town square, only about 75 of the town's inhabitants turned out to hear an oration about their reform mission. At that point, Edwards lost his temper and criticized the community, telling them that they were slaves for taking so little interest in politics. For this scolding, the army received only 87 cents when they passed the collection hat. Complicating matters for the Hoganites was the decline in press coverage. By the time the army left Omaha, news dispatches had shifted to coverage of the Pullman strike that had tied up railway traffic radiating out of Chicago and away from the industrial army movement. The violent and disruptive nature of that strike also had the impact of alarming rural people and turning them against the working class in general.

Hogan's navy continued to receive the cold shoulder when they reached other major stops in Missouri. At Kansas City, Mayor Webster Davis refused to permit the men to land within the city limits and stationed mounted police along the waterfront to enforce his order. When the men complained after receiving only a meager handout from the city (flour, bread, and coffee that amounted to enough for one meal), police warned them that they would be arrested for vagrancy and sent to the workhouse if they were caught inside city limits. At Jefferson City the story was the same as the mayor and city council donated only a small amount of flour, bacon, and bread. By the time the men arrived at St. Louis during the final week of July, they were half-starved and demoralized. The only organized group to offer them any help was the small Socialist Labor Party which held a public rally that netted the army $11.80. When other donations totaled only two dozen loaves of bread and a few bundles of clothes, it looked like the great adventure had reached its end.

After 60 days on the river and having traveled 2,670 miles, the movement ended at its final encampment at Carondelet on the south side of the city. After waiting hopelessly for several days for additional donations to continue their journey, the men convened a council to discuss their next move. The decision was finally made to let the crew of each boat make their own future plans. Five of the crews voted to continue down the Mississippi River to Cairo or New Orleans and then travel from there by land to Washington. The others agreed to sell their boats, divide the money, and go their own way. The men also agreed to divide the $435 in the company's treasury (mostly money that had been donated by an anonymous Iowa philanthropist). At that point, the men sent J.D. Sullivan (the navy's treasurer), John Edwards, and Edward H. Hogan (no relation to William) to town to get the cash. They never returned.

Betrayed and abandoned by their leaders, the navy broke up. A few decided to head down the Mississippi. Others continued east

5. Hogan's Montana Army

toward Washington. Most of the men apparently decided to return to Montana, hopping boxcars as their mode of transportation. The day after the theft of the navy's treasury, police arrested Edward Hogan for public drunkenness. While in jail, he confessed to having taken $145 of the navy's money (his portion of the split). As for the other traitors, Sullivan, he said, had headed for Denver, while Edwards had fled to another western city. As for William Hogan, Judge Knowles finally released him from jail after serving half of his six-month sentence, aided by a petition signed by 10,000 of Butte's citizens.

6

Scheffler's Portland Army

The Pacific Northwest in the early 1890s was a region dominated by a few industries—mining, lumbering, and agriculture—that were especially prone to market fluctuations and to the dictates of the seasons. As a result, thousands of workers might be drawn to one job market when demand for labor was high, only to be released when that demand abruptly dropped off. When this happened, the unemployed worker would often head to the region's major urban centers looking for temporary employment or assistance from charities that might get them through a difficult time. In these urban centers, the seasonally unemployed would come into contact with the underemployed laboring masses that were already there and what might be called the itinerant "tramp" who often drifted from place to place. But the lines differentiating the temporarily unemployed from those who lived a truly transient existence on the margins of society were often blurred. As a result, many charity administrators and municipal officials often employed the term "tramp" to deny charity to all itinerants.

Portland, Oregon, was one urban center that had a formal charity network in place. But rather than viewing unemployment as a byproduct of the region's economic structure, charity workers, reformers, and municipal authorities commonly equated unemployment with moral failings—the genuine desire of some to avoid work and to dissipate their limited funds in brothels and saloons. This attitude generated an ongoing discussion about who was entitled to relief and allowed charity workers to separate a city's married, permanent residents (regarded as worthy applicants for assistance) from young, single, unemployed male workers who were often considered to be part of the "vagrant horde."[1] During hard times, like the depression that began in 1893, the anxiety of the residents of a city like Portland regarding the "tramp

6. Scheffler's Portland Army

menace" grew as the numbers of unemployed men wandering the city's streets increased, even though many of those newly unemployed were workers from the skilled trades and crafts.

The growing dilemma for people like Thomas Nelson Strong, the president of the City Board of Charities in Portland (CBC), was how to aid the "deserving" who needed assistance without encouraging the "undeserving" to continue to live a life of dependence that, it was believed, would destroy their self-respect. For others, like Arthur J. Brown, head of the First Presbyterian Church of Portland, the greater fear was that Portland might become a "rendezvous for all the shiftless and fraudulent of the whole Northwest, who will eagerly flock to places which seem to promise a maximum of relief with a minimum of investigation."[2]

When Coxey armies of unemployed laborers began to form across the West in the spring of 1894 with the intention of marching on Washington, many of the movement's supporters were itinerants who had migrated to the region's urban centers in search of a job. As the Coxey movement gained momentum on the West Coast, the Portland press turned more hostile and joined municipal officials in dismissing the movement as a collection of tramps and vagabonds. The *Evening Telegram* proclaimed that the Coxey movement was "largely comprised of tramps and hobos," constituted nothing more than a "mobilization of bandits," and represented "a menace to law and order." The *Oregonian*, the city's dominant newspaper under the conservative direction of Harvey W. Scott, found the movement "grotesque in the extreme ... made up of tramps and hobos, whose only anxiety was to evade police and avoid the work offered them."[3] At a time when many middle-class Americans equated the working classes in general and labor unions in particular with social agitation and possibly social revolution, the rise of industrial armies only heightened those fears.

Some Portland officials and newspaper editors tried to blame neighboring California for exacerbating the problem by encouraging their unemployed workers to head north. Encouraged or not, the first Coxey army in Oregon actually did come from California. This group, comprised of some 50 men organized in San Francisco in early April 1894 by Charles E. Kain, originally planned to travel through Oregon to Seattle where they intended to link up with a similar contingent of Coxeyites before heading east. Moving north on Southern Pacific freight cars, the army passed through Ashland, Roseburg, Cottage

"Work, give us work"

Grove, and Salem where a local newspaper described the men as "quite respectable; they look to be just what they claim—hard-working men in search of work."[4] Picking up a few recruits along the way, the group numbered close to 60 by the time it reached Portland. Upon arrival, however, they received word that the Seattle industrials had already started their march to the nation's capital. No longer motivated to move north, Captain Kain chose to keep his men in Portland while he tried to arrange for transportation to the east.

Kain's men proceeded to the East Side flats near Sullivan's gulch where they immediately raised the American flag and set to the task of establishing a well-ordered camp. Captain Kain and a few other leaders soon met with Mayor Eugene Shelby, Chief of Police Charles H. Hunt, and CBC President Strong who offered to provide the men with four meals if they would then leave town. After initially maligning the men as a "regiment of dirty vagrants," the mayor offered the men work, but not the type they wanted. The mayor proposed that the men could be put to work breaking rock for a downtown street repair project and that in return for six hours of work the city would provide vouchers for two meals and one lodging. This work-relief project was reluctantly agreed to by CBC President Strong, who commented: "We can furnish help and work to worthy, industrious men who have families to support, but we are not in favor of feeding an organized, crack regiment of dirty vagrants roaming aimlessly from one place to another."

The suggestion only angered Captain Kain, who responded: "We are all honest workingmen—not vagrants. We are out of work. We don't want any man to follow us if he can get work at living wages." As historian Dmitri Palmateer noted, to Kain, "nonremunerative or low-paying jobs—especially chopping wood, breaking rock, and other jobs provided by charities—perpetuated itinerants' marginalized status."[5] Kain told Strong, "We have been living all winter on Salvation Army soup tickets; we are tired of that. We want work—work, sir at honest wages—at wages on which we can support a family."[6] The message from Captain Kain was clear. The unemployed men in his group were victims of economic circumstance, and, acknowledging their identity as productive laborers, honest workingmen, not tramps. When asked by Strong why he was in Portland, Kain replied that his men were heading to Washington "for the purpose of showing the national authorities the actual condition of the unemployed in this country." "We are starving in a land of plenty! Why?"[7] The following

6. Scheffler's Portland Army

day Kain accepted a job in his trade, house painting, and left the army he had helped organize.

Kain's replacement was Jack Short, also an original organizer of the group, who was described as an honest looking fellow, but one who demonstrated little ability as a leader. When Captain Short asked city officials for additional provisions (the men had been given 150 pounds of meat, 3 sacks of potatoes, 10 pounds of coffee, and 100 loaves of bread) while the army continued to negotiate for rail transportation, he was turned down. The *Oregonian* agreed completely with the decision: "Neither the mayor nor the city council has any legal right to feed tramps.... The chief of police has no right to buy bread, beef and coffee for free distribution among an army of sturdy beggars." Editorially, the *Oregonian* argued that the industrial army was concealing its "bare indecency of beggary" behind the "pretense of political agitation."[8] City leaders, however, perceived of a larger problem and feared that more cooperation would only establish a bad precedent and encourage additional armies to come into the city. City officials had, in fact, received a report that another army of 600 men was about to leave Oakland, California, and head north. When appeals to Governor Sylvester Pennoyer for assistance in securing transportation on the Northern Pacific failed, the army found itself in a difficult situation.

In the meantime, a local group in Portland with connections to the Central Labor Council, decided to form its own army. J.B. Smith, apparently an experienced labor organizer, came up from San Francisco to lead the organizing effort. Leaders of this new organization, selected by Smith, held a secret meeting in the Central Labor Council Hall and drafted a program of action. The plan was to organize 12 companies of 60 men. On April 19, 400 local recruits held a public meeting at the Third Street plaza where leaders gave speeches explaining the purpose of the movement—in essence a living protest to present conditions, and a request for government action during moments of economic distress to provide employment to willing workers. Meanwhile, organizers set up a central recruiting station on the sidewalk at the northeast corner of Third and Burnside streets. Each new recruit was given a small piece of red, white, and blue ribbon and a card inscribed with the number of his company and regiment. Two days after the mass rally in the plaza, J.B. Smith resigned his leadership position, stepping aside for S.L. Scheffler,[9] an unemployed stonemason by trade, who assumed command of the group.

"Work, give us work"

The make-up of the nearly 500-man army undoubtedly surprised many. According to Anton Conrad, a tinsmith who left the army because he found work at his trade in Portland, its ranks included 14 watchmakers and jewelers, 37 clerks and bookkeepers, 40 machinists, twelve engineers, 8 shoemakers, 7 tailors, 9 bakers, 11 professional cooks, 25 waiters, 3 bookbinders, and 13 shopkeepers. He also noted that "there are more good men in the industrial regiment of Portland than any outsider would believe. Most of those with whom I became intimate were like myself, victims of unfortunate circumstances, who never looked forward to such hard times in this country as we are having."[10] The goals of this new body were simply stated and again expressed the regional orientation of those involved. As one official put it: "What we want is plenty of work and free silver. If we get the latter, the former will come without the bidding."[11]

When the two groups of industrials agreed to merge under Scheffler's command as the Portland army, they faced the cold realization that the Union Pacific and Northern Pacific railroads (the lines linking Portland with Omaha and Kansas City) were not as cooperative as the Southern Pacific had been. Unable to gain access to a train in Portland, the combined army of more than 500 men left the city on April 25, sent off by a crowd of over 500 supporters. Marching eastward along the Union Pacific line, the army reached Troutdale, about 15 miles up the Columbia River, that night. When the army reached the small town, a railroad stopping point and a likely spot to catch a passing freight train, they received a hearty welcome from the local residents. The Union Meat Company donated meat, local merchants contributed flour and potatoes, and town officials allowed the men the use of a livery stable and some vacant buildings for quarters. The following day, members of the army made their first bold move and occupied the local telegraph office and train depot so that they might track train movements and watch for a likely freight to hop. Although the Coxeyites in the telegraph office continued to relay all messages and conduct business in a responsible manner, one loyal employee slipped away to a nearby town and notified Union Pacific officials of the takeover.

Protesting the invasion of their property in Troutdale, Union Pacific officials were able to get Judge Charles B. Bellinger to issue an injunction to have the men cease their trespass on company property. U.S. Marshal Henry C. Grady was given the order to assemble his deputies and proceed to Troutdale to serve the injunction. Responding

6. Scheffler's Portland Army

to the court's order, the Coxeyites quietly vacated the property. But after Grady and his men had returned to Portland, they disregarded the injunction and reoccupied the train depot. Feeling that he had been left in the lurch, Sheriff Penumbra Kelly wired Governor Pennoyer requesting that he send the state militia to Troutdale to protect private property, specifically that of the Union Meat Company which felt that its supply of meat might be confiscated by the army.

Governor Pennoyer, currently running for the U.S. Senate as a Populist and sympathetic to the plight of Portland's industrial army, refused the request. In doing so, he informed Sheriff Kelly that "[t]his is a civil and not a military government, and it is your duty to exercise the civil power to quell any disturbance when it occurs, and not to call upon the militia before it occurs."[12] Upon hearing of the governor's refusal to send state troops, Marshal Grady decided to assume charge of the situation. He then wired U.S. Attorney General Richard Olney and made the argument that the lack of action by the state necessitated that federal troops be placed on alert.

Marshal Grady's telegram to Attorney General Olney began a process that would become a pattern in future conflicts involving the nation's railroads, the federal government, and the various traveling armies of the unemployed. Olney was a staunch defender of law and order and a former railroad attorney. In addition to advising and defending rail corporations, he sat on the board of directors of several major railroads. As historian

Attorney General Richard Olney, ca. 1913. President Grover Cleveland appointed Olney, a former Boston railroad attorney, to be attorney general in 1893. While in office, Olney utilized the court injunction and the deployment of federal troops to curtail the industrial army movement and break the strike by Pullman workers in 1894. His actions earned him the enmity of labor unions. Wikimedia Commons.

H.W. Brands noted, "By inclination and association, Olney saw the world much as the railroad managers did."[13] It was easy for him to envision thousands of unemployed workers marauding across the country, hijacking trains, and headed down a slippery slope toward anarchy.

Although it was understood that train theft was normally considered to be a state rather than a federal crime, most railroads (the Great Northern was the lone exception) west of the Mississippi River were in federal receivership as a result of the depression. Looking to capitalize on this unique situation, Olney initially sought to employ U.S. marshals to arrest members of the industrial armies that commandeered trains for violating federal court orders that guaranteed unobstructed operation of railroads that were vital to national security. But asking a force of U.S. marshals to arrest and physically restrain industrial armies that sometimes numbered more than 1,000 men proved to be a problem. Local and state law enforcement personnel and U.S. marshals and federal posses simply could not halt train thefts by themselves.

It also became quickly apparent that many citizens and more than a few local authorities sympathized with the industrial armies and refused to interfere with the Coxeyites who passed through their towns. Complicating matters for federal enforcement was the popular perception in the West that railroads had long been symbols of greed, power, and corruption. It was also very expensive to raise and maintain posses whose recruits were often of questionable quality. Olney's only alternative was to arrange federal military intervention.

When an industrial army threatened or seized a train belonging to a railroad in federal receivership, Olney could seek an injunction from the nearest federal judge forbidding such action. If an industrial army refused to abide by the court's order, which most did, federal marshals would be asked to make a pro forma attempt to arrest the leaders for contempt of court. If that attempt failed, for any of a variety of reasons mentioned above, Olney could then request that President Grover Cleveland order Secretary of War Daniel S. Lamont to intervene with troops under the authority of RS 5298 to "enforce the faithful execution of the laws of the United States ... in whatever State or Territory thereof the laws of the United States may be forcibly opposed, or the execution thereof forcibly obstructed."[14] The task of enforcing the federal injunction would then fall to the Commanding

General of the U.S. Army, John M. Schofield, who would then send instructions to the appropriate departmental (regional) commander under his direction.

Back in Portland, Marshal Grady proceeded to take the next step in the enforcement process. He and his 16 deputies joined with 30 deputies under the command of Portland Chief of Police Hunt and immediately left for Troutdale on an eastbound train. The plan was for this expanded contingent to join Sheriff Kelly's own five-man local police force and evict the industrials from the Union Pacific depot at Troutdale. But when Grady arrived at the scene, he saw that Scheffler's men had already deserted the station and were lined up to march with gear on their backs. It looked like they were preparing to move on. With no property to rescue, and with local residents haranguing him for his unwarranted intervention, Grady had no choice but to back down, withdraw his men, and return to Portland.

Embarrassed by the scene at Troutdale, Grady defended his inability to expel Scheffler's army by claiming that 300 of the 500 men in the army carried weapons. He then concocted a scheme with Union Pacific officials whereby a train of empty box cars would be sent to Troutdale, each car carrying a posted copy of the court's injunction. Knowing that the empty train would be too appealing for the men to resist, he could then maneuver them into violating the law. The plan worked perfectly. After Scheffler's men boarded the train, the engineer immediately side-tracked it, uncoupled the engine from the box cars, and then drove off without them. Having ingeniously placed the Portland army in contempt of court for trespassing on Union Pacific property, Grady then proceeded to wire Attorney General Olney:

> Five hundred men ... have taken possession of freight train of the Union Pacific Railroad at Troutdale, Oregon. Said railroad in the hands of receivers appointed by U.S. courts.... Have no arms for deputies and find the people in sympathy with the men. Am therefore obliged to call on you for U.S. troops.... The situation is critical and the men are desperate. Please advise.[15]

In response, Olney instructed Brigadier General Elwell S. Otis, commander of the Department of the Columbia at Vancouver, Washington, to give Grady as much military support as may be necessary to carry out the order of the U.S. court. Interestingly, Grady's urgent telegram reporting the theft of a train was actually sent when the army was in possession of only a set of box cars that had no locomotive to pull them.

"Work, give us work"

Even though the men had not yet made off with a train, Grady continued to plot. This time he persuaded General Manager E. Dickinson of the Northern Pacific and Superintendent Robert Baxter of the Union Pacific to travel to Troutdale by special train. The train would be disguised as a freight and sent to Troutdale under the pretense of picking up a supply of beef for Portland. Scheffler's men had been informed that the train was coming. When it arrived on April 28, they immediately took possession of the engine. Within 20 minutes they had replaced the company's engineer and fireman with their own men, sidetracked the private car carrying the railroad officials, and coupled the engine to the idle boxcars. With 500 Coxeyites piled into the empty freight cars, the train pulled out of town and began to race down the Columbia River Gorge.

The army had fallen into a trap and all that was left was for Grady to close it. He immediately wired Attorney General Olney and requested that he appeal to President Cleveland to authorize military assistance. By order of the president, General Schofield directed General Otis to assist Grady in capturing the hijacked train. While General Otis requested two troops of the 4th Cavalry (about 112 men) stationed at Fort Walla Walla to intercept the hijacked train from the east, Grady contacted Portland for a fast train to carry his posse in pursuit of the stolen train from the West. Much like Hogan's train hijacking in Montana, which had taken place only days before, the chase was on.

Scheffler's train stopped briefly in The Dalles to take on coal, but the stop allowed Grady's pursuit train to get closer. Proceeding rapidly from the east, the troops from Fort Walla Walla chose to make their stand at Arlington. When they arrived at the depot in the late afternoon, they marched down the line about a quarter of a mile, placed torpedoes on the tracks, and then hid behind some boxcars and sand dunes running along the side of the tracks. When the captured train approached, a flagman waved it to a stop. At that moment, the torpedoes exploded, and the soldiers rushed the train without incident. After nearly eight hours and a distance of 120 miles, the chase was over. When Marshal Grady arrived in his pursuit train, he ordered that all the men in the army be lined up and searched. His men collected three revolvers, a few butcher knives, and some shaving razors, hardly the arsenal of an armed band of desperados. Grady ordered the soldiers to give the captured men water but no food. The 507 prisoners were then taken back to Portland to stand trial.

6. Scheffler's Portland Army

When Scheffler's industrial army got off the train in Portland only 434 men could be accounted for. Apparently, about 75 men had managed to drop off the train during the night. The 52 men that Grady identified as leaders of the army were placed in city and county jails, while the remainder of the men were confined in boxcars in the Union Pacific yards and closely guarded by 25 soldiers. As the leaders were marched off to jail a crowd of about 1,000 sympathizers gathered to cheer them on, shouting "Keep up your courage boys; we're with you."[16]

Following the arrival of the captured Coxeyites, a rally was held in the Third Street plaza where Populist orators delivered pro–Coxeyite speeches before a crowd of about 1,500 sympathizers. The weight of the public demonstration on behalf of the army seemed to have an impact on the legal proceedings. When the "leaders" were brought into court for their hearing on April 30, L.B. Cox, the attorney for the Union Pacific, declined to press for any specific punishment because, he said, the offense (violation of the injunction) had been against the dignity of the court. Left to his own discretion, Judge Charles Bellinger chose to be lenient. He lectured the men on the seriousness of what they had done and warned them that a second offense would not be treated lightly. Then, after receiving a promise from Scheffler and his men that they would obey the orders of the court in the future, he ordered the men released. Despite having been thwarted in their attempt to hijack a train and having been chastised by Judge Bellinger, 3,000 of the city's workers still felt compelled to stage a parade in their honor after their release. Accompanied by a brass band and banners, the marchers moved through downtown Portland shouting, "Down with the marshals and up with the Coxeyites!"[17]

After the judge's decision on April 30, about 100 of the men decided to abandon the effort to get to Washington and resigned from the army. But about 350 of the industrials who remained in camp seemed determined to continue their march. The following day, the remaining Coxeyites participated in the International Labor Day parade in the city where more than 3,000 men and 100 women marched in line. Following the event, the press reported that there were no riots or violent demonstrations of any kind. Despite that fact, Marshal Grady sent Attorney General Olney a telegram the following day in which he stated: "Affairs here are bordering on insurrection; fully anticipate trouble; have no equipment for special deputies in such event. Can you wire me requisition on Gen. Otis, Vancouver, for

50 rifles—also side arms and 150 rounds of ammunition?"[18] No action was taken. It seemed that Grady had overstepped in his zealous desire to curb all "radical" activity in Portland.

When news of Jacob Coxey's arrest in Washington, D.C., on May 1 reached Portland, a few more of Scheffler's men became discouraged and dropped out. A rumor began to circulate that the industrial army was about to break up. Actually, those still determined to march were breaking up into small groups of 10 to 25 and, during the first week of May, began hopping eastbound freights at night. When the railroad employees seemed to ignore their presence on the trains, the men assumed that the Union Pacific had tacitly agreed to assist them in reaching Kansas City. But Union Pacific officials had another plan in mind. As the army rode east across the Snake River bridge into Idaho, they also entered the district of Federal Judge James H. Beatty, known to be a willing ally of the railroad. With a judge willing to issue new injunctions and to empower new squads of federal marshals to halt the army's reckless crusade, officials of the Union Pacific certainly must have anticipated that an end to train stealing was near.

As soon as the advance guard of Scheffler's army moved into Idaho, officials of the Union Pacific issued orders to throw them off its cars. When larger groups persisted in their attempts to steal a ride, the railroad simply stopped its trains. When the men climbed off the trains, deputy U.S. marshals were directed to read them the injunction that had been issued by Judge Beatty on May 8 prohibiting them from stealing rides or hijacking trains and to inform them that they would be arrested if they tried to do so. These actions had the effect of stranding Scheffler's army at various points all along the rail line in Idaho. Then, after listening to criticism from townspeople along the route who objected to having the problem dropped at their doorstep, Union Pacific managers reversed course and agreed to haul Coxeyites in small groups.

As various elements of Scheffler's army continued across southern Idaho, they followed the route of the Union Pacific–owned Oregon Short Line through Weiser, Payette, Caldwell, Nampa, and Pocatello. About 100 men were put off at Weiser, but citizens donated 30 dollars to feed them and then cheered as the men departed the following day carrying the American flag. A similar response greeted the men in Payette where the mayor paid for two hearty meals and a lunch for the men to take with them the next day. The following day, a 37-man contingent of Scheffler's Portland army arrived in Caldwell aboard one of

6. Scheffler's Portland Army

the Short Line trains. The stop in Caldwell was supposed to have been a short one, but orders came down from Union Pacific headquarters that the train was to be sidetracked as long as the men remained on board. Blocked from proceeding, the army set up camp on an old circus ground back of the Pacific Hotel where they unfurled the American flag. Noted Idaho politician William Borah, who happened to be in Caldwell at the time, described the men as "very determined" to reach Washington but "peaceable and quiet."[19] He had expected to see an unruly band of hobos, but was surprised to find them educated and well-dressed. Soon after their arrival, a deputy U.S. marshal from Boise appeared on the scene to read Judge Beatty's order, to which the men paid little attention.

Realizing that the Coxeyites could be with them for a while, Caldwell's citizens called a public meeting in the town's new opera house where they expressed sympathy for the industrials and censured the Union Pacific for bringing destitute men into their community and then abandoning them while providing no provision for their care. Surprised by the public hostility it had aroused by its action, Union Pacific officials again retreated from their previous position and had a locomotive back down the track from Nampa the next day to pull the sidetracked cars, with the men on board, out of town. Before the Coxeyites departed, merchants and prominent citizens alike contributed 10 to 25 dollars' worth of flour, bacon, and potatoes or similar amounts of cash. The *Caldwell Tribune* editorially commented that the Coxeyites had no reason to complain about their treatment in Caldwell. "Everything possible was done for their comfort and they went away well fed and hopeful.... That public sentiment is largely with them there is no question."[20] The *Index* of nearby Emmett, Idaho, was of the opinion that many people in the state shared the army's anger and noted that "these 'armies' pointing their way to Washington seems to be a spontaneous condemnation of unwise, unjust and class legislation" recently passed by Congress, legislation that many believed unfairly benefited the rich at the expense of workers and small farmers. "It is not strange," said the editors, "that Coxeyism is here. It is strange it delayed its coming so long."[21] The residents of Caldwell seemed to share the general feeling of resentment toward the growing power of the railroads and other corporate monopolies. "Stealing trains nowadays," observed the *Spokane Chronicle*, "is almost as popular as stealing railroads was a few years ago."[22]

"Work, give us work"

It was obvious that the progression of the various contingents across the state would be increasingly difficult. A few days later, when a group of Scheffler's army boarded a train at Nampa, Idaho, they again met resistance. Railroad crews, given orders to sidetrack any train carrying Coxeyites, refused to move the train and called in local law enforcement to arrest the men and take them to Boise for trial. Another large group of industrials jumped a train headed for Pocatello, where they planned to regroup and pick up about 30 new recruits. In anticipation of their arrival, local residents collected 400 pounds of meat and 400 loaves of bread. But when city officials heard that an unexpectedly large group of men was about to arrive, they asked the Union Pacific to take the train through without stopping. Undeterred, sympathizers forwarded the anticipated provisions to the nearby town of McCammon where the men picked them up before proceeding to Montpelier.

At Montpelier, Idaho, a division point on the Union Pacific line, about 250 industrials climbed off the train for what they thought would be a brief rest stop. Once again sending mixed signals, railroad officials ordered crews to sidetrack all trains carrying Coxeyites. That meant that several hundred men in Scheffler's army were now stranded in Montpelier. The next day, a group of about 50 men, not wishing to sit around until their meager provisions ran out, stole an engine and raced across the border to the town of Cokeville in neighboring Wyoming. Believing that they were now safe from the jurisdiction of Idaho authorities, the men rested while Scheffler went ahead to solicit supplies. Unbeknownst to Scheffler and his men, one trainload of marshals was heading west from Cheyenne to meet them, while another was speeding east from Boise.

The next morning the remaining 200 industrials stranded in Montpelier climbed aboard an eastbound mail train. Following orders, crewmen uncoupled the engine and left the men sitting in the rail yard. They were soon surprised to see a special train carrying Joseph Pinkham, U.S. marshal for Idaho, 30 of his deputies, and the Union Pacific division superintendent E.E. Calvin roll into town. Marshal Pinkham again read Judge Beatty's restraining order and warned the Coxeyites that anyone trying to board a train would be shot. At a hastily called town meeting, the mayor and a group of citizens asked the marshal to allow the Coxeyites to move on. Marshal Pinkham responded that he was bound to carry out the mandate of the

6. Scheffler's Portland Army

court and again read Judge Beatty's restraining order. He then asked those assembled if they would be willing to help arrest any men who chose to violate the law. At that point, saloonkeeper John F. O'Conner rose from his seat and shouted that he would never help arrest men whose only crime was that they were destitute. After the audience gave O'Conner a vigorous round of applause, the meeting adjourned.

Unsure what the next step would be, Coxeyites and deputies continued to confront each other in the rail yard. When a freight train pulled into town that afternoon, a decision had to be made. Should the men seize the opportunity, challenge Marshal Pinkham, climb aboard, and risk being shot? At that moment, Dick Williams, a local constable, climbed on top of one of the cars and shouted "Follow me. I'll lead you to Washington. I'll take you out."[23] Emboldened by that act, the industrials immediately rushed to climb aboard the train.

At that point, things began to get out of hand. Pinkham's deputies immediately arrested Williams and dragged him off to jail. Defiant, Williams shouted: "Just wait a minute, boys, and I'll be back. We'll take this train out then, and if these sons of bitches follow us they will follow a trail of blood." When Williams, who was also the town jailer, refused to surrender his keys, Pinkham and his deputies placed Williams under arrest in superintendent Calvin's special train car. When the angry crowd surged toward the car, 30 deputies pointed their Winchesters out the windows, while Marshal Pinkham again warned that he would shoot the first man who tried to board the car. At that moment, Jack Westfall, a Bear Lake County deputy sheriff, ripped open his shirt, pointed to his chest, and shouted, "Shoot me. I'd just as ... [soon] die as see that man taken away from here." He then turned to the crowd and yelled, "Come on boys, we'll get him."[24] Excited by Westfall's bravado, men grabbed coupling pins, rocks, and any other weapon they could get their hands on and rushed toward the car. But before they were able to ascend the steps, the train jerked forward and pulled out of the depot. Outnumbered and sobered by the angry crowd, Marshal Pinkham decided to return to Pocatello with his lone prisoner and request the assistance of federal troops.

Looking to make a run for it, the Coxeyites in Montpelier took an engine from the roundhouse, added five empty boxcars, and quickly steamed east to join their confederates in Wyoming. But time was running out. Wyoming's federal marshal J.P. Rankin and eight newly-sworn-in deputies were able to surprise and arrest the

"Work, give us work"

Coxeyites camped at Cokeville where they were then taken to Green River. At that point, deputies were also able to arrest another advance guard of train-stealers. Although a few industrials managed to slip away, about 200 of Scheffler's men were taken into custody and locked in empty boxcars. The protesters were guarded by a contingent of deputies and backed by about 250 soldiers who had been hurriedly dispatched from Fort Russell (near Cheyenne) at the request of John A. Riner, Wyoming's federal judge, to protect the property of the Union Pacific Railroad.

As in other instances where large bodies of industrials had been placed under arrest, federal officials were not sure what to do with them. Judge Riner actually made the trip to Green River but decided to have only 15 of the so-called ringleaders taken back to Cheyenne. When it looked like Judge Riner might let the rest of the men go free, startled Union Pacific officials sent a wire to Attorney General Olney asking that he write to the federal judge in Idaho and stress

Coxeyites at morning roll call in camp on the edge of Green River, Wyoming, May 16, 1894. Troops were called in from Fort Russell in Cheyenne to guard the protesters until the proper warrants could arrive and they could be sent back to Idaho for trial. Album A 12-005 79-20-3. Sweetwater County Historical Museum.

the "importance of holding entire army which committed outrage at Montpelier and hearing cases of all of them and imposing adequate punishment to make example such as will have effect of deterring others from like action." Olney's abbreviated instructions to the judge followed their request to the letter stating, "important that entire commonweal army arrested for lawlessness at Montpelier should be tried and adequately punished. Unwise to discharge any of them."[25] Judge Beatty agreed to the request and proceeded to provide Marshal Pinkham with warrants to arrest the Coxeyites and have them brought back to Boise for trial. Pinkham then wired Riner, "Hold the army that captured the train at Montpelier yesterday until I arrive with warrants for them. I waive no jurisdiction over them. The outrage against the law and the right of property was too vicious. I want them back."[26]

On May 16, Pinkham, supplied with official warrants and accompanied by a dozen deputies and 25 soldiers from Fort Boise, traveled to Green River to collect the troublesome Montpelier hijackers. Confined in sealed coaches and placed under heavy guard, the prisoners were transported to Boise for trial. The number of those taken into custody was actually increased by the arrest of 57 additional train-stealers who were picked up in Nampa on the return. Back in Boise, Scheffler and Montpelier troublemakers Dick Williams, John O'Connor, and Jack Westfall were taken to the Ada County jail, while the rest of the men were held in a roundhouse and some empty boxcars.

When the Boise trial finally commenced in late May, no-nonsense federal Judge James Beatty set a clear precedent for judges to follow in other states when dealing with train hijackers. Beatty was a hard-liner who regarded the Coxeyites as "deluded people" on a misadventure and, as he informed Attorney General Olney, "I feel that this wild crusade *must be stopped* at once before more dangerous complications arise."[27] He also resented the lenient decision of Judge Bellinger in Portland and that Oregon had seemingly allowed its unemployed to be foisted on the people of Idaho.

Under pressure from the directors of the Union Pacific and from Attorney General Olney to take harsh action and punish all the men and not just the ringleaders, Judge Beatty, on June 5, rendered his verdict and surprised everyone by its severity. The judge called the movement a conspiracy, which meant that the men had knowingly worked together to steal trains. He acknowledged that the Coxey movement included some good men, but also noted that during the trial he had

"Work, give us work"

Members of Scheffler's Portland Army, with federal troops standing guard, board a train in Green River, Wyoming, to head back to Boise, Idaho. At their trial, Judge James Beatty found them guilty of contempt for violating the court's injunction. He sentenced Scheffler to six months in the county jail, while the remainder of his army received sentences of from thirty to sixty days. May 1894. Album A 12-005 79-20-3. Sweetwater County Historical Museum.

seen too many faces "which bore the indelible stamp of the criminal."[28] He found every defendant guilty of contempt of court and sentenced everyone to prison. Scheffler and the outspoken Dick Williams got six months in county jails, while the remainder of the men received sentences of from 30 to 60 days to be carried out at a place yet to be determined. The judge held out the hope of early release for prisoners who agreed to leave the state.

Judge Beatty still had to find a place to confine 185 prisoners. His rather sinister yet ingenious solution was to create a special prison encampment that the men would have to construct themselves. The site he selected for the new prison was in the desolate prairie wilderness at the western border of Idaho where the Union Pacific Railroad crossed the Snake River from Oregon. According to historian Gerald Eggert, the "board shed" in Boise where the prisoners had been held

6. Scheffler's Portland Army

was to be taken apart and rebuilt at the remote site. The costs related to this bizarre order would be further reduced because the prisoners would do their own cooking.[29] Choosing this site for the prison so close to Judge Bellinger's district sent a clear message that he disapproved of the Oregon judge's earlier decision. It also served as an example to discourage any additional Coxeyites from coming into Idaho from Oregon. As Beatty explained to Attorney General Olney, "I get them started *back* instead of *forward* and hope to continue them westward to their place of starting."[30]

On June 12, Pinkham's deputies, armed with rifles and six-guns, took the Coxeyites to the Boise railroad station, herded them like cattle into 10 box cars, and nailed the doors shut to prevent escape. The prisoners were then taken to a desolate expanse of sand and sage on the Snake River near Hells Canyon. Some of the men called the enclosure "Camp Pinkham," others called it "Camp Despair." Supporting the movement of the prisoners were two infantry companies that would be stationed at the camp to help the guards in case there was trouble. And there was in fact trouble. Prisoners, much like

View of Scheffler's Portland Army at their prison camp by the Snake River in Idaho. After Judge James Beatty found all 185 members of Scheffler's Army guilty of contempt of court, he ordered them to construct their own prison encampment at a remote site on the Oregon-Idaho border. Photograph shows men, canvass tents, and train crossing the bridge from Oregon into Idaho, June–July 1894. Denver Public Library, Western History Collection, X-21555.

those incarcerated in Japanese relocation camps during World War II, divided into two groups—cooperators and resisters. Deputies tried to segregate the two hostile factions on opposite sides of the railway track, but insults and abuse continued, especially when cooperators won special privileges and early releases. One group of resisters actually tunneled 70 feet from beneath its barracks before guards discovered their attempted escape route.

In the end, Judge Beatty's harsh punishment seemed to be as much psychological as it was symbolic. Over the next two months, the judge released a few of the men at a time, apparently thinking that spacing their release would prevent the Portland army from reforming. He also made an arrangement with the Union Pacific to transport the men west upon their release. Judge Beatty's unprecedented action of sentencing an entire army of men to prison may have served as an example for Nebraska's federal Judge Elmer S. Dundy who, just weeks later, would employ a similar tactic to crush the last of the western Coxey armies from Salt Lake City and Denver who had commandeered a Union Pacific train near Ogallala.

7

THE NORTHWESTERN INDUSTRIAL ARMIES OF CANTWELL AND JEFFRIES

When Washington became a state on November 11, 1889, it was riding the crest of a boom. Seattle, recovering from a devastating fire earlier that year that leveled 30 blocks of the central part of the city, was rebuilding in brick and stone at a feverish pace. New commercial buildings could be seen changing the cityscape and city planners were widening streets and beginning to pave them with bricks rather than the old, creosoted wood planks. With an economy boosted by timber, coal, and agricultural production, Seattle had begun to emerge as a shipping center with a thriving waterfront. Tacoma, with a similarly based economy, saw its fortunes boosted by a transcontinental rail link established in 1883. Spokane, located in the remote southeastern part of the state but linked to the East by both the Great Northern and Northern Pacific Railroads, was becoming a major transportation center.

The state's population, especially in its major cities, reflected its accelerated growth, increasing nearly fivefold during the decade. Seattle's population increased from 3,553 in 1880 to nearly 43,000 by 1890, while Tacoma could boast of 36,000 residents (more than 35 times its total in 1880). Spokane, with an economy fueled by mining, wheat, and timber, saw its population increase from 356 to more than 19,000 in the span of 10 years. The newcomers from the East who migrated to the state to find jobs in railroad construction, agriculture, mining, and lumbering assumed that they had reached the promised land.

The Panic of 1893 was not the first depression in the United States, but it was the first one to send the economy of the Pacific Northwest reeling. News that the Philadelphia & Reading Railroad

"Work, give us work"

had declared bankruptcy on February 20, 1893, sent a signal that the economy might be in trouble. Then, in April, Secretary of the Treasury John G. Carlisle announced that the nation's gold reserves had fallen below the "acceptable" level of $100 million, a sign that falling silver prices had spooked investors into a stampede to convert their silver dollars into gold. The final blow arrived on May 4 when the National Cordage Company, known to many as the "rope trust," failed. The failure touched off a trading panic the following day. The Panic, and the depression it spawned, soon began to take its toll. By the end of 1893, more than 15,000 business venturers and 642 banks had failed and between two and three million workers had lost their jobs. Before the depression of the 1890s was over, almost one-third of the nation's railroad milage would pass through receivership.

The economic collapse had a devastating impact on the Pacific Northwest; 32 Washington banks failed in little more than seven months in 1893. There were 17 more bank failures in 1894 and another 18 in 1895. Many businesses were forced to shut their doors as well. The repeal of the Sherman Silver Purchase Act caused mines to close all over the West and ended mining expansion in Okanogan County in north central Washington. Branch railroads serving the mines also failed, adding to the numbers of unemployed. Men, dependent on weekly wages, were either laid off or forced to accept severe pay cuts. Lumber interests were hurt as well when overextended and financially strapped railroads reduced timber shipments out of Washington by a third. Seventy-five percent of the shingle plants operating in the state in 1893 would be out of business two years later. When railroads reduced shipments, stopped new construction, and cut back on maintenance more men found themselves joining the ranks of the unemployed. Coinciding with the Panic and compounding problems was the state's first severe crop failure which intensified the economic burdens on farmers and added to the number of unemployed.

Tens of thousands of others, on what historian Carlos Schwantes has termed the "wageworkers' frontier," were thrown out of work.[1] Local governments occasionally instituted some sort of street improvement work paying bare subsistence wages, but cities like Tacoma just did not have the money. In a time of laissez-faire—where the federal government assumed no responsibility for unemployment or even made any attempt to measure it, did not take action to increase spending or expand the money supply, declined to bail out

7. The Northwestern Industrial Armies of Cantwell and Jeffries

manufacturers or banks or extend emergency credit to businesses in trouble, and refused to provide destitute people with food or shelter—many workers found that their labor could no longer cover the bare necessities of life. Unemployed men walked the streets looking for work.

On April 7, 1894, about 200 of Seattle's unemployed laboring men, described as "all sturdy, active fellows, neatly dressed and with earnest, serious faces," met in a vacant Northern Pacific Railroad storage building at the corner of South Second and Weller streets and organized as the Northwestern Industrial Army.[2] Newspapers reported that the men had been following the progress of Coxey's and Fry's armies with close interest. The men elected Henry Shepard, an unemployed surveyor, as their leader. Shepard was a short, soft-spoken man with a mustache and side-whiskers who did "not impress one as being a great general."[3] The goal of the new association was to join together in a march across the country to Washington, D.C., to protest current conditions. Shepard had no radical agenda, he merely asked the 72 men who signed up that first day to pledge to recognize only honest working men and to refrain from any association with drunkards, thieves, and convicts. The following night, more than 800 people attended a public meeting held at the same location. According to one reporter, "the hall was crowded to suffocation, the passageway at the rear of the room was filled and a large crowd filled the street for half a block."[4] Commander Shepard introduced the other officers, explained the aims of the association, and recorded the names of several hundred new recruits.

To attract public attention and hopefully gain donations and additional recruits, Shepard's Seattle army staged parades through the city on April 14 and 18 led by the Rialto Band. One of several banners carried by the marchers read "Gold at a Premium—Humanity at a Discount." Citizens and businesses rallied behind the cause and donated food and some money. In response, the army's numbers grew to nearly 450. As the army's membership rapidly increased, the leaders scurried to find rail transportation to Washington, D.C. As it was common practice for unemployed workers to hop trains in the Pacific Northwest, the leaders hoped that the Northern Pacific might provide free transportation. Railroad officials, however, refused to carry any Coxeyites. Instead, they reportedly made a counteroffer. Because the members of the American Railway Union had struck and its train tracks were in poor condition (obstructed by uncleared rock and dirt slides), the company offered to provide a train for the army if it would work to clear the track on its way to St. Paul. That offer, seen as an attempt to use the unemployed as strikebreakers, was quickly rejected with the statement that their objective was to "uphold the dignity of labor and not degrade it."[5]

On April 14, about 1,000 unemployed men gathered in the National Theater, a rundown venue at Twelfth and A streets in Tacoma, to organize a similar industrial army. Included in the ranks were sawmill and shingle mill workers, loggers, railroad workers, miners, a sailor, a teamster, a printer, a baker, a boilermaker, and a blacksmith. Assuming leadership of this second body was Frank P. Cantwell, perhaps Tacoma's most recognizable personality. An occasional prize fighter, he had previously been employed as a saloon bouncer for Harry Morgan, owner of the Theatre Comique, a dance-hall on Tacoma's Pacific Avenue, and known as the head of the local underworld. At the time, he was married to Dora Charlotte, usually called Charlotta, the wealthy widow of his former boss.

Cantwell, known to most as "Jumbo," was a giant of a man with a booming voice and boisterous personality. He was also, like Carl Browne, a natural showman and an easy mark for reporters who wanted to sensationalize the movement. A typical speech from Jumbo was a mix of humor, profanity, and populism. Nevertheless, as one reporter noted, "There is something magnetic about him." Another agreed with that assessment, "His language is not very Emersonian, but he does know how to talk to the commonwealers."[6] Instead of Browne's curious buckskin attire, Cantwell outfitted himself in a tailor-made, $90, navy-blue uniform consisting of a long, double-breasted coat with epaulets and shiny brass buttons, dark trousers with blue stripes down the legs, and a broad-brimmed black hat with braid. More striking in appearance was Cantwell's attractive, tall, blonde, well-mannered wife Charlotta, who usually wore somber black dresses adorned with conspicuous diamond jewelry. Ironically, it would be Charlotta that would rise above her connection to the criminal underworld to become one of the truly remarkable leaders of the western Coxeyites.

Partly as a result of the intercity rivalry between Seattle and Tacoma, Cantwell's group looked to maintain its independence from Shepard's army and boldly announced their own sweeping agenda. The Tacoma army wanted the government to fund a liberal education

7. The Northwestern Industrial Armies of Cantwell and Jeffries

for all, construct a canal in Nicaragua, restrict immigration, and develop farmlands through extensive irrigation. The odd assortment of demands actually reflected the unique needs of Washington's laborers. A canal across Central America would expedite shipping and provide an economic benefit to the Puget Sound region; potential homesteaders would benefit from subsidized irrigation projects; and every working-class family would benefit from greater access to education.

The request for restrictions on immigration, a growing national concern, was especially strong in the Pacific Northwest where the importation of cheap Chinese labor was a sore point among native-born workers and a recurring issue during hard times. Equally provocative was the group's leader who was not averse to using brazen rhetoric to attract attention. When calling for men to join his army, Cantwell remarked: "If Cleveland and both houses of the national Congress know that the people throughout the country are calling through hungry stomachs for work and bread, and the government can put these men to work upon public improvements and does not, then it is a traitor to the wants of the people."[7]

Unfortunately, Cantwell had no better luck in negotiating with the railroads than Shepard had. Jumbo had begun by publicly stating that his men would not walk and requested free transportation. When officials of the Norther Pacific turned him down, he offered to pay $1,000 for a train of 20 boxcars to take 300–400 men as far as St. Paul, Minnesota. When railroad officials rejected that offer, Cantwell raised it to $10,000. But railroad officials again refused, saying that they would not haul men as freight. Undaunted, and never short of bravado, Jumbo responded, "We ain't too good to steal a train. Them fellas in Congress has broke the law. Why can't we?"[8] At that point, Charlotta proposed that the railroad ship one cow in each boxcar and simply carry 30 or 40 men to care for it. That idea was also rejected.

Based on prior conversations between Shepard and Cantwell, the two separate Washington state armies planned to converge at Puyallup, a small railroad junction just south of Tacoma. Thousands of Seattle residents gave Shepard and his 700-man army a rousing send off when they marched out of the city on April 25. As one reporter described the scene: "Every house, gate-post and fence was alive with spectators, who spoke words of encouragement to the men with canteens and blankets on their backs."[9] With shouts of "On to

"Work, give us work"

Washington!," Tacoma's industrial army with Jumbo Cantwell riding in a buggy at its head and accompanied by his St. Bernard dog marched out of town toward Puyallup in military formation two days later. Some 600 individuals were part of the original marching column. Three hundred were recruits dedicated to the journey, whereas the rest were sympathizers who had agreed to remain in Tacoma as a home guard to assist in caring for wives and children left behind. As the army departed, Cantwell worked the crowd for cash donations, while several wagons carrying provisions accompanied the army on its route. It was reported that the Tacoma army had $2,000 in its treasury at the outset. Neither "general" imagined that they would be stuck in Puyallup for nearly 10 days.

On April 25, just as the two armies were set to begin their marches to Puyallup, Brigadier General Elwell S. Otis gave instructions to the commanding officers at Fort Walla Walla and Fort Spokane in Washington and Fort Sherman in Idaho to hold their companies in readiness. The order was prompted by the massing in Portland, Seattle, and Tacoma of armies of the unemployed who, it was feared, might try to commandeer trains in their eagerness to move toward Washington, D.C. Just one day before, a contingent of industrials in Butte, Montana, under the command of William Hogan had stolen a freight train from the Northern Pacific yards, piled 300 men into six empty coal cars, placed an unemployed engineer at the throttle, and headed east. As previously noted, due to bankruptcies caused by the depression most of the major railroads were in the hands of receivers under the control of the United States federal court system.

As the numbers in the emerging armies began to approach the thousands, it became apparent that the court, with the civil force at hand, would not be able to execute its orders and that troops would have to provide military assistance at some point. The fear of a train seizure in the Pacific Northwest became a reality on April 28 when Solomon Scheffler's Portland army stole a Union Pacific train at Troutdale, Oregon. Military authorities now worried that the example of train stealing in Oregon, coupled with Hogan's capture of a train in Butte, Montana, might encourage other groups in the region to take similar action. As a result, on April 29, General Otis directed the commanding officer at Fort Sherman to proceed with his entire infantry force to Spokane and set up camp on the line of the Northern Pacific Railroad. At the same time, the bulk of the garrison stationed at the

7. The Northwestern Industrial Armies of Cantwell and Jeffries

Vancouver, Washington, barracks made ready for departure for the cities on the Puget Sound.

When the two industrial armies converged on Puyallup at the base of the Cascades, railroad officials became alarmed regarding the potential danger to their property. Feeling that they had just cause, they persuaded Judge Cornelius Hanford to issue a restraining order prohibiting interference with Northern Pacific trains and to authorize U.S. Marshal James C. Drake to hire extra deputies to protect railroad property. In short fashion, Drake employed scores of deputies at $5 a day to man all trains operating in the area to prevent any Coxeyites from boarding and sent a dozen deputies into Puyallup to guard railroad property there. Other deputies soon patrolled the train yards in Seattle, Ellensberg, Yakima, and Spokane. At Puyallup, deputies were armed with Winchester rifles and carried copies of Judge Hanford's restraining order.

Looking to bolster the spirits of the men stranded in Puyallup, Mary Hobart, a fiery Populist orator, took the opportunity to condemn the escalation of force. Directing her comments at the deputy marshals in the audience, she advised them to go home and let the Commonwealers take a train and proceed on their way. "Us wimmen is tired of populatin' the world to have our sons shot down by you Russian Hessians."[10] For its part, the Northern Pacific only allowed trains to move out of Puyallup in daylight. Further heightening tensions was a rumor that officials of the Northern Pacific had ordered crews to plant explosives in the bank of a cut near Buckley, Washington, and intended to set them off and block the track should either army commandeer a train.

Compounding problems for the industrial armies that were growing impatient during their extended stay in Puyallup was the temper of the local residents who were becoming irritated at having 1,100 to 1,300 uninvited guests in town. As a result, citizens called a meeting to address the problem and invited Governor John Hart McGraw to attend. Unlike Governor Pennoyer in Oregon, Governor McGraw was not in sympathy with either the current march or the larger industrial army movement. Three thousand people crowded into the local opera house for the May 2 meeting, which reporters described as a gathering almost devoid of any semblance of order. When finally given the opportunity to speak, Governor McGraw, a spirited little man with a bald head, waterfall mustache, and rimless pince-nez, told the men that he could not force the railroad to carry them. He also reminded the men that economic conditions in the East were as bad as in the West, and that the army was, as Coxey had discovered, unwanted by authorities in the nation's capital. He advised the men to send a small delegation and for the rest to go home. At that point, E.J. Jeffries, spoke up from the audience: "It is said we should go home. We have no homes. Where is it we should go? Back to Seattle, where the judge would vag us in twenty-four hours? No, we want to go east, and there demand redress of our wrongs from the chief executive of this nation."[11]

Undeterred by the governor's unsupportive attitude, Jumbo Cantwell took the floor and declared that his men had been lured west by the railroad—with the promise of jobs in a booming economy—and that now they would make the railroad carry them back. The comment touches on a point raised earlier. Many workers had come west expecting to find unbounded opportunity, but hard times thwarted their "unrealistic aspirations and expectations and made them susceptible to the notion that they must fight to regain their inheritance."[12] As labor historian Herbert Gutman noted, "Aspirations and expectations interpret experience and thereby help shape behavior."[13] It has been argued that this "clash between unrealistic dreams and harsh reality" often give rise to militant unionism, violence, and "radical crusades" like those conducted by the armies of the unemployed in 1894.[14]

As the tenseness of the situation at Puyallup increased, the Seattle army found that it had its own internal leadership problem to deal with. When compared to the dynamic Jumbo Cantwell, the rather lackluster Henry Shepard increasingly appeared to many of his men as not the man to lead them on a national crusade. Some in the ranks grumbled that he was becoming too dictatorial in trying to impose military discipline, and that he was usurping the powers of the executive committee. The final break came when Shepard was charged with not being open in his accounting of the army's cash reserve. As rumors began to circulate that Commander Shepard was planning to run off with the army's treasury, he was asked to give an accounting of the funds that had been donated to the army. When he could only produce 43 cents in the treasury, the men demanded his resignation. To guard against any future abuse of authority, the Seattle men created a supreme council to oversee finances and to do so in a more transparent fashion. Replacing Shepard was Edward J. Jeffries, a tall, thin,

7. The Northwestern Industrial Armies of Cantwell and Jeffries

28-year-old attorney and one of the original Seattle organizers. Born in Detroit, Michigan, Jeffries had learned a trade as a typesetter on several hometown newspapers before deciding to attend the University of Michigan Law School. He was admitted to the bar in 1889. After that, he moved his family to the Pacific Northwest where he became active in various agrarian reform organizations and was currently an ardent Populist.

On May 3, about 120 members of Cantwell's army hopped a slow, 15-car freight hauling shingles and lumber and eight empty cattle cars headed in the direction of Buckley, just east of Puyallup. When the train reached Buckley, the stationmaster wired Tacoma that a train had been hijacked by Coxeyites. U.S. Marshal Drake immediately called out all available deputies and ordered a locomotive and a passenger car so that he could give pursuit. Soon after that a second wire reached Drake reporting that the train had not been hijacked. Superintendent Joe McCabe had ordered the engineer to pull the train onto a siding at Palmer and uncouple the locomotive. The engineer then returned to Buckley, leaving the men stranded. At that point, Marshal Drake canceled his call for a special and purchased tickets for himself and 26 deputies to Palmer on a regular night train.

When the train stopped briefly at Puyallup, and to the surprise of everyone aboard, Jumbo Cantwell boarded the train with a first-class ticket. At every stop, when a number of industrials tried to climb aboard, Jumbo worked to boost the men on, while deputies worked with the conductor and the brakeman to throw them off. As the train pulled away, Jumbo could be heard shouting: "Spokane or bust, boys, Spokane or bust. I'm with you."[15] When the train reached Palmer, Cantwell found his sidetracked army shivering under wet blankets and huddled around a bonfire. Fortunately, the deputies left to guard them unlocked the train depot and allowed the industrials to spend the night around the pot-belly stove. General Cantwell, on the other hand, spent the night in the Hot Springs Hotel. A number of reporters referred to such leaders, which would have included Jacob Coxey, as "featherbed" generals.

Realizing that it would be impossible to travel as one large unit, Cantwell and Jeffries decided that in order for their armies to make the 400-mile march to Spokane, a natural reorganization point where the Great Northern and the Northern Pacific lines converged before they entered Idaho, they would have to break up into smaller bands and travel as the opportunity presented itself. The usual mode of travel was to climb on the top of the cars or, on passenger trains, cling to the end of a baggage car that had no opening into the next car. There, on the "blind," they had a better chance of being unnoticed once the train picked up speed. Braver travelers often used squares of wood to serve as seats to ride under the cars on the brake beams. It was a dangerous way to travel and, as one reporter noted, "It fills your whiskers with sand and your eyes with cinders."[16] It did, however, keep one out of the rain. But traveling in small squads presented other problems. Progress was slow, the terrain rugged and sparsely inhabited, and the men lacked money and provisions. It was only a matter of time before tired, hungry, and demoralized marchers with thousands of miles yet to go would attempt to quicken their movement by boarding east-bound trains and seizing railroad property.

It was almost a certainty that the fragmented armies, numbering more than 1,000 and soon scattered along the Northern Pacific track from the Stampede Tunnel (which the Northern Pacific attempted to close to men on foot, forcing them to climb the old switchback trail over the pass) to Pasco in central Washington, would encounter trouble all along their route. Once over the Cascade Mountains, the preferred route for the Coxeyites was east to Ellensburg on the arid side of the state, south to Yakima, then southeast to Pasco, and, finally, northeast across a sparsely populated expanse of sand and sagebrush to Spokane. Near Pasco, the Northern Pacific operated the only bridge across the Columbia River, which was now guarded by federal marshals.

The first contingent of Coxeyites reached Yakima on May 3, two days after Jacob Coxey's ill-fated march in Washington, D.C. It was reported that the men turned down a job offer of 75 cents a day plus board to work in the hop fields, saying that they needed to get to Washington instead. They moved on the next day in an empty freight car. A few hours later a much larger group arrived and made camp at the north end of the town. The following day a freight train brought even more. Sixty of these Coxeyites had made news when they captured a single gondola car at Cle Elum on the Northern Pacific mainline east of the Cascade Tunnel. Lacking a locomotive, the men shoved the heavy car to the mainline and then started it on the 28-mile down grade to Ellensburg under its own momentum. To avoid any accidents, the division superintendent ordered all the trains sidetracked so that the gondola would have the right of way. At Ellensburg, this group

7. The Northwestern Industrial Armies of Cantwell and Jeffries

Western entrance to the Stampede Tunnel. In Washington, more than a thousand Coxeyites became scattered along the Northern Pacific track in the central part of the state. In an effort to inhibit their progress, officials of the Northern Pacific attempted to close the Stampede Tunnel to force the men to climb the old switchback trail over the pass. Photo by Frank Jay Haynes, 1890. Wikimedia Commons.

joined another group of their comrades. By May 6 there were some 200 industrials in the small town. A Chinese restaurant served the men food, a baker allowed them to bake bread in his ovens, townspeople donated flour, farmers brought in wagon loads of potatoes, and two butchers contributed beef.

Seeing the futility of any further progress on the rails, a small number of men decided to shift their mode of transport from rail to boat and float down the swift-moving Yakima River. It took the men a day to build a flat-bottomed boat, 6 feet wide by 20 feet long, nailed together with 40-penny-spikes, caulked and pitched, and braced with 2 × 6 boards. The following morning, 18 men boarded the boat and set off. But about four miles downstream, they encountered an eddy that tossed the boat against a large log in the middle of the river and overturned it. Four men drowned in the mishap, while the remaining 14 survivors were left desperately clinging to the log in the river. One of the men was finally able to swim ashore and rushed back to Ellensburg get assistance for the stranded men. Rescuers then worked for three

"Work, give us work"

Guarding Coxey's Army, Northern Pacific depot, Ellensburg, Washington, April 1894. Two Washington State Militia men stand with rifles next to the last passenger car of the Northern Pacific Railroad locomotive. The militiamen were guarding members of the Northwestern industrial armies of Frank "Jumbo" Cantwell and Edward J. Jeffries. While in Ellensburg, members of these armies were arrested and kept in a makeshift corral near the county courthouse. Frank J. Haynes was the official photographer for the Northern Pacific Railroad. Courtesy of the Ellensburg Public Library.

hours trying to get a rope to the men on the log. Finally, after tying one end of the rope to a tall pine tree and then using a system of pulleys, they were able to haul each of the men to the top of the tree and then to the ground by ladder. By the end of the ordeal, some of the men had been on the log in ice cold water for about nine hours. The incident ended any thought of going down the Yakima River by boat.

Another group of Coxeyites encamped north of Yakima kept to themselves, coming into town only to pick up food donated by local sympathizers. Peaceful distancing ended, however, when a deputy marshal struck one of the marchers with a cane. When it looked like the Coxeyites might do harm to the deputy in retaliation, reinforcements were called in. The scuffle then moved to the train station where the army tried to board a freight train and marshals tried to pull them off.

7. The Northwestern Industrial Armies of Cantwell and Jeffries

At that point, a number of Yakima residents began to yell encouragement to the Coxeyites, and some began to throw stones at the marshals. In an attempt to get away from the mob that seemed to be inciting the marchers to violence, marshals ordered the train to pull out of the station. When the train started moving in reverse, many of the industrials thought they were being taken back to the coast. In an attempt to halt the engine, men tried to set the train's brakes while the marshals used clubs to knock them off the cars. With emotions running high, some of the marshals fired their guns, wounding three of the marchers and shooting John Jolly, one of their own deputies, by mistake. After the confrontation, deputies under the command of Marshal W.C. Chidester, who had accidently shot himself in the thigh during the melee, proceeded to arrest 154 industrials for attempting to steal rides on trains and 18 Yakima residents for inciting the men to riot.

The following day another group of men boarded two cattle cars at Ellensburg and came down the line with the idea of liberating their

Hundreds of unemployed men who joined the Northwestern industrial armies to march on Washington, D.C., in May of 1894 wait at the North Yakima train depot for an eastbound train. These men had had problems in Ellensburg. They had more in Yakima where fights, shooting, and arrests resulted. Taken to Seattle under armed guard for trial, twenty-nine Coxeyites received 60-day sentences. Courtesy of the Yakima Valley Museum.

comrades being held at Yakima. But deputies at Yakima had received a telegram warning them that 150 men were on their way and that they were armed with rifles. About 50 deputies quickly responded to intercept the hijacked train. They were able to do so when they barricaded a bridge by placing rails across the track. At that point, the men were ordered to throw up their hands. Those on the top of the cars complied, but those at the back of the train decided to make a run for it. In the mayhem, shots were fired and three Coxeyites were wounded. Those not injured were arrested and taken to join their fellow marchers in custody. In the end, nearly 200 men, guarded by 32 deputy marshals, were placed in two boxcars without water or adequate ventilation (they had to carve air holes into the sides of the cars with pocket knives) and transported to Spokane. Hundreds of demonstrators met the train at the depot where they demanded that the men be given food and water. Ultimately transferred to passenger cars, the industrials were taken back to Seattle to stand trial.

The return of so many Coxeyites to Seattle as prisoners created another tense situation and mob demonstrations in support of the arrested marchers followed. Sensing that the situation was slipping out of control, Judge Hanford requested the assistance of federal troops to enforce the orders of the court. Once again, President Cleveland authorized military assistance under RS 5298. Responding to that request, General Otis dispatched five companies of the 14th U.S. Infantry Regiment from the Vancouver Barracks to Seattle to restore peace. Eventually, 111 Commonwealers were found guilty of violating the court order not to interfere with railroad property. Before Judge Hanford sentenced some of the men to 60 days in the McNeil Island penitentiary, he gave them a lecture on opportunity.

> The people that came to this Northwest country when my father did found here no railroads, nor steamboats, nor manufacturing industries to give employment and afford wages ... when they met with hard times, instead of ... making demands upon the government for relief, they planted potatoes and peas and cabbage, and preserved themselves and their families from starvation. They set out fruit trees which bore fruit a good deal quicker than any extraordinary measures by which it is proposed to obtain relief by coercion from the congress of the United States will ever bring it.[17]

Surely some of the propertyless, industrially employed wage-earners awaiting sentencing must have been appalled by the judge's naïve, pre-industrial vision of the United States in 1894. According to one

7. The Northwestern Industrial Armies of Cantwell and Jeffries

account, as the convicted men were led to the city dock in manacles, they broke into song. The chorus of that song went:

> So sing along, march along,
> Come along, march along
> While the air is pure and balmy
> And every mother's son
> Will march to Washington,
> And join General Coxey's Army.[18]

After skirmishes along the route in central Washington, scattered detachments of Cantwell's and Jeffries's armies began to reassemble in Spokane. At that important rail hub, the Coxeyites were able to pick up some additional recruits when a local army led by James Dolphin fell apart. With so many industrials in town, authorities began to fear a return of the mob violence that had taken place in Seattle after the return of the men arrested at Yakima. As a result, the U.S. district judge for the state of Washington requested the assistance of troops to enforce the orders of the court. In response, the War Department ordered troops to be stationed along the line of the Northern Pacific in eastern Washington and neighboring Idaho.

In assessing the situation in Spokane, Cantwell and Jeffries decided to again break up the army into smaller groups, hop freights when possible, and then regroup at some distant point. Jumbo opted for his men to follow the Great Northern route through Montana to Great Falls where they would rendezvous. Jeffries, on the other hand, decided on the Northern Pacific route through southern Montana to Butte and Helena. If everything went well, and the two armies managed to cross 1,500 miles of mountains and prairies, they would ultimately regroup in Minneapolis–St. Paul were the two rail lines once again converged.

Even in the face of all the precautions taken by the military, some of the constantly moving detachments of the industrial armies managed to pass into Montana. Believing they were now beyond the reach of the military, the men began to commandeer trains on a regular basis. In most cases, the troops, working in conjunction with Montana's Marshal William McDermott, were able to pursue and recover the stolen trains and arrest the hijackers. The pattern of train stealing and eventual capture continued in the region and by the end of May, Marshal McDermott held approximately 300 prisoners in custody in western Montana. As the Secretary of War noted in his annual report for 1894, the prompt action of the troops "soon disintegrated and scattered the fragments of these so-called industrial armies. Of the 3,000 or 4,000 men who composed them, the small proportion which passed beyond department lines could do but little mischief, lost their importance, and escaped from observation."[19]

The increased incidence of train stealing (one estimate was that the "industrials" commandeered some 40 trains at various points) elicited different responses from different sections of the country. In the East, the *Nation*, no friend of the Coxeyites, was outraged: "Trains have been stolen by organized mobs, and the same public that called for vengeance upon the Jesse James gang and other express robbers, has weakly said of these industrial train robbers, 'Poor fellows, they are out of work and must do something." In the West, a Populist newspaper in the state of Washington viewed things differently: "It is hard to make the masses believe that any wrong has been committed by a human being in attempting to get a free ride in a box car, when this same public has watched so-called railroad kings steal entire railroads and read in the monopolistic press such men designated as 'Napoleons of finance,' etc."[20]

When Jumbo Cantwell's half-starved army finally straggled into Great Falls, Montana, they were a sorry lot. Many of the men's clothes were in rags and some wore ruined shoes wrapped in gunnysacks. Sensing that the army was in dire straits, Jumbo and Charlotta decided to switch roles. Jumbo would now travel ahead as the army's advance agent, and Charlotta would assume the day-to-day leadership of the men. It was at that moment that Charlotta became the army's angel. She spent a great deal of her fortune renting empty buildings to provide shelter for 1,260 men. She obtained food from butchers and bakers and persuaded church groups to donate second-hand clothing and shoes. She took over Salvation Army headquarters at night and staged fund-raising rallies. Charlotta, accompanied by her six-year-old daughter Mabel from her earlier marriage, were the main attractions, often singing the songs of the Coxey movement to raise money for food.

Charlotta managed to get the remnants of her Tacoma army back on the road and traveled ahead of the men as they moved east. Reaching St. Cloud, Minnesota, she addressed a huge crowd at a picnic sponsored by the American Railway Union. She eventually raised enough money to hire a freight train to carry the men on to Minneapolis. Charlotta rode in the caboose with her daughter, while her

7. The Northwestern Industrial Armies of Cantwell and Jeffries

troops filled the boxcars. At Minneapolis, the army split into groups. The larger body continued on to Washington while others either pursued the rumors of jobs or just drifted off on their own. It was not long before Charlotta's good deeds and devotion to the cause reached the Coxeyites camped in Washington, D.C. As the *Washington Post* reported, "The men of the army are anxious to see her and admire her for her bravery and self-devotion to the cause."[21] But Charlotta would never actually make it that far. In repairing the army's flagging morale and restoring their physical health, she compromised her own. She managed to get as far as Chicago before her health finally gave out. On the advice of a physician, she headed back to Tacoma, telling reporters that she planned to rejoin her "boys" when her health improved.

Jeffries' main army reached Missoula, Montana, on May 21 with 100 men. Smaller groups continued to come into town almost daily over the next two weeks. As they had done earlier for Hogan and his men, the citizens of Butte, Montana, provided Jeffries and his men with a warm welcome when they reached town on May 27. The Butte Home Guard had secured a $10,000 treasurer's bond to help the Seattle men and other armies passing through the town. The bond was to be retired through the contribution of one dollar a month from each subscriber and comprised about 75 percent of Butte's business and working men. Jeffries complimented residents with having the best organized town in the country and promised the townspeople that he would add the unlimited coinage of silver to his list of demands from Congress. Jeffries's Seattle group left Butte on June 5.

Cantwell arrived in Minneapolis on June 16 with between two and three hundred men. Two days later, the *Anaconda Standard* reported that Jumbo "engaged in a controversy" with the mayor and the chief of police and was placed under arrest and subsequently fined for disorderly conduct.[22] The newspaper reported that most of Cantwell's advance detachment had deserted. Those who stayed loyal to Jumbo remained at their camp on the outskirts of the city. Carrying a letter of introduction from the Spokane Trades Council, Jumbo was able to win the support of organized labor in the Twin Cities. With the aid of their donations and some new recruits, he soon had a renewed army of 200 men whom he proceeded to lead across Minnesota and Wisconsin. But the journey was not an easy one. At La Crosse, Wisconsin, the army commandeered a stock train and rode to Milwaukee where police awaited their arrival. After having surrounded the train and locked the doors, the police then moved the train a few miles down the track and left the men there for some time without food. Farther down the line near Racine, Wisconsin, a squad of railway policemen employed by the Chicago & Northwestern clubbed the passing Coxeyites. Traveling on his own from Chicago by regular coach, Jumbo and a few of his followers finally reached Washington in time for Fourth of July festivities. Bands of his men would continue to trickle into the capital over the next several weeks.

Jeffries waited for a time in the Twin Cities to collect the remainder of his men who had had a tough time with federal deputies while traveling across North Dakota. One episode offered a glimpse of their travail. On June 15, the *Oakes Republican* reported that a band of armed men had captured a Northern Pacific train east of Bismarck. When the train stopped at Dawson, the engineer stepped down from the engine to enter the telegraph office. At that moment, about 50 men swarmed over the engine. They uncoupled the locomotive and one car from the rest of the train and ordered the fireman to assume the duties of engineer. A small number of deputy marshals attempted to stop the train seizure, but they were outnumbered. It was reported that one of the deputies was shot in the melee. As the engine sped off to the east, Marshal William Daggett wired Colonel E.S. Miller, commander of the North Dakota National Guard at Jamestown, to ask for help. Miller immediately appointed deputies and boarded a train to head west. The hijackers found themselves in a trap. Colonel Miller and his men were approaching from the east and Marshal Daggett and his men were closing in from the west. Desperate not to be caught, the hijackers abandoned the stolen engine and fled into the woods. The two posses were able to surround the train-stealers, place them under arrest, and return them to Bismarck for trial.

From St. Paul, Jeffries decided to make a detour and move the remainder of his army north to Duluth. He had read about the trouble that Cantwell had encountered in Wisconsin and was concerned that rail lines to Chicago would be tied up due to the Pullman Strike. Knowing something of the terrain from his youth, Jeffries planned to proceed to Duluth and hire a boat to take his men across the Great Lakes to Cleveland or Buffalo. The route also had the advantage of passing through towns that had not grown tired of a continuous stream of industrial armies.

With a few hundred dollars that had been donated by organized

7. The Northwestern Industrial Armies of Cantwell and Jeffries

labor and wealthy mine owners in Montana and additional cash contributions from members of the International Typographical Union of which he was a member, and through public speaking engagements, Jeffries raised enough money to pay for 400 members of his army to travel across Lake Superior on a steamer to Marquette on Michigan's upper peninsula. From Marquette, the army proceeded by chartered boxcars to the Straits of Mackinac, which the men crossed by boat before hiking 16 miles to Cheboygan. From that point, and only after a great deal of persuasion, the Michigan Central Railroad agreed to haul the men south to Bay City. Citizens there and in nearby Saginaw gave the Coxeyites a warm welcome and raised $400 for the army to charter a lumber schooner that would take them to Detroit and then on to Cleveland.

At both Detroit and Cleveland, however, the army received a cold shoulder. Few residents donated food or clothing, while the generosity of organized labor also proved disappointing. In Cleveland, police officers would not let Jeffries speak in the public square and no one bothered to find the army a place to camp for the night. "Well, this is the meanest place we have struck yet," grumbled one member of the army.[23] Responding to the slight, Jeffries' men covered their mouths with handkerchiefs and strips of cloth and paraded through the downtown streets with a banner that read: "Free Speech in Cleveland." The demonstration attracted attention and brought the men some assistance.

From Cleveland, it was overland to Pittsburgh during the last week of July. After 50 men who had boarded a train at Ravenna were ordered off at gunpoint and then taken to jail, several hundred of their fellow marchers set up camp on the courthouse lawn and dared the police to arrest them. As Jeffries commented: "The only force we ever use is the force of numbers." That same idea directed his larger vision: "If we can get a million men there [in Washington] we can just swarm all over the Capitol grass and everything else. What could they do? Arrest us? Let them arrest. For everyone they could arrest there would be ten to take his place."[24]

Jeffries's army passed through Pittsburgh with 430 men, but being the seventh or eighth army to reach that city meant that their welcome was less than enthusiastic. From Pittsburgh, the army walked 60 miles southeast to Connellsville, a railway town and coke-producing center in the mountains. Refusing to walk further, the men climbed aboard a Baltimore & Ohio freight train. At that point a fight broke out between the Coxeyites and railroad crewmen and train detectives. Men swung clubs and heavy links of chain and threw coupling pins and pieces of scrap iron. Jeffries fought alongside his men. More than 100 Coxeyites were arrested and taken to Uniontown, the county seat, for trial. Sixty-five of the men were sentenced to pay either a five-dollar fine or spend five days in jail.

The men served the time. Upon their release, the army continued on to Washington, finally reaching the capital on August 6. Jeffries and several of his associates took steps to organize a permanent industrial army, but their efforts did not get further than drawing up a program. Decidedly Populist in nature and far broader than good roads or reclaiming arid land in the West, their platform called for direct legislation (the initiative, referendum, and recall), nationalization of the railroads, free coinage of silver, compulsory education for children, and repeal of tramp and vagrancy laws.

By the time that Cantwell and Jeffries reached Washington in July and August only fragments of the earlier armies remained. Local authorities were losing patience with the shabby camps of half-starved men in their midst. On August 9, Maryland Governor Frank Brown ordered 40 special policemen to raid a camp near Bladensburg and arrest the men there for vagrancy. After a sham trial in which the men were not even provided with an attorney, they were all sentenced to three months in the Maryland House of Correction. Two days later, Virginia Governor Charles T. O'Ferrall evicted Coxeyites from another encampment at Rosslyn. Under orders from the governor, militiamen drove the marchers back into the District of Columbia where commissioners there eventually chartered railway coaches to take the men back to one of the major cities in the Midwest. Those who had trekked from the Pacific Northwest were provided with transportation to Minneapolis–St. Paul. After that some of the men headed to North Dakota to harvest wheat, while others hopped boxcars and headed back to the Pacific coast.

Not much is known about Jumbo Cantwell after he reached Washington. When Harry Holmes, one of the men under Charlotta's direction, returned home months later, he praised Charlotta but cursed Jumbo for exploiting his men while he went around giving lectures that fattened his "wad." According to Holmes and others, Jumbo stole the army's treasury ($3,000) and then fled to South America, although the story was never confirmed.

Jeffries showed better. On his way home from Washington, he told a reporter from the *Spokane Chronicle* that the march was "an educational campaign, meant to sow discontent as we went along."[25] Back in Seattle, he promoted a self-help program called the Industrial Cooperative Society. The organization helped 150 men survive the winter of 1894–95. The men lived communally and pooled whatever wages they were able to earn. As one Populist journal that supported the idea commented: "Self-help through cooperation is at present the only remedy for a plundered and degraded people."[26] Jeffries eventually returned to Detroit where he became a judge and something of a legend as a champion of the underdog while on the bench. Charlotta remained in Tacoma until 1902 when the probate of her first husband's estate was finally completed. By the time she paid the legal fees, she was broke. After that, she just disappears from the records.

On August 1, Fry, Galvin, Vinette, Cantwell, Kelly, Jennings, and three other leaders of the various armies who still had men in Washington made a final appeal to Congress to address the unemployment problem in the nation which they called a "Petition of the Unemployed." The petition, accompanied by a draft of "A Bill to Provide Work for American Citizens" that was introduced in the U.S. Senate by Senator William Peffer of Kansas, stated that it represented millions of unemployed or partly unemployed and underpaid workingmen who have "naught but their ability to labor to provide for themselves and families, and the average wealth possessed by them would not purchase a decent coffin." It also noted that the unemployed had waited hopefully for private and public enterprise to offer them work, but that their current condition had tested their loyalty to the laws of the land "as witness the violent outbreaks that are becoming so alarmingly frequent."[27]

This, they explained, was the reason why thousands of members of the various industrial armies were currently in jail who from hunger were forced to trespass on railroad property or to borrow transportation in an emergency. Listed in the petition were a number of demands that included: immediate employment on public works at fair wages or else national assistance to supply their own wants by cooperative industry; the free coinage of silver and a legal-tender currency issued directly to the people; and the immediate curtailment of foreign laborers until there is a demand for their labor or until the serfdom of the wage earner is abolished. This final "petition in boots" also failed to gain any consideration from Congress.

8

THE INDUSTRIAL ARMIES OF COLORADO AND UTAH

The repeal of the Sherman Silver Purchase Act during the Panic of 1893 had a devastating effect on the mining states of the Rocky Mountain West and none more severely than Colorado. By September 1893 the Colorado Bureau of Labor Statistics reported that 377 businesses had failed, 435 mines had closed, and 45,000 people in the state were out of work. As the price of silver plummeted, mining companies laid off workers and reduced the wages of those who managed to hold on to their jobs. With an overabundance of workers, mine owners could easily replace men unwilling to accept a cut in pay. As the economic downturn intensified, and as mines and smelters shut down, thousands of unemployed men began to pour into Denver in the hope of finding work. The state was already suffering economically even before the Panic. Several years of harsh winters and summer droughts had hurt Colorado farmers as well. With agriculture in distress, mines closing, and stock prices falling, banks closed, businesses failed, and farms fell to foreclosure.

As the unemployed flooded into Denver, they found there were no steady jobs and very little help. The Denver Trades and Labor Assembly set up Camp Relief for a few weeks during the summer of 1893, while the city appropriated some money for street paving and employed a number of married men at $1.50 for eight hours of work. Rescue missions tried to provide food and shelters. One gospel mission opened a wood yard where in exchange for three hours of work an unemployed worker could obtain three meals and one night's lodging. The mission employed about 100 men per day. But charity organizations could not keep up with the growing demand and, as a result, were forced to concentrate their efforts on helping women and children. The People's Tabernacle operated one of Denver's largest relief

8. The Industrial Armies of Colorado and Utah

efforts. They provided winter clothing, some medical attention, ran a free bathhouse, and offered shelter for the homeless, but it, too, was forced to limit assistance to those who had been living in the city for more than 60 days. Several other groups organized community gardens in an effort to supplement general food insufficiency.

With the city increasingly unable to take care of the jobless and homeless, railroads began offering free transportation for those wishing to leave the mile-high city. As the crisis deepened in the late spring of 1894, when numerous industrial armies descended upon the city, the unemployed gathered at River Front Park along the South Platte River and created an enormous tent city. Desperate for a way to ease the crisis, the Denver Chamber of Commerce made a gift of lumber to the homeless there, apparently in the hope that they would build rafts and just drift away. During the first week of June 1894, unemployed Coxeyites camped at the site made a desperate attempt to do just that.

The first of several Coxey armies to emerge in Colorado was led by William Grayson, a Scot who claimed to have once been in the British army. Grayson had little trouble generating recruits among Denver's unemployed. News of the advance of Kelly's 1,500-man army from Ogden to Omaha on a Union Pacific freight train undoubtedly piqued interest and added to Grayson's recruits. The idea must have certainly excited Denver's officials as well as they could now hope to export at least a portion of their burdensome social problem.

On April 17, 1894, one hundred men in Grayson's army went to the yards of the Burlington & Missouri River Railroad and climbed into empty boxcars hoping to begin their journey to the nation's capital. The yardmaster, looking to have some fun with his uninvited guests, moved the cars from track to track for several hours before it became obvious that the cars were going nowhere. Foiled in their first attempt at train-hopping, the men then made their way to the Union Pacific yards where they spent the night in the roundhouse. In the morning, the men again climbed into some empty cars that they believed were about to be sent to Julesburg in northeastern Colorado where the Denver branch line joined the Union Pacific main line to Omaha.

Once again, the yardmaster played a trick. When the train was ready to leave, he had crewmen cut the train in two, drop out the cars loaded with Coxeyites, and then reconnect the train. The train moved out before Grayson's men understood what had happened. After lingering in the yards all morning trying to figure out their next move,

"Work, give us work"

the Coxeyites finally decided to head out across the rolling prairie on foot. They walked as far as Evans just outside of Greeley. From that point, they were able to ride in wagons furnished by the locals in the towns through which they passed as they moved northeast toward the Nebraska border.

Trouble seemed to follow Colorado's first industrial army. At Julesburg, the men deposed Grayson and elected Barney Hudson to be their new leader. But when he got drunk in North Platte, Nebraska, and landed in jail, they elected Henry Bennett to replace him. Bennett was a soft-spoken Virginian and a painter and paper-hanger by trade. He appeared to be well-liked by the men. Under his direction, the army reached Ogallala, Nebraska, on May 2, having walked 35 miles in two days. By the time the army neared Kearney, Nebraska, they numbered 78 men. Town officials, who had greeted Kelly's army nearly a month earlier, were unsure what to do with these new arrivals. After some discussion, it was decided to give the men enough food for one meal and hope that they would move on. To that end, the town council approved an order for 50 loaves of bread, 15 pounds of coffee, 20 pounds of sugar, 12 dozen eggs, and 50 pounds of bacon. They also allowed the army to camp in the brick works just west of town.

Kearney had a strong Populist organization and quite a few towns-people who sympathized with the Coxeyites. As a show of solidarity, those interests invited the army into town for a small celebration. The men readily accepted and marched into town with flags flying. The following morning, furnished with wagons supplied by their local supporters, Bennett's army set out toward Shelton. As the men crossed the town's main street, they paused to give three cheers for Kearney. Newspapers reported the army leaving Hastings, Nebraska, on May 14.

Bennett and his men eventually followed a course that took them through much of Nebraska before descending into northeastern Kansas on their way to St. Joseph, Missouri. At that point they hoped to build rafts and float down the Missouri River. Bennett did get his men as far as Kansas City, but deserted them at that point, absconding with the army's treasury of $108. The money had been raised at a local Populist convention to purchase boats for the continuance of their journey. There is some evidence that a core of the men from Bennett's group voted to continue, and that "Mother" Mary Jones, traveling a day or two ahead of the men, served as their advance agent giving speeches and soliciting money and supplies all the way to St. Louis.

8. The Industrial Armies of Colorado and Utah

In an interview given to a reporter from the *Topeka State Journal*, the so-called "Mother of the Commonweal" noted that, as a member of the Home Guard unit in Chicago, it was her work "to help the army along."[1]

In Colorado, the interest in marching to Washington was as strong as any state and especially so amongst unemployed miners. With talk of joining Coxey's army in the air, a second contingent of 50 Colorado Coxeyites organized the Cripple Creek Industrial Army under the command of John Sherman Sanders on April 27, 1894. The formal articles of organization called for Congress to enact legislation that would be beneficial to the general mass of working people; restore the free and unlimited coinage of silver at 16 to 1; and pass an irrigation bill much like that called for by Charles T. Kelly that would reclaim desert land. Such a measure was seen as a way to create jobs for the unemployed and generate opportunity for willing homesteaders.

Cripple Creek was one of the largest towns in the gold mining region of the state. When the Panic of 1893 and the repeal of the Silver Purchase Act caused the price of silver to plummet, newly laid-off silver miners moved into the gold mining district looking for work. The surge in surplus labor encouraged mine owners either to lower wages or to demand that workers put in longer hours for less pay. When conditions became intolerable in the winter of 1894, union men, led by the Western Federation of Miners (WFM), began a strike that essentially closed the mines for months. When Sanders was later asked by a Kansas reporter to describe the men in his army, he remarked: "The men with me are nearly all from the silver districts. They came to Cripple Creek to get work but found the strike on and refused to take the place of strikers for they are all union men."[2] With little hope of a settlement in sight, and with the real prospect that mine owners would soon try to reopen the mines with strikebreakers, a number of men decided that an organized march to protest conditions was their best option.

The 29-year-old Sanders was an electrician and a "practical" miner who had worked in mines all over the West and had been employed at Cripple Creek for several years. He was described as a man with some education, well-mannered, and quiet and dignified in his bearing. By the time the "brigade" marched out of Cripple Creek and Victor on May 4 with flags flying and drums beating, it had grown into an "army" of nearly 300 men, soon to be augmented by other unemployed miners from Coal Creek, Florence, and Pueblo. The

"Work, give us work"

Florence & Cripple Creek Railway provided a free train for the army to Cañon City, and the Denver & Rio Grande Railroad carried the men in similar fashion on to Pueblo. While his men rested, Sanders requested that the Missouri Pacific provide free transportation for his men as they moved east. The reply from company officials was that they would agree to carry the men only if they paid full passenger fares. Fearing that Sanders's men might try to capture a train, Missouri Pacific officials gave the order for workers to run the company's good engines and passenger cars out of town. The only pieces of equipment left behind were an old Denver & Rio Grande Western switch engine whose boiler leaked badly and a number of flatcars.

Seeing no way out of his dilemma, Sanders told his men, now increased by the addition of new recruits to 450, that the railroad had given him permission to borrow the old engine. Sanders was fortunate in that among his men were three locomotive engineers, five firemen, three telegraph operators, and one civil engineer. The men coupled the engine to the flatcars, loaded their tents, and climbed aboard, although there was little more than standing room to be had. With the men waving their flags and a crowd cheering them on, the train begin to steam east across the plains toward Kansas at a high rate of speed.

Unlike Hogan's capture of a train from a corporation (Northern Pacific) that was in receivership and could request protection from the federal courts, the solvent Missouri Pacific did not have that luxury. As a result, the railroad tried in every way to stop the hijacked train without federal assistance. Officials ordered engines to be wrecked at several cuts along the way to block the track and stop the stolen train. As in Montana, they had crewmen place obstructions on the tracks and ordered linemen to drain the water tanks along the route. After a run of about 20 miles, Sanders' men encountered their first derailed engine, overturned by company employees to block their passage. Undaunted by the obstruction, the men found tools in a section foreman's shack, tore up the tracks from behind the train, re-laid them around the wrecked engine, and continued, taking enough rails with them to discourage any pursuit. When the engineer, a veteran on the line named Lewellyn, discovered that he was running low on water near Ordway, the men formed a line much like an old-time fire brigade and replenished the tender from a nearby irrigation ditch using buckets, dinner pails, and coffee pots. When the industrials encountered a second wrecked engine lying across the track, they once again built around the obstacle.

8. The Industrial Armies of Colorado and Utah

Five miles west of Chivington, Colorado, the army encountered its third wreck. Crews of the Missouri Pacific had removed spikes from the rails and overturned a boxcar. They then proceeded to fire up an engine and, with a good head of steam, crash it into the boxcar and effectively block the track. Because the overturned engine was too heavy to move without machinery, the men set to work chopping up the boxcar, burning the wood to give them light while they labored to relay track around the wreckage. Once the road had been cleared, the train stopped in Chivington only long enough for the men to get something to eat. While in town, the local telegraph operator informed Sanders that the track was clear to Scott City, Kansas, and that the water tanks were full. Ominously, the operator also reported that a federal marshal and a considerable number of deputies were waiting at that point to arrest them.

Officials of the Missouri Pacific had sent a request to Kansas Governor Lorenzo Lewelling asking for his help in recovering the road's stolen property. But the Populist governor, who only a few weeks earlier had spoken of the Coxey movement as "a spontaneous uprising of the people" and "an earnest and vigorous protest against the injustice and tyranny of the age," did not feel that the situation required calling out the state militia.[3] Instead, he recommended to his constituents that they petition Congress to give the industrials food, shelter, and a fair hearing. Blocked by the governor, attorneys for the railroad then decided on a different tactic. Even if the road was not in receivership, the Coxeyites could be seen as committing a federal offense if it could be shown that the army's actions had disrupted the movement of the U.S. mail. Actually, Sanders and his men had been careful to take sidings so as not to delay trains carrying the mail, but the attorneys for the Missouri Pacific persuaded a federal judge in Kansas to issue a warrant for their arrest.

At Horace, Kansas, Sanders and his men were finally able to abandon their rusty old switch engine and seize a first-class locomotive, but their wild ride was almost over. As the army approached Scott City on May 10, they noticed that 50 feet of track in front of the station had been torn up and that a large number of deputies were lined up on the station platform. Newspapers reported that most of the deputies had Winchesters while others had double-barreled shotguns and revolvers. Each of the deputies reportedly carried 50 rounds of ammunition. The game was up. After a journey of 220 miles, Sanders and his intrepid Colorado contingent surrendered peaceably to Marshal S.T. Neely and a posse of 40 deputies who had been sent to intercept them. There were no guns found among the captured men. Accompanying the special train were reporters from the *Topeka Capital*, the *Kansas City Star and Times*, the *Chicago Times*, and the *Denver News*. After a supper furnished by local sympathizers, the men were loaded onto passenger coaches to be taken to Topeka. Sanders appeared to be nonplussed about the arrest. He was convinced that his army had not obstructed the mail and felt that a Populist governor would be sympathetic to their point of view. Besides, being allowed to ride in Pullmans to the Kansas capital was a quick way to advance his army another 300 miles closer to its destination.

After an all-night journey to Topeka, a huge crowd greeted the train at the station early the next day. As the men waved to the crowd of sympathizers, excited onlookers coaxed Sanders out onto the rear platform to have his picture taken. The townspeople brought cookies, dishpans full of bread, and plugs of chewing tobacco, and passed these through the train windows to the men. Governor Lewelling provided the army with 50 tents to form a camp in the rail yards. Local citizens were allowed to visit the camp and nearly 2,000 did so with many bringing additional food for the Coxeyites.

No one was quite sure as to what should be done with such a large number of prisoners. A federal judge in Denver who had declined to issue an injunction to stop the men in Colorado commented that he did not see how a chain of flatcars was in any way connected to the U.S. mail. Speaking for the men, the *Rocky Mountain News* editorially argued that Sanders and his men had not committed a crime of criminal trespass because they had not removed the train from railroad property. The editors added that if the commandeered train had delayed the mail, it was because the railroad had ditched its equipment and blocked the track at numerous points in an effort to stop the Sanders train. In one last jab at the railroad's logic, the editors joked that "perhaps the federal statute making it a criminal offense to 'walk on the grass' may extend to the prairies of Kansas."[4]

In the meantime, federal authorities seemed to be in no hurry to rush the case to trial and test their new legal theory. Unlike other cases where hijackers were tried for contempt of court, the men in this case would be tried before a jury of their peers. Even the U.S. attorney for Kansas seemed to be at a loss on how to proceed, stating: "My

8. The Industrial Armies of Colorado and Utah

object ever since the arrest has been to disband and disorganize this body of men."[5]

After two days in Topeka, the men were transported further east to the Fort Leavenworth military installation on the Missouri River. At that point, the court set a bond of $300 for Sanders and $250 for each of the 350 men with him. Little else was done. Instead of a speedy trial, the men spent the next month as loosely guarded prisoners. They lived in tents pitched in the shade trees or bedded down in abandoned railway cars on the grounds and ate regular military meals rather than prison food. The atmosphere was relaxed and friendly and the prisoners fraternized with soldiers and deputies. Sanders, who thought that charges would eventually be dropped, was even released on his own recognizance. He took the opportunity to tour Kansas as a lecturer for the Populist party.

When a rumor began to circulate that President Cleveland did not want the army to reach Washington, and that he had instructed the court to find the men guilty, some of the men began to worry. Because such a verdict would most likely mean time in jail, about 30 men decided to slip past their guards in small numbers and escape. Once on the "outside," they reassembled on the railroad tracks and then caught a train to Kansas City. It was thought that some of the men joined the remnants of Bennett's army in Kansas City and continued their journey down the Missouri River.

On June 18, a jury returned a verdict in the trial of the Sanders' train-stealers, taking less than an hour to find the men guilty of obstructing the U.S. mail. When news of the decision reached the camp of the Coxeyites at Leavenworth, there was quite a commotion, and a number of the prisoners decided to attempt an escape. During the confusion, about 40 of the industrials managed to get away. The presiding judge ordered the remaining men to pay fines and serve short jail sentences. The convicted men were then divided into squads and sent to county jails scattered throughout the state. Like the action of Judge Beatty in Idaho, the staggered and scattered release of the prisoners was seen as a way to prevent the army from re-forming. Sanders had promised to reassemble his army, but he never did.

Even after the misadventures experienced by the armies of Grayson-Bennett and Sanders, Coloradoans had not lost their fascination with the Coxey crusade. One reason for this was the activism of Denver's Home Guard. As in other states, the organization was created to provide moral support and financial aid to local Coxeyites while on the road and economic support to families left behind. The Denver Home Guard, in cooperation with the local Ladies' Relief Corps and organized labor, claimed to represent 10,000 Coxeyite sympathizers in the city. Their weekly meetings kept local interest in the industrial army concept alive, and they were not shy about firing off a protest letter to Lafayette Pence, their Populist congressman in Washington, or marching through the streets of town armed with pro–Coxey banners.

It seemed to many locals that Denver had become a mecca for the unemployed, not only from within Colorado but from neighboring states/territories as well. The virtual suspension of all silver mining in Colorado produced a steady stream of the unemployed into Denver and intensified the burden on that community. Toward the end of May, hundreds of unemployed workers were arriving in the city every

Coxey's Army demonstration in Denver, Colorado. Creator: Forman, no date. The Denver Home Guard, a moral and financial support group formed to assist men on the march and families left behind, in cooperation with the local Ladies' Relief Corps and organized labor, claimed to represent 10,000 Coxeyite sympathizers in the city. This photograph underscores their enthusiasm. Denver Public Library Special Collections, Call # X-21550.

8. The Industrial Armies of Colorado and Utah

day. Following orders from Colorado Governor Davis Waite, the Colorado militia loaned the men cooking utensils and several hundred tents. It was not long before a tent city had sprung up along the banks of the South Platte in an area known as River Front Park. In a short time, the population of the tent city grew to nearly 1,500, the largest encampment of unemployed anywhere in the United States.

Soon to join Denver's swollen tent city were members of Henry Carter's industrial army from Salt Lake City. The depression badly damaged Utah's economy which was dependent upon agriculture, transportation, and mining. As it had elsewhere in the country, farm income dropped severely in the territory with wheat selling for as little as 30 cents a bushel. Similarly, railroad construction, which had helped fuel a speculative boom in the territory in the 1880s, came to a halt. But the most serious problem impacting the territorial economy was the closing of the mines. Silver production dropped by a third and copper production by one-half of what they had been before the depression, while salt production declined by over 90 percent. In mid–February 1894, fifteen hundred unemployed men gathered in downtown Salt Lake City to ask city and county leaders to provide work on the roads and on construction for the new state capital that was about to start. By one report, more than 4,000 of the 9,000 laboring men in Salt Lake City were out of work in the spring of 1894.

In mid–April, several hundred unemployed men in Salt Lake City, excited by newspaper accounts of the arrival of Kelly's 1,500-man industrial army in Ogden, decided to organize their own contingent and chose Henry Carter, a young carpenter, as their leader. While negotiations with officials of the Rio Grande Western Railroad regarding transportation east continued, the Utah army of the unemployed, numbering about 500, paraded out of Salt Lake City on April 30 to an encampment in Murray, Utah. Sympathetic crowds estimated at four to five thousand lined the streets to cheer them on. But not everyone was elated. The *Salt Lake Tribune* ran a humorous story about one woman who resented that her husband had joined up. Accompanied by a friend, the two ladies drove to the army's camp outside Salt Lake City, stormed passed guards, and exited dragging a man in tow. After a heated exchange between the couple, the wife slapped her husband and proclaimed that she would "thrash" any man who would desert his wife and children "to follow a 'will-o'-the-wisp' across the deserts of the West."[6]

From the outset, General Carter found himself under a great deal of pressure. On May 4, newspapers announced that negotiations with the Rio Grande Western Railway had broken down and that company officials stated that they would not carry the army at any price. Carter placed the blame on Democratic officials in Washington and local politicians whom he charged had pressured the railroad into refusing to transport his men to prevent them from reaching the nation's capital in protest. He charged that the railroad had initially offered to carry the army to Grand Junction, Colorado, for $500, to Denver for $1,000, and to Kansas City for $1,500 before the governor and other Democratically appointed territorial officials intervened to have the road rescind its offer. That same afternoon, Carter spoke before a crowd of six to seven hundred people in downtown Salt Lake City and excoriated the larger forces that seemed to be blocking his advance:

> I speak to you as a representative of the toilers, the producers of the American nation. We here are a small branch of the 2,000,000 unemployed, down-trodden workingmen of America.... Their voices rein in a hoarse-swelling chorus, sounding throughout the nation a protest against plutocracy and the corporate power that has ground them into the dust and made them slaves in this land of the free and home of the brave.... We are willing to work, but we cannot obtain it.... We will not starve without making one supreme struggle to better our condition.... We are going to Washington, and don't you forget it, and we are not going to walk either.[7]

Carter also had to deal with stories in the press that could affect the way the public viewed his crusade. On May 7, the *Salt Lake Tribune* reported that the firm of Kilpatrick and Collins, railroad contractors, had floated an offer to employ the entire industrial army at $1.50 per day on railroad construction work in Montana. Similar offers had been made to Fry's army when it reached East St. Louis (digging trenches for the laying of pipe) and when a contingent of the Northwest armies arrived in Yakima (harvesting crops). Rejection of such offers, real or fake, could convince some sympathizers who might see the action as an unwillingness to work to stop contributing supplies and rations. In responding to the report, Carter stated that a formal offer of employment had never been made, and that he considered it a "scheme to disband the army." "We have in our ranks," he noted, "men of all trades and many professions, and to ask them to go into the wilds of Montana and work as common laborers is an insult to them."[8]

After more than a week wasted in fruitless negotiations with railroad officials, Carter ordered his restless army to march from its

8. The Industrial Armies of Colorado and Utah

camp at Murray to Lehi where it set up camp about a mile from the Rio Grande Western tracks and close to the Union Pacific line. Joining Carter's men at Lehi were about 250 men who had marched from California. The following day the group started toward Provo where, in the early hours of May 12, about 40 men captured a westbound Union Pacific train and switched it to the eastbound tracks of the Rio Grande Western. The men then drove the train to the Provo station where employees of the railroad intervened, throwing a switch and derailing the engine and the coal tender. While the insurgents set about the task of restoring the engine to the track, they were surrounded by 40 armed deputy U.S. marshals. Ultimately, "General" Carter and 27 of his "lieutenants" and "colonels" were arrested and taken to the Utah penitentiary. After hearing the charges against Carter and a number of his officers, Judge S.A. Merritt of the Utah Supreme Court fined Carter $100 and sentenced him to five days in jail. Others connected to the hijacking received smaller fines but similar five-day jail terms.

A week after the trial, however, the *Ogden Standard* published a transcript of a telegram that allegedly had been sent by Judge H.W. Smith, a colleague, to Merritt before he had even heard the Carter case. "It is all-important," read the message, "that they be found guilty and held for contempt, because we have detectives among them, and they intend to carry things with a high hand if their leaders are discharged, and it seems to be the understanding among them that they will disband if their leaders are held.... A special effort will be made to get Carter off. It should not prevail. He is the most guilty of all, although there may be some difficulty in showing it." Merritt allegedly wired back, saying: "I appreciate the situation and concur in your reasoning." When the story broke in the press, the editor of the *Salt Lake Tribune* remarked: "The like of this was probably never before written by one judge to another. It is a direct call on Judge Merritt to find the accused guilty whether they are guilty or not."[9] When interviewed, Smith denied that he had sent the message, but Merritt admitted that the correspondence had taken place. Populist sympathizers were quick to condemn the exchange, calling it an example of "judicial infamy" and "the most damning evidence yet brought out, showing the corruption of the courts."[10] For others, who thought that train stealing should be stopped, it did not seem to matter.

After the incident with the stolen train at Provo, Carter's men adopted a policy much like that of Cantwell and Jeffries in

"Work, give us work"

Washington. They would break up into small groups of 40 or 50 and then surreptitiously jump aboard trains headed east. On May 16, the first group of 50 arrived in Pueblo, Colorado, on a freight. Apparently, the Rio Grande agreed to carry the men rather than have any more delays or trouble on their line. Two days later, an advance guard of 100 men from Carter's army arrived in Denver from Pueblo on a Denver and Gulf stock train. Ten days later, 375 additional Coxeyites reached Denver via the Denver & Rio Grande. Two hundred of these men were part of the Utah contingent under the command of Henry Carter, while the remainder were from Stockton, California. The California Coxeyites had been on the road for 49 days and had suffered tremendous hardships crossing the Utah deserts. The combined group joined their comrades at the already over-crowded River Front encampment.

Coxey Army Scenes. Participants in one of the western industrial armies have a meal in camp as they pass through Colorado. An American flag is staked in the ground, laundry hangs on a clothesline, 1894. Online Collection, CHS Scan # 20030902, History Colorado.

8. The Industrial Armies of Colorado and Utah

The rapidly growing numbers at the camp alarmed Denver's conservatives. Even though steps had been taken to maintain law and order in the tent encampment, many in the city regarded the camp as an eyesore and a catch-all for tramps and hobos that would only lead to begging on the streets and petty theft. They were also angry with Governor Waite for welcoming the industrials to the state, when he must certainly have known that the railroads would refuse to take them out. Denver's sizeable Home Guard, however, offered a significant counter to any thought of a forced removal. But Denver's relief agencies quickly found themselves in a predicament. They simply could not keep feeding the rising number of unemployed that just kept coming into the city. As one exasperated official of the Denver Home Guard commented: "The home reserve was not formed to support men from Utah and California and all the other places, but was to take care of the people of Denver."[11] During the first week of June, donations dropped off and the quantity and quality of the free meals declined. Soon, those encamped at the river were reduced to a diet that amounted to little more than bread and coffee. With railroads refusing to relax their no-transit posture and their train yards heavily guarded, the situation had reached a crisis point.

Then, just as the situation appeared to be hopeless, someone came up with an idea. Why not boat down the Platte? Kelly's men had turned into sailors when stranded in Des Moines, and Hogan's men had decided to raft down the Missouri River after being detained in Montana. Eager to push this idea forward, the Denver Chamber of Commerce agreed to provide provisions for the trip, while others promised to donate lumber and materials to build the boats. At certain times of the year the Platte River would have been too shallow for any type of navigation, but recent heavy rains and snow melt had swollen the river and made the idea seem feasible if perhaps a bit more dangerous. Scouts sent to survey the river downstream reported that a squadron of small boats could conceivably make the journey.

Following the advice of those who claimed to have some shipbuilding expertise and using their own sweat equity, Denver's Coxeyites were able to construct 100 flat-bottomed boats that looked like smaller versions of Kelly's Des Moines River scows. Optimists in the group planned to ride these vessels all the way to Kansas City and hoped to make the trip in 12 days. To raise funds for their journey, the men charged the city's curious citizens 15 cents to watch them conduct competitions—a tug of war, bicycle races, and a baseball game. The main attraction, however, was in watching the men build boats. Some sawed planks, others hammered nails, and still others caulked seams. Each boat was given a name when completed such as "General Coxey" and "Keep Off the Grass." But some who had inspected the boats at close hand were not so confident about the "navy's" prospects. "The boats are not so formidable looking and they do not look any too seaworthy either," remarked one reporter. To the critical eye, the boats appeared to have been hastily constructed from material that was too light and flimsy for anything other than a brief afternoon sail on a lake. When reporters asked one officer about the upcoming departure, he replied in words that proved to be prophetic: "We don't expect to have much of a picnic."[12]

The first boats of the Denver Coxeyites set off on June 4. Two days later an advance group of 150 men started out for nearby Brighton where they would wait for General Carter and the main body of men who would follow the next day. Minor incidents on the water marred the first day. The small boats did prove to be trickier to maneuver than envisioned, and it did not take much for a hidden piling or half-submerged log to cave in the hull of a flimsy craft. Many were surprised to find that the river was a bit more dangerous than expected.

Coxey's Army. View of a collection of men from various western industrial armies by the South Platte River in Denver, Colorado, June 1894. Photograph shows men building flat bottom boats at River Front Park. Rapidly flowing river current and dangerous snags are shown in foreground. Denver Public Library Special Collections, Call # X-21551.

8. The Industrial Armies of Colorado and Utah

Men who happened to fall overboard found it difficult to swim to shore against the strong current and had to be rescued by spectators. Although many laughed at the floundering sailors, those who could not swim were not that amused. Maybe the boats were not as safe as first thought.

As Carter and the main body of men set out, well-wishers shouted "On to Washington" for encouragement. But this would not be a day of good fortune. The current was just as strong and dangerous as the day before, but this time a strong crosswind made the small boats impossible to steer. In narrow portions of the river, where water flowed at a rate of 15 to 20 miles an hour, a boat that was not under control could easily overturn or crash into some obstacle. One boat with five men on board, none of whom could swim, crashed into the pilings of a railroad bridge. While the panicked "sailors" cried for help, one of their comrades sank beneath the water and disappeared. For the others, the swift current swept them into a cluster of submerged branches and logs. As one local newspaper reported, "Snags shattered the clumsy crafts and cast the ... mariners into quicksands.... How many disappeared in these traps will never be known."[13] As rescuers tried to free one man, the body of another washed up on a sandbar. Several other bodies were sighted at a nearby bridge.

Another hidden danger was barbed wire fencing (used to keep cattle from escaping when the water in the river was low) that was submerged at places in the rain-swollen river. Boaters caught in the wire had their scows torn apart and often found themselves ensnared in the fencing. In the aftermath, a *Rocky Mountain News* reporter commented: "The marks of the unfortunate fleet are visible at every hand. Broken oars are plentiful along the banks and crushed boats are to be seen at irregular intervals. Blankets and wearing apparel are hung to many a wire fence or lodged on the branches of trees hanging into the water."[14]

The original plan was to have a pilot boat travel ahead of the fleet to mark sandbars and hidden snags with red flags, while the rest of the boats would follow in single file. One expert oarsman was to travel with each boat, and lifelines were to be at the ready at dangerous places on the river. But none of these precautionary steps seemed to have been taken and it was obvious that there were too many men and too much baggage in the shallow-draft boats. Lamenting the mistakes that were made, and perhaps looking to shift some of the blame,

General Carter commented: "This whole river business was a mistake and was undertaken against my advice, and those who started did so without orders. Those of us who are left have but little provision."[15]

When the survivors finally stumbled into Brighton, the townspeople found them places to bed down for the night and fixed them breakfast the next day. After that everyone was in rescue mode and rumors were plentiful. Someone reported having seen a man wearing a blue coat with epaulets sink beneath the water. If true, that could only have been General Carter. Another report came in that the body of a black man named Roberts had been found. But no sooner had these reports come in than in walked Roberts and General Carter. Although some estimated that the death toll might have approached 40, only six bodies were ever recovered. Some of those who escaped the horrors of the Platte placed blame on the railroads for forcing them to take to the river in the first place. Applying the same logic, other critics might have placed some of the blame on local officials who eagerly supported the idea in perhaps an overzealous move to rid the city of an economic burden. Others directed their anger at General Higginson, the leader of the advance guard, for poor planning and for possibly being inebriated at the time. Most, however, agreed that the immediate cause of the disaster was the poor design of the boats themselves, which were ill-suited to the task.

After the disaster, an internal dispute amongst the survivors caused the army to split into three separate groups. General Carter continued to lead the Utah contingent, while General Adams was chosen to lead the Colorado group (ex-general Higginson had been demoted to quartermaster). Captain Benning was elected commodore of the navy and led perhaps 150 men who were willing to give the Platte a second try and set out again in their flimsy craft. They did agree, however, to reduce the number of occupants in each boat. The men in the armada of 27 boats slowly made their way down the river into Nebraska and reached the Platte River bridge south of Kearney on June 26. A delegation came into town to solicit supplies which were provided and hauled to the bridge.

Having to contend with its third industrial army, town officials decided to deal with the men at a distance. The men said they had been making about 40 miles a day when they were not hassled by deputies. Farmers along the way had provided the men with some food and they supplemented what was given with fish caught from the river.

8. The Industrial Armies of Colorado and Utah

The following day, the navy floated off toward Grand Island. Several weeks later, a greatly reduced group of 27 men finally reached the Missouri River just south of Omaha. It was probably this small contingent that joined-up with Hogan's boaters after they left Omaha following Fourth of July celebrations.

Choosing to follow a different course, several hundred Coxeyites under two different commanders decided to abandon the river and proceed on foot following the Union Pacific train route. To make sure the men did not have a change of heart and decide to return to the city, Denver officials and the ever-helpful Home Guards sent a large donation of food ahead to Fort Morgan. When the men arrived at Fort Morgan, however, they were surprised to learn that the carload of provisions had been sent even farther down the line. It was not until the Denver marchers reached Julesburg near the Nebraska border, about 100 miles from Ft. Morgan, that they finally caught up with the promised provisions.

At Julesburg, however, an incident occurred that changed the course of the march. Some of the men decided to commandeer a locomotive and a line of boxcars. But in their hurray to get moving, they ran the train through an open switch and off the track. Undeterred, the Coxeyites immediately set to work putting the box cars back on the track, but the 60-ton engine proved too heavy for even several hundred men to lift. Fearing that any further delay in trying to get the engine back on track would lead to their capture, the men involved in the attempted hijacking began to split up. One group of about 200 men decided to capture the first train through and head toward Ogallala, Nebraska. Another group of 100 men led by General Adams hired two teams to haul their provisions and started across country toward the Burlington & Missouri line but changed their minds and headed toward Big Springs, Nebraska, on the Union Pacific line instead. The balance of the army chose to camp by the river.

Early that evening, Marshal Jones arrived in Julesburg from Denver with 120 deputies and arrested about 70 men presumed (mistakenly) to be part of the group that had been involved in the foiled attempt to hijack a train. These men were taken back to Denver for trial. Sensing that the army was now hopelessly fragmented, and tired of men who would no longer follow orders, General Carter decided to abandon the effort and return to Salt Lake City. The deputies who remained behind in Julesburg immediately set out in pursuit of Adams and his men.

Officials of the Union Pacific anticipated that remnants of the "Denver" army, now strung out along the rail line in southwestern Nebraska, would continue to attempt to commandeer trains. In response, they readied a special train in Omaha to carry 100 deputy marshals west to apprehend any suspected train-stealers that might have eluded the lawmen from Denver. On June 15, about 200 Coxeyites captured an east-bound freight train at Big Springs, Nebraska, but deputies were able to halt their progress when they arrived on a west-bound train. Following orders from Nebraska's federal judge, Elmer S. Dundy, the heavily armed deputies arrested the men without incident. Following a directive from Attorney General Richard Olney, Dundy ordered the ringleaders brought to Omaha for trial. Then, in a surprise move, he directed that the remaining prisoners be transported in sealed boxcars to a recently abandoned military barracks at Fort Sidney in western Nebraska. According to a dispatch from Sidney to the *Indianapolis Journal*, the men were confined in a small building inadequate to house half their number. They were allegedly forced to sleep without blankets on bare floors. Their food was poor and many of the men were sick. The dispatch noted that the men had been confined to this "pen of filth" for two weeks waiting their farcical trial, described as an example of "kangaroo justice," to begin, and still had not been told what the charges were.[16]

After being held for two weeks in that remote location, Judge Dundy finally arrived to hold court at the site. The judge charged the Denver Coxeyites with contempt of court and, with little foundation, for obstructing the mails. He summarily found the men guilty, but chose not to sentence them as might be expected. Instead, Judge Dundy simply allowed the prisoners to remain confined at the fort for several more weeks. Following the example of federal judges in Idaho and Kansas, he then released the men in groups of five over the next month to prevent any chance that they might try to regroup. Upon their release, each Coxeyite was provided with enough rations for two days.

Conclusion

The most prominent protest movement to emerge during the depression of the 1890s was the colorful 400-mile march by an army of unemployed men from Massillon, Ohio, to Washington, D.C., led by an eccentric businessman by the name of Jacob Coxey. He called his march a "petition in boots." Although the saga of Coxey's army was well-chronicled by the 40-or-so reporters who marched with it, it was only part of a much larger story that did not get the same attention in the national media. Beginning in late March 1894, other armies of the unemployed began their own self-generated pilgrimages from depressed urban areas along the West Coast, from empty mining camps in the Rocky Mountains, and from the forests and fields of the Pacific Northwest. They started from cities like Los Angeles, San Francisco, Portland, Seattle, Tacoma, Salt Lake City, and Denver, and from more isolated towns like Reno, Butte, and Cripple Creek, Colorado.

The tremendous amount of publicity surrounding Coxey soon led the public to associate all other industrial armies with him and to call them "Coxey armies." The goal of each effort, although their specific demands differed and the distance they had to travel varied, was to reach the nation's capital where they would join together in numbers predicted to exceed 100,000. They hoped that the size and scope of their demonstration, coupled with their obvious determination, would call attention to the extent of unemployment in the country and impel the federal government to take immediate action to respond to the economic crisis.

The initial reaction to the formation of Coxey armies on the part of a majority of conservative-minded members of the middle- and upper-classes, most politicians in Washington, and almost all popular journals was to regard the entire procession with contempt and to shower it with ridicule. To these critics, Coxeyism was, as one editor

Conclusion

commented, "a movement curiously adapted for reflecting to every crank and visionary and reformer a justification of his own particular hobby."[1] Other newspaper editorials took a similar position. To the *Portland Oregonian,* the Coxeyites were the "anti-work army," to the *Townsend Leader,* the "industriless industrials," and to the *Spokane Chronicle,* a "battalion of bums." The *Tacoma Ledger* called them a "horde of loafers," the *Everett Times,* "an army of tramps," and the *Seattle Post-Intelligencer,* a "band of organized vagrants" most of whom "would not saw wood to pay for breakfast."[2] Its leaders were deluding their followers, encouraging lawlessness, threatening property, and inciting outbreaks of disorder. Followers were either tramps, vagabonds, or hobos, and, considered together, were nothing more than mobs falsely claiming to represent the people.

Others, however, saw things differently. Journalist W.T. Stead, a close observer of the movement, noted that the "Coxeyites, ridiculed by the classes, have the sympathy of the masses." "Coxey and his tatterdemalion followers," said Stead, "are laughable enough no doubt to those who from the stalls of full-fed comfort can only see the ludicrous side of weltering misery; but to the masses who suffer it is not surprising that they should appear in another and much more serious light. For they are ... the peripatetic advertisers of social misery."[3] In a similar vein, writer Ambrose Bierce derided the "pickpocket civilization," a society in which the affluent few exploited the labor of others and stymied the kind of useful public policy advocated by Coxey under the doctrine of laissez-faire.[4]

Coxey's initial march inspired others to form their own "armies," although their agendas and composition differed. Whereas critics liked to portray Jacob Coxey's "army" as a mixture of tramps, charlatans, and utopian reformers, the eastern press and the Cleveland administration came to view the industrial armies from the West (which included a large number of unemployed miners and railroad construction workers) "in a different light from Coxey's outfit." "Unlike the latter, the industrial armies that formed on the Pacific Coast and moved eastward along the transcontinental railroads were truly proletarian in nature."[5] One contemporary commentator made a similar comparison: "A different class of beings from Coxey's followers are these western crusaders. In the main they are stalwart young fellows, hardened by exposure and full of animal life; harder men to deal with than the meek, listless Coxey Commonwealers."[6]

8. Conclusion

In addition, the numbers, at times approaching 2,000 in one army, were much more formidable. One newspaper counted 13 different groups of Coxeyites, primarily from the West, numbering more than 5,000 marchers on the road at one time during the spring of 1894. Jack London, a temporary member of Kelly's army and a self-proclaimed "tramp" himself, estimated that there were 5,000–10,000 members of the various armies of the unemployed out of the 40,000–60,000 tramps in the country.[7]

Those "armies" were not without their supporters. Those who came to view the marchers simply as unemployed workers looking for work joined them in spirit and provided food, shelter, and wagon transportation for the men along the way, or maintained home guard units to care for family members left behind. Crowds turned out with brass bands and banners to cheer the industrials as they marched through town on foot or sped by on a captured train. Others banded together to intimidate federal marshals and their deputies who sought to halt their progress. In Council Bluffs, Iowa, a group of sympathizers led by a number of women actually stole a train themselves in an effort to help Kelly's army advance.

It was apparent to a number of observers at the time that Coxeyism was a manifestation of a serious social-economic malaise in the country. One Los Angeles reporter described the general unease as a "simmering, seething cauldron of discontent." "You find it," he stated, "on every hand wherever you go; whether east of the Rockies or beyond them, whether on the coast or on the sound.... You hear it on streetcorners, nay, ... you *see* it there in the hundreds of idle men who are all day, and late into the night, standing about telegraph poles in the business centers, waiting for something to turn up."[8]

For many who had recently migrated from the East, it seemed like the West no longer symbolized a field of opportunity as had been previously assumed. To many workers, it seemed as if they had been lured west under false pretenses. Now in trouble, the nation's producers—farmers and industrial workers—felt increasingly abandoned by the nation's "power elite." Even Richard Olney, who played such a key role in curtailing the Coxey movement, understood the changes taking place when he observed that those hardest hit by the depression felt "a sense of wrong—a conviction that they do not have fair play—that society by its very constitution necessarily works injustice and inequality, favoring a few with not only abundance, but with a

Conclusion

superfluity of blessings, while excluding the great majority not merely from the luxuries, but almost from the decent comforts of life."[9]

Coxey's march on Washington certainly captured public interest, but it also sparked a national debate not just over the past but over the future course of America as well. As W.T. Stead commented at the time: "And now ... we have Coxeyism ... to proclaim to the world the need for action other than that of *laissez-faire*."[10] Coxeyism forcefully raised the public question of what the proper role of the federal government in American society should be. When Jacob Coxey first proposed his plan for assisting the unemployed by having the government create jobs to build roads or construct other public works projects, he was anticipating New Deal–sponsored work relief programs that would come 40 years later. But asking for such things in the 1890s was seen by many as not only eccentric but also as threatening basic American values. "Coxeyism teaches a bad lesson," read one newspaper editorial, "the most dangerous lesson indeed that can be taught to the American people—the lesson of dependence on the Federal government."[11]

Many traditionalists likened the idea to paternalism and found it distasteful in that it appeared to undermine individual initiative. To such critics, the Coxeyites seemed to want something they had not earned. Equally disturbing were their demands that suggested that unemployment stemmed not from laziness, defects in character, or personal misfortune, as commonly assumed, but rather from larger, systemic problems in the economy. If this were true, what did it mean for traditional virtues like self-reliance and individual initiative? If the government assumed a greater responsibility for individual well-being, could this not corrupt America's basic character?

Coxeyite supporters saw things differently. There was a difference, they argued, between asking for bread and asking for jobs. They were not compromising the idea of individual initiative. They were merely asking for the opportunity to pursue it. They also noted the irony in the argument that asking for the government to offer assistance was somehow un–American. Didn't high tariffs protect manufacturers? Didn't federal land grants assist the development of railroads? Didn't the governmental philosophy of laissez-faire actually create an unregulated economic environment that businessmen regarded as conducive to promoting their self-interests? Why shouldn't the same concern be shown to workers? As the editor of one

8. Conclusion

Midwestern periodical commented, in words that seem eerily relevant today, "Can any reasonable mind reject the general proposition that labor as well as capital has claims which governments are bound in duty and self-interest to respect and, within reasonable limits, to allow.... Why should not government apply to the labor market the same business common sense which it applies to the money market for the prevention of disaster?"[12]

Economist Thorstein Veblen observed at the time that the industrial army movement represented a new way of thinking. To Veblen, it signified a recognition on the part of the working class of its "vital economic relation to the general [federal] government, and through the general government to all the rest of the community, without intermediation of any lower or local body."[13] Arthur Vinette, a member of Fry's industrial army and a carpenter by trade, discovered that in city after city traveling artisans found a surplus of labor and a scarcity of jobs. As he commented in an article published in *The Carpenter*, his trade magazine: "From Ohio to Missouri, tramping over the plains, scaling the snow-clad Rockies, a pitiless fate follows in his footsteps.... He follows the wide valleys, he is on the line of every railroad, but somehow or other, there is always a surplus crop of his tribe." Finally reaching the Pacific coast and encountering the same dilemma, he concludes, "Alas, the promised land is a myth."[14]

As economist Anne Mayhew noted, "Experience in industry had convinced the unemployed marchers that the availability of jobs was not determined locally, but, rather, that jobs were created through a national mechanism [the nationally integrated self-regulating market created by railways and industrialization]."[15] The men who marched with the various industrial armies in 1894 truly believed that "if they were ready and willing to work productively, then by rights they should be able to make a living by doing so; and that, if impersonal market forces did not afford them this opportunity, they were entitled to a remedy from their government."[16]

One other significant impact that the national protest of the unemployed had in 1894 was to cause the federal government to alter the way in which it dealt with domestic disorders. When Coxey decided to mount his protest, he envisioned it as a "petition in boots." In other words, Coxey and his followers, with some difficulty, could actually walk the 400 miles from Massillon, Ohio, to Washington, D.C. But for the industrial armies that formed along the West Coast and in the

Conclusion

Rocky Mountains, that was impossible. As Carlos Schwantes noted, "It was a far greater distance from any point on the Pacific Slope to the nation's capital than that traveled by medieval Europe's crusaders to the Holy Land."[17] In order to overcome that obstacle, railway transportation was indispensable. As W.T. Stead commented, "The petitions in boots really came to mean petitions on wheels."[18] To make that possible, the leaders of the various industrial armies would have to ask the railroads for free passage or at least to transport their men at greatly reduced rates. When the railroads refused to carry riders for anything other than full fare, the various armies often commandeered trains. In doing so, they saw the action as a necessity of transportation and regarded it as borrowing rather than stealing.

The temporary expropriation of railroad property by the various industrial armies during the spring and early summer of 1894 triggered governmental alarm. To the Cleveland administration and to property owners in general, this was unacceptable. Equally unnerving was the thought of having possibly 100,000 unemployed men converging on the nation's capital. With a fear of the so-called tramp menace already embedded in the culture, and with almost all the major national magazines running articles that portrayed the various industrial armies in a negative light, it was easy to excite alarm. In an age when most middle-class Americans still equated the working classes and labor unions with subversion and worker agitation with social revolution, the cross-country marches of numerous industrial armies convinced many that catastrophe was imminent.

When police arrested Jacob Coxey for walking on the capitol grounds, it was actually the beginning of a concerted effort to prevent other western armies, that had already clashed with U.S. military forces for more than a week, from descending upon Washington. To many businessmen and property owners, and to President Grover Cleveland and Attorney General Richard Olney and other conservative-minded politicians in both political parties, it was time to take forceful government action. Secretary of State Walter Q. Gresham, for one, stated that he "regarded the armies as lawless bands infected with anarchist doctrines who portended much trouble," while Attorney General Olney foresaw in the industrial armies "the first symptoms of impending industrial revolution."[19] To such defenders of the status quo, the actions of the industrial armies conjured up memories of the Paris Commune of 1871 where a violent insurrection

8. Conclusion

had demonstrated where "mob rule" might lead or the images of violence and destruction that had been such a part of the Great Railway Strike of 1877.

In the spring of 1894, train theft was commonly regarded as a state and not a federal crime. Usually, these lawless acts would have been dealt with by local law enforcement agencies or by state militias. But some western states had no militia, while others had only inadequate forces. However, because most railroads that operated in the western United States were under the custody of federal courts as a result of the depression, there was a legal opening for federal intervention. Initially, Attorney General Olney thought he could control the hijacking of trains by empowering U.S. marshals to arrest violators using the legal pretext that the continued and unobstructed operation of the railroads was vital to national security. But Olney quickly realized that U.S. marshals and federal posses could not alone stop the progress of industrial armies that might number up to 1,500 men. Complicating matters was the realization that many citizens, who had long resented the railroads as symbols of greed and uncontrolled power, and many local authorities actually aided and abetted the industrial armies in their journeys. Even a few Populist governors such as Hogg in Texas, Waite in Colorado, Lewelling in Kansas, and Pennoyer in Oregon turned a deaf ear to any requests from the railroads to have their state militias intervene. Assessing these difficulties, Olney decided that federal *military* intervention was his only viable option.

When an industrial army stole a train belonging to a railroad in federal receivership, the receivers (managers) of a threatened railroad would ask for an injunction from the federal judge in whose jurisdiction the incident occurred forbidding the action. If the industrial army ignored the injunction, as was usually the case, then federal marshals would be called out to make a formal attempt to arrest the leaders for contempt of court or, as occurred in Kansas, for obstructing the U.S. mail. When such attempts failed, Attorney General Olney would request President Cleveland to order the Secretary of War Daniel S. Lamont to intervene with troops under the authority of RS 5298 to enforce the execution of the laws of the United States wherever they may be "forcibly" opposed or obstructed. The task of carrying out the enforcement of these orders fell to Commanding General of the U.S. Army John M. Schofield who then issued orders to one of his eight regional commanders.

Conclusion

The deployment of troops throughout the West helped bring an end to the seizure of trains, which in turn defused the volatile Coxey movement as the Cleveland administration had intended. Train stealing was not only stopped, but, as Attorney General Olney stated, "very large numbers of almost desperate men who would otherwise have found their way to Washington were compelled to remain at home.'"[20] By the early summer of 1894 most of those who had attempted to commandeer trains were in prison. In the process, however, a precedent had been set. As the Coxey movement was losing its momentum, the great Pullman strike was just beginning, and the practice by which the attorney general would ask the federal courts for an injunction to prevent or frustrate a labor organization and its strike activities would be employed again as a basic strategy.

When the federal government met the challenge of Coxeyism with a new policy of government by injunction, corporate America learned that they would have to lean on the federal government and the federal courts to maintain their freedom of action. When railroads met hostility from townspeople in the small mining and railroad towns of the West who demonstrated their loyalty to workers and their sympathy for the various armies of the unemployed, they perceived that resistance as a new threat to their power. Similarly, when they reached out to local or state authorities to deal with rebellious Coxeyites or striking workers, they were often rebuffed. To overcome this localized opposition, the railroads turned to the federal laws and courts. It was rather ironic that many critics who denounced the efforts of Coxeyites to expand the function of the federal government as paternalistic, would fail to see that federal protection of the railroads was something very similar.

Chapter Notes

Preface

1. Quoted in Donald L. McMurry, *Coxey's Army: A Study of the Industrial Army Movement of 1894* (Seattle: University of Washington Press, 1929), 281.
2. T. B. Veblen, "The Army of the Commonweal," *Journal of Political Economy* 2 (June 1894): 458.
3. Lucy G. Barber, *Marching on Washington: The Forging of an American Political Tradition* (Berkeley: University of California Press, 2002), 220.

Introduction

1. Carlos A. Schwantes, *Coxey's Army: An American Odyssey* (Lincoln, NE: University of Nebraska Press, 1985), x.
2. Donald L. McMurry, *Coxey's Army: A Study of the Industrial Army Movement of 1894* (Seattle: University of Washington Press, 1929), 277.
3. Douglas W. Steeples and David O. Whitten, *Democracy in Desperation: The Depression of 1893* (Westport, CT: Greenwood Press, 1998), 53.
4. McMurry, *Coxey's Army*, 10.
5. Henry Frank, "The Crusade for the Unemployed," *Arena* 10 (July 1894): 241–42.
6. McMurry, *Coxey's Army*, 6.
7. Quoted in Ray Stannard Baker, *American Chronicle: The Autobiography of Ray Stannard Baker* (New York: Charles Scribner's Sons, 1945), 19.
8. Schwantes, *American Odyssey*, 18.

Chapter 1

1. Douglas W. Steeples and David O. Whitten, *Democracy in Desperation: The Depression of 1893* (Westport, CT: Greenwood Press, 1998), 50, 53.
2. Quoted in Benjamin F. Alexander, *Coxey's Army: Popular Protest in the Gilded Age* (Baltimore: Johns Hopkins University Press, 2015), 23–24. See also *Congressional Record* (House, February 17, 1887), 49 Cong., 2d Sess., vol. XVIII (Washington: Government Printing Office, 1887), 1875.
3. Quoted in Alexander, *Coxey's Army*, 36.
4. Quoted in Samuel Reznek, "Unemployment, Unrest, and Relief in the United States during the Depression of 1893–97," *Journal of Political Economy* 61 (August 1953): 332.
5. Quoted in John L. Thomas, *Alternative America: Henry George, Edward Bellamy, Henry Demarest Lloyd and the Adversary Tradition* (Cambridge, MA: Belknap Press), 172.
6. Alexander, *Coxey's Army*, 35–36.
7. Edward Bellamy, "The Program of the Nationalists," *Forum* 17 (March 1894): 89.
8. Quoted in Alexander, *Coxey's Army*, 47.
9. Philip Dray, *There is Power in a Union: The Epic Story of Labor in America* (New York: Anchor Books, 2010), 192.
10. W. T. Stead, "'Coxeyism': A Character Sketch," *Review of Reviews* 10 (July 1894): 48
11. Dray, *Power in a Union*, 193.
12. Stead, "Coxeyism," 47.
13. *Ibid.*, 52.
14. Carlos A. Schwantes, *Coxey's Army: An American Odyssey* (Lincoln, NE: University of Nebraska Press, 1985), 46.

Chapter Notes

15. *Ibid.*, 44.
16. Philip S. Foner, *History of the Labor Movement in the United States*, Vol. II. (New York: International Publishers, 1955), 242.
17. Stead, "'Coxeyism,'"54.
18. Henry Vincent, *The Story of the Commonweal* (London: British Library, 1894 reprint ed.), 70.
19. Jerry Prout, *Coxey's Crusade for Jobs: Unemployment in the Gilded Age* (DeKalb, IL: Northern Illinois University Press, 2016), 83.
20. Jerry Prout, "Coxey's Challenge in the Populist Moment" (Ph.D. diss., George Mason University, 2012), 278–79.
21. Quoted in Schwantes, *Coxey's Army*, 69.
22. Mentioned in Ray Stannard Baker, *American Chronicle: The Autobiography of Ray Stannard Baker* (New York: Charles Scribner's Sons, 1945), 22.
23. Donald L. McMurry, *Coxey's Army: A Study of the Industrial Army Movement of 1894* (Seattle: University of Washington Press, 1929 reprint ed.), 104–5.
24. Alexander, *Coxey's Army*, 68.
25. Journalist Ray Stannard Baker, who had watched the melee unfold, picked up as many beads as he could find and returned them to Browne when he visited him in the District jail later that day. Speaking in tears, Browne responded, "You're the only friend I've got left in the world." Quoted in Baker, *American Chronicle*, 25.
26. Dray, *Power in a Union*, 193.
27. Quoted in H. W. Brands, *The Reckless Decade: America in the 1890s* (New York: St. Martin's Press, 1995), 175.
28. Foner, *History of the Labor Movement*, 243.

Chapter 2

1. Newspapers often spelled Fry's last name as Frye.
2. Quoted in Henry Vincent, *The Story of the Commonweal* (London: British Library, 1894 reprint ed.), 163
3. Carlos Schwantes, *Coxey's Army: An American Odyssey* (Lincoln, NE: University of Nebraska Press, 1985), 87.
4. Henry Frank, "The Crusade of the Unemployed," *Arena* 10 (July 1894), 242.
5. Vincent, *Story of the Commonweal*, 163.
6. Quoted in Frank, "The Crusade of the Unemployed," 243.
7. Quoted in Schwantes, *Coxey's Army*, 92.
8. Quoted in Vincent, *Story of the Commonweal*, 166.
9. *Ibid.*, 168.
10. Quoted in Donald L. McMurry, *Coxey's Army: A Study of the Industrial Army Movement of 1894* (Seattle: University of Washington Press, 1929 reprint ed.), 133.
11. Quoted in Schwantes, *Coxey's Army*, 93.
12. *Ibid.*
13. *Ibid.*, 94.
14. Quoted in Robert C. Cotner, *James Stephen Hogg: A Biography* (Austin: University of Texas Press, 1959), 425–26. See also *El Paso International Daily Times*, March 29, 1894.
15. Quoted in Schwantes, *Coxey's Army*, 95.
16. *Ibid.*, 97
17. Henry Winfred Splitter, "Concerning Vinette's Los Angeles Regiment of Coxey's Army," *Pacific Historical Review* 17 (February 1948): 31.
18. The Farmers' Alliance was an agrarian movement of the 1870s and 1880s that sought to improve economic conditions for farmers through the creation of cooperatives. The organization played a leading role in establishing the Populist Party in the early 1890s.
19. *Topeka State Journal*, June 19, 20, 1894.
20. Quoted in Schwantes, *Coxey's Army*, 267.
21. McMurry, *Coxey's Army*, 6.

Chapter 3

1. Newspapers often spelled Kelly's name as Kelley.
2. Quoted in Donald L. McMurry,

Chapter Notes

Coxey's Army: A Study of the Industrial Army Movement of 1894 (Seattle: University of Washington Press, 1929; reprint ed. 1968), 152.
3. Ibid.
4. William D. Haywood, *Big Bill's Book: The Autobiography of William D. Haywood* (New York: International Publishers, 1929; rev. ed. 1958), 51–52; Peter Carlson, *Roughneck: The Life and Times of Big Bill Haywood* (New York: W. W. Norton & Co., 1983), 44, 51–52.
5. John Gary Maxwell, *Robert Newton Baskin and the Making of Modern Utah* (Norman, OK: University of Oklahoma Press, 2013), 262.
6. *Salt Lake Tribune*, April 9, 1894.
7. Quoted in Carlos A. Schwantes, *Coxey's Army: An American Odyssey* (Lincoln, NE: University of Nebraska Press, 1985), 105.
8. *Salt Lake Tribune*, April 9, 1894.
9. Quoted in Schwantes, *Coxey's Army*, 106.
10. Franklin Folsom, *Impatient Armies of the Poor: The Story of Collective Action of the Unemployed, 1808–1942* (Niwot, CO: University Press of Colorado, 1991), 158.
11. Schwantes, *Coxey's Army*, 103.
12. Quoted in *ibid..*, 109.
13. The account of the Ogden standoff was taken largely from Henry Vincent, *The Story of the Commonweal* (London: British Library, 1894 reprint ed.), 127–29; McMurry, *Coxey's Army*, 156–60; and Schwantes, *Coxey's Army*, 104–10.
14. Quoted in Gene E. Hamaker, "The Commonweal Comes to Kearney, 1894," *Buffalo Tales* 2 (May 1979): 2–3.
15. *The Outlook*, 49 (April 1894): 733.
16. Ibid.
17. Quoted in Vincent, *Story of the Commonweal*, 137.
18. Quoted in Schwantes, *Coxey's Army*, 121.
19. Joseph T. Duryea, "The 'Industrial Army' at Omaha," *The Outlook* 49 (May 5, 1894): 782.
20. Vincent, *Story of the Commonweal*, 154–55.
21. Quoted in Carlos Schwantes, "Soldiers of Misfortune, Pt. 1," *The Annals of Iowa* 46 (Winter 1983): 503.
22. Quoted in Schwantes, *Coxey's Army*, 123.

Chapter 4

1. Donald L. McMurry, *Coxey's Army: A Study of the Industrial Army Movement of 1894* (Seattle: University of Washington Press, 1929; reprint ed. 1968), 174.
2. Jack London, "Tramping with Kelly through Iowa: A Jack London Diary," *Palimpsest* 52 (June 1971): 317, 318.
3. *Ibid.*, 320–21.
4. McMurry, *Coxey's Army*, 175.
5. Jack London, "The March of Kelly's Army," *Cosmopolitan* 43 (October 1907): 644.
6. Henry Vincent, *The Story of the Commonweal* (London: British Library, 1894 reprint ed.), 151–52.
7. London, "Tramping with Kelly," 339.
8. Quoted in Carlos A. Schwantes, *Coxey's Army: An American Odyssey* (Lincoln, NE: University of Nebraska Press, 1985), 140.
9. The story of Kelly's march from Van Meter to Des Moines is taken from Schwantes' excellent summary in *Coxey's Army: Am American Odyssey*, 139–41.
10. Statistics are from McMurry, *Coxey's Army*, 187–88.
11. Quoted in Carlos A. Schwantes, "Soldiers of Misfortune (Pt. 2)," *The Annals of Iowa* 46 (Spring 1983): 578.
12. London, "The March," 644.
13. William J. Petersen, "Jack London and Kelly's Army," *Palimpsest* 52 (June 1971): 307–08.
14. London, "The March," 645, 646.
15. Schwantes, *Coxey's Army*, 192.
16. Quoted in Schwantes, "Soldiers of Misfortune (Pt. 2)," 587.
17. London, "The March," 647–48.
18. Charmian London, *The Book of Jack London*. Vol. 1. (New York: The Century Co., 1921), 161.
19. Schwantes, *Coxey's Army*, 194–95.
20. *Ibid.*, 228.
21. Schwantes, "Soldiers of Misfortune (Pt. 2)," 589.

Chapter 5

1. Thomas A. Clinch, "Coxey's Army in Montana" *Montana, The Magazine of Western History* 15 (Autumn 1965): 5.
2. Quoted in Michael P. Malone, *The Battle for Butte: Mining and Politics on the Northern Frontier, 1864–1906* (Seattle: University of Washington Press, 1981; Helena, MT: Montana Historical Society Press, 1995), 55.
3. Carlos A. Schwantes, *Coxey's Army: An American Odyssey* (Lincoln, NE: University of Nebraska Press, 1985), 150.
4. Benjamin F. Alexander, *Coxey's Army: Popular Protest in the Gilded Age* (Baltimore: Johns Hopkins University Press, 2015), 88.
5. Quoted in Schwantes, *Coxey's Army*, 152.
6. *Philipsburg Mail* (Granite County, MT), April 26, 1894.
7. Newspapers occasionally spell Haley's name as Hailey.
8. Quoted in Schwantes, *Coxey's Army*, 159.
9. Quoted in *ibid.*, 160–61.
10. Quoted in Gerald G. Eggert, *Railroad Labor Disputes: The Beginnings of Federal Strike Policy* (Ann Arbor: University of Michigan Press, 1967), 142.
11. Philip Dray, *There is Power in a Union: The Epic Story of Labor in America* (New York: Anchor Books, 2010), 167–68.
12. *Anaconda Standard*, May 1, 1894.
13. Quoted in Carlos A. Schwantes, "Coxey's Montana Navy: A Protest against Unemployment on the Wageworker's Frontier" *Pacific Northwest Quarterly* 73 (July 1982): 100.

Chapter 6

1. Dmitri Palmateer, "Charity and the 'Tramp'": Itineracy, Unemployment, and Municipal Government from Coxey to the Unemployed League," *Oregon Historical Quarterly* 107 (Summer 2006): 231.
2. Quoted in *ibid.*, 233.
3. Quoted in *ibid.*, 234.
4. Quoted in Herman C. Voeltz, "Coxey's Army in Oregon, 1894," *Oregon Historical Quarterly* 65 (September 1964): 272 fn. 21.
5. Palmateer, "Charity and the 'Tramp,'" 236.
6. Quoted in Voeltz, "Coxey's Army," 273 fn. 23.
7. Quoted in Palmateer, "Charity and the Tramp," 237, 238.
8. Quoted in *ibid.*, 239.
9. Newspapers often spelled Scheffler's name as Sheffler or Shreffler.
10. Quoted in Voeltz, "Coxey's Army," 270 fn. 14.
11. Quoted in Edrie Lee Vinson, "General Jacob Sechler Coxey and His Relationship to the Industrial Armies of the Pacific Northwest," Thesis, Carroll College, 1973, 53–54.
12. Quoted in Franklin Folsom, *Impatient Armies of the Poor: The Story of Collective Action of the Unemployed, 1808–1942* (Boulder, CO: University Press of Colorado, 1991), 176.
13. H. W. Brands, *The Reckless Decade: America in the 1890s* (New York: St. Martin's Press, 1995), 151.
14. Clayton D. Laurie and Ronald H. Cole, *The Role of Federal Military Forces in Domestic Disorders, 1877–1945* (Washington, D.C.: Center of Military History, U.S. Army, 1997), 118.
15. Quoted in Voeltz, "Coxey's Army," 283.
16. Quoted in *ibid.*, 287.
17. Carlos A. Schwantes, *Coxey's Army: An American Odyssey* (Lincoln, NE: University of Nebraska Press, 1985), 199.
18. Quoted in Voletz, "Coxey's Army," 290.
19. Quoted in J. Anthony Lukas, *Big Trouble* (New York: Simon and Shuster, 1997), 412.
20. Quoted in *ibid.*
21. *Index* (Emmett, Idaho), May 19, 1894. See also Lukas, *Big Trouble*, 412.
22. Quoted in Carlos A. Schwantes, "Law and Disorder: The Suppression of Coxey's Army in Idaho," *Idaho Yesterdays* 25 (Summer 1981): 12.
23. Quoted in *ibid.*, 19.
24. Quoted in *ibid.*
25. Quoted in Gerald Eggert, *Richard*

Chapter Notes

Olney: Evolution of a Statesman (State College, PA: Penn State University Press, 1991), 125.

26. Salt Lake Tribune, May 16, 1894.

27. Quoted in Eggert, Richard Olney, 125.

28. Quoted in Schwantes, "Law and Disorder," 23.

29. See Eggert, Richard Olney, 126.

30. Quoted in Schwantes, "Law and Disorder," 24.

Chapter 7

1. For a detailed discussion of this topic see: Carlos A. Schwantes, "The Concept of the Wageworkers' Frontier: A Framework for Future Research," Western Historical Quarterly 18 (January 1987): 39–55; Carlos A. Schwantes, "Images of the Wageworkers' Frontier," Montana, The Magazine of Western History 38 (Autumn 1988): 38–49.

2. Seattle Post-Intelligencer, April 8, 1894.

3. Quoted in Bruce A. Ramsey, The Panic of 1893: The Untold Story of Washington State's First Depression (Caldwell, ID: Caxton Press, 2018), 101.

4. Seattle Post-Intelligencer, April 10, 1894.

5. Quoted in Edrie Lee Vinson, "General Jacob Sechler Coxey and His Relationship to the Industrial Armies of the Pacific Northwest" (Thesis, Carroll College, 1973), 70.

6. Quoted in Ramsey, Panic of 1893, 102.

7. Post-Intelligencer, April 16, 1894.

8. Quoted in Murray Morgan, Puget's Sound: A Narrative of Early Tacoma and the Southern Sound (Seattle: University of Washington Press, 1979), 283.

9. Post-Intelligencer, April 26, 1894.

10. Quoted in ibid.., April 30, 1894.

11. Quoted in Morgan, Puget's Sound, 287.

12. Carlos Schwantes, "Protest in a Promised Land: Unemployment, Disinheritance, and the Origin of Labor Militancy in the Pacific Northwest, 1885–1886," Western Historical Quarterly 13 (October 1982): 386.

13. Herbert Gutman, Work, Culture, and Society in Industrializing America: Essays in American Working-Class and Social History (New York: Vintage Books, 1976), 29.

14. Quoted in Carlos Schwantes, "Images of the Wageworkers' Frontier," Montana: The Magazine of Western History 38 (Autumn 1988): 38.

15. Quoted in Morgan, Puget's Sound, 288.

16. Quoted in Ramsey, Panic of 1893, 106.

17. Post-Intelligencer, May 23, 1894.

18. Morgan, Puget's Sound, 284.

19. United States War Department, "Annual Report of the Secretary of War for the Year 1894," Vol. 1 (Washington, D.C.: Government Printing Office, 1894), 155.

20. Quoted in Carlos A. Schwantes, Coxey's Army: An American Odyssey (Lincoln: University of Nebraska Press, 1985), 196.

21. Quoted in ibid.., 244.

22. Anaconda Standard, June 19, 1894.

23. Quoted in Schwantes, Coxey's Army, 241.

24. Quoted in ibid.., 242.

25. Quoted in Ramsey, Panic of 1893, 110.

26. Quoted in Schwantes, Coxey's Army, 257.

27. Donald L. McMurry, Coxey's Army: A Study of the Industrial; Army Movement of 1894 (Seattle: University of Washington Press, 1929 reprint ed.), 253–54.

Chapter 8

1. Topeka State Journal, June 28, 1894.

2. Ibid., May 26, 1894.

3. Quoted in Donald L. McMurry, Coxey's Army: A Study of the Industrial Army Movement of 1894 (Seattle: University of Washington Press, 1968), 273.

4. Rocky Mountain News, May 12, 1894.

Chapter Notes

5. Quoted in Carlos A. Schwantes, *Coxey's Army: An American Odyssey* (Lincoln, NE: University of Nebraska Press, 1985), 204.
6. The humorous story and quote are from the *Salt Lake Tribune*, May 2, 1894.
7. *Ibid.*, May 4, 1894.
8. *Ibid.*, May 8, 1894.
9. McMurry, *Coxey's Army*, 224–25; *Ogden Standard*, May 28, 1894; *Salt Lake Tribune*, May 28, 1894.
10. Quoted in McMurry, *Coxey's Army*, 224.
11. Quoted in Schwantes, *Coxey's Army*, 270.
12. Quoted in *ibid.*., 215.
13. *Rocky Mountain News*, June 9, 1894.
14. *Ibid.*
15. *Ibid.*
16. Quoted in McMurry, *Coxey's Army*, 215.

Conclusion

1. Quoted in Donald L. McMurry, *Coxey's Army: A Study of the Industrial Army Movement of 1894* (Seattle: University of Washington Press, 1968), 263.
2. Quoted in Bruce A. Ramsey, *The Panic of 1893: The Untold Story of Washington State's First Depression* (Caldwell, ID: Caxton Press, 2018), 100.
3. W. T. Stead, "Coxeyism: A Character Sketch," *Review of Reviews* 10 (July 1894): 47, 52.
4. Quoted in Philip Dray, *There is Power in a Union: The Epic Story of Labor in America* (New York: Anchor Books, 2010), 194.
5. Jerry M. Cooper, *The Army and Civil Disorder: Federal Military Intervention in Labor Disputes, 1877–1900* (Westport, CT: Greenwood Press, 1980), 106.
6. Shirley Plumer Austin, "The Downfall of Coxeyism," *Chautauquan* 19 (July 1894): 452.
7. See Douglas W. Steeples and David O. Whitten, *Democracy in Desperation: The Depression of 1893* (Westport, CT: Greenwood Press, 1998), 88.
8. John E. Bennett, "Is the West Discontented: Is a Revolution at Hand?" *Arena* 81 (August 1896): 400.
9. Quoted in Carlos A. Schwantes, *Coxey's Army: Am American Odyssey* (Lincoln, NE: University of Nebraska Press, 1985), 20.
10. Stead, "Coxeyism," 47.
11. Quoted in Dray, *Power in a Union*, 195.
12. Quoted in McMurry, *Coxey's Army*, 280–81.
13. T. B. Veblen, "The Army of the Commonweal," *Journal of Political Economy* 2 (June 1894): 459.
14. Quoted in Jules Tygiel, "Tramping Artisans: Carpenters in Industrial America, 1880–90" in Eric H. Monkkonen ed., *Walking to Work: Tramps in America, 1790–1935* (Lincoln: University of Nebraska Press, 1984), 96.
15. Anne Mayhew, "Polanyi's Double Movement and Veblen on the Army of the Commonweal," *Journal of Economic Issues* 23 (June 1989): 559.
16. Benjamin F. Alexander, *Coxey's Army: Popular Protest in the Gilded Age* (Baltimore: Johns Hopkins University Press, 2015), 4.
17. Schwantes, *Coxey's Army*, 84.
18. Stead, "Coxeyism," 49.
19. Clayton D. Laurie and Ronald H. Cole, *The Role of Federal Military Forces in Domestic Disorders, 1877–1945* (Washington, D.C.: Center of Military History, United States Army, 1997), 117.
20. Quoted in *ibid.*. 118.

Bibliography

Alexander, Benjamin F. *Coxey's Army: Popular Protest in the Gilded Age.* Baltimore: Johns Hopkins University Press, 2015.
Annin, James T. *They Gazed on the Beartooths,* Vol. 2. Billings, MT: Reporter Print Co., 1964.
Arrington, Leonard. "Utah and the Depression of the 1890s." *Utah Historical Review* 29 (January 1961): 2–18.
Austin, Shirley Plumer. "The Downfall of Coxeyism." *Chautauquan* 19 (July 1894): 448–52.
Baker, Ray Stannard. *American Chronicle: The Autobiography of Ray Stannard Baker.* New York: Charles Scribner's Sons, 1945.
Barber, Lucy G. *Marching on Washington: The Forging of an American Political Tradition.* Berkeley: University of California Press, 2002.
Bellamy, Edward. "The Program of the Nationalists." *Forum* 17 (March 1894): 81–91.
Bennett, John E. "Is the West Discontented: Is a Revolution at Hand?" *Arena* 81 (August 1896): 393–405.
Berman, David R. *Radicalism in the Mountain West, 1890–1920: Socialists, Populists, Miners, and Wobblies.* Boulder: University Press of Colorado, 2007.
Blasi, Brigida. "The Wyoming March of Coxey's Army." *WyoHistory.org* (May 31, 2022). https://www.wyohistory.org/encyclopedia/wyoming-march-coxeys-army.
Brands, H.W. *The Reckless Decade: America in the 1890s.* New York: St. Martin's Press, 1995.
Braniff, Annie. "Historic Events I've Lived Through: Kelly's Army on the March, in 'Kelly's Army Crosses Iowa.'" *Iowa Heritage Illustrated* 88 (Summer 2007): 93–95.
Butcher, Carol. "A Stolen Train." *Dakota Datebook* (June 15, 2020): 1–2. http://news.prairiepublic.org/post/stolen-train.
Caldbick, John. "Panic of 1893 and Its Aftermath." HistoryLink.org Essay 20874. https://www.historylink.org/file/20874.
Clayton, John. *Stories from Montana's Enduring Frontier: Exploring an Untamed Legacy.* Charleston, SC: The History Press, 2013.
Clinch, Thomas A. "Coxey's Army in Montana." *Montana, the Magazine of Western History* 15 (Autumn 1965): 2–11.
Closson, Carlos C., Jr. "The Unemployed in American Cities." *Quarterly Journal of Economics* 8 (January 1894): 168–217.
Cooper, Jerry M. *The Army and Civil Disorder: Federal Military Intervention in Labor Disputes, 1877–1900.* Westport, CT: Greenwood Press, 1980.
Cotner, Robert C. *James Stephen Hogg: A Biography.* Austin: University of Texas Press, 1959.
Dray, Philip. *There Is Power in a Union: The Epic Story of Labor in America.* New York: Anchor Books, 2011.
Duryea, Joseph T. "The 'Industrial Army' at Omaha." *The Outlook* 49 (May 5, 1894): 781–83.

Bibliography

Eggert, Gerald G. *Railroad Labor Disputes: The Beginnings of Federal Strike Policy*. Ann Arbor: University of Michigan Press, 1967.

———. *Richard Olney: Evolution of a Statesman*. State College: Penn State University Press, 1991.

Feder, Leah Hannah. *Unemployment Relief in Periods of Depression: A Study of Measures Adopted in Certain American Cities, 1857 through 1922*. New York: Russell Sage Foundation, 1936.

Folsom, Franklin. *Impatient Armies of the Poor: The Story of Collective Action of the Unemployed, 1808–1942*. Boulder: University Press of Colorado, 1991.

Foner, Philip S. *History of the Labor Movement in the United States, Vol. II: From the Founding of the American Federation of Labor to the Emergence of American Imperialism*. New York: International Publishers, 1955.

Frank, Henry. "The Crusade of the Unemployed." *Arena* 10 (July 1894): 239–44.

Gipe, George A. "Rebel in a Wing Collar." *American Heritage* 18 (December 1966): 25–29. https://www.americanheritage.com/rebel-wing-collar#4.

Gordon, John Steele. "The Other Great Depression." *American Heritage* 42 (May/June 1991). https://www.americanheritage.com/other-great-depression.

Guarneri, Carl J. *The Utopian Alternative: Fourierism in Nineteenth-Century America*. Ithaca, NY: Cornell University Press, 1991.

Gustaitis, Joseph. "Coxey's Army." *American History Illustrated* 24 (March/April 1994): 39–45.

Gutman, Herbert G. "The Failure of the Movement by the Unemployed for Public Works in 1873." *Political Science Quarterly* 80 (June 1965): 254–76.

———. *Work, Culture, and Society in Industrializing America: Essays in American Working-Class and Social History*. New York: Vintage Boons, 1976.

Hamaker, Gene E. "The Commonweal Comes to Kearney, 1894." *Buffalo Tales* 2 (May 1979): 1–6. http://www.bchs.us/BTales_197905.html.

Haywood, William D. *Bill Haywood's Book: The Autobiography of William D. Haywood*. New York: International Publishers, 1929; rev. ed. 1958.

Hoffman, Charles. "The Depression of the Nineties." *Journal of Economic History* 16 (June 1956): 137–64.

Hooper, Osman C. "The Coxey Movement in Ohio." *Ohio State Archaeological and Historical Society Publications* 9 (1901): 155–76.

Howard, Oliver Otis, Thomas Byrnes, and Alvah H. Doty. "The Menace of 'Coxeyism.'" *The North American Review* 158 (June 1894): 687–705.

Hunt, Herbert, and Floyd C. Kaylor. *Washington West of the Cascades*. Chicago: S.J. Clarke Co., 1917.

Laurie, Clayton D., and Ronald H. Cole. *The Role of Federal Military Forces in Domestic Disorders, 1877–1945*. Washington, D.C.: Center of Military History, U. S. Army, 1997.

Lennon, John. "Can a Hobo Share a Box-Car? Jack London, the Industrial Army, and the Politics of (In)visibility." *American Studies* 48 (Winter 2007): 5–30.

London, Charmian. *The Book of Jack London*. Vol. 1. New York: The Century Co., 1921.

London, Jack. "Hoboes That Pass in the Night." *Cosmopolitan* 43 (November 1907): 190–97.

———. "The March of Kelly's Army." *Cosmopolitan* 43 (October 1907): 643–48.

———. "Tramping with Kelly through Iowa: A Jack London Diary." *Palimpsest* 52 (June 1971): 316–46.

Lukas, J. Anthony. *Big Trouble*. New York: Simon & Schuster, 1997.

Malone, Michael P. *The Battle for Butte: Mining and Politics on the Northern Frontier, 1864–1906*. Helena: Montana Historical Society Press, 1981, reprinted 1995.

Maxwell, John Gary. *Robert Newton Baskin and the Making of Modern Utah*. Norman: University of Oklahoma Press, 2013.

8. Bibliography

Mayhew, Anne. "Polanyi's Double Movement and Veblen on the Army of the Commonweal." *Journal of Economic Issues* 23 (June 1989): 555–62.
McMurry, Donald L. *Coxey's Army: A Study of the Industrial Army Movement of 1894.* Seattle: University of Washington Press, 1929, reprint ed. 1968.
_____. "Industrial Armies of the Commonweal." *Mississippi Valley Historical Review* 10 (December 1923): 215–52.
Mecham, Kirke, ed. "Bypaths of Kansas History: Scott City *Republican,* May 17, 1894." *Kansas Historical Quarterly* 11 (February 1942): 100–10.
Morgan, Murray. *Puget's Sound: A Narrative of Early Tacoma and the Southern Sound.* Seattle: University of Washington Press, 1979.
Palmateer, Dmitri. "Charity and the 'Tramp': Itineracy, Unemployment, and Municipal Government from Coxey to the Unemployed League." *Oregon Historical Quarterly* 107 (Summer 2006): 228–53.
Petersen, William J. "Jack London and Kelly's Army." *Palimpsest* 52 (June 1971): 289–315.
Pierce, J Kingston. "Panic of 1893: Seattle's First Great Depression." HistoryLink.org Essay 2030. https://www.historylink.org/file/2030.
_____. "The Panic of 1893: The Northwest Economy Unraveled as the 'Gilded Age' Came to a Close." *Columbia: The Magazine of Northwest History* 7 (Winter 1993–94): 1–7.
Plumb, George E., comp. *The Daily News Almanac and Political Register for 1895.* Chicago: Chicago Daily News Co., 1895.
Prout, Jerry. "Coxey's Challenge in the Populist Moment." Ph.D. diss., George Mason University, 2012.
_____. *Coxey's Crusade for Jobs: Unemployment in the Gilded Age.* DeKalb: Northern Illinois University Press, 2016.
_____. "Populism and Populists: The Incoherent Coherence of Coxey's March." *American Journal of Economics and Sociology* 78 (May 2019): 593–619.
Ramsey, Bruce A. *The Panic of 1893: The Untold Story of Washington State's First Depression.* Caldwell, ID: Caxton Press, 2018.
Rezneck, Samuel. "Unemployment, Unrest, and Relief in the United States During the Depression of 1893–97." *Journal of Political Economy* 61 (August 1953): 324–45.
Schwantes, Carlos A. "The Concept of the Wageworkers' Frontier: A Framework for Future Research." *Western Historical Quarterly* 18 (January 1987): 39–55.
_____. *Coxey's Army: An American Odyssey.* Lincoln: University of Nebraska Press, 1985.
_____. "Coxey's Montana Navy: A Protest Against Unemployment on the Wageworkers' Frontier." *Pacific Northwest Quarterly* 73 (July 1982): 98–107.
_____. "Images of the Wageworkers' Frontier." *Montana The Magazine of Western History* 38 (Autumn 1988): 38–49.
_____. "Law and Disorder: The Suppression of Coxey's Army in Idaho." *Idaho Yesterdays* 25 (Summer 1981): 10–26.
_____. "Protest in a Promised Land: Unemployment, Disinheritance, and the Origins of Labor Militancy in the Pacific Northwest, 1885–1886." *Western Historical Quarterly* 13 (October 1982): 373–90.
_____. "Soldiers of Misfortune (Pt. 1)." *The Annals of Iowa* 46 (Winter 1983): 487–509.
_____. "Soldiers of Misfortune (Pt. 2)." *The Annals of Iowa* 46 (Spring 1983): 567–92.
_____. "Western Women in Coxey's Army in 1894." *Arizona and the West* 26 (Spring 1984): 5–20.
Shaw, Albert. "Relief for the Unemployed in American Cities." *Review of Reviews* 9 (January 1894): 29–37.
Splitter, Henry Winfred. "Concerning Vinette's Los Angeles Regiment of Coxey's Army." *Pacific Historical Review* 17 (February 1948): 29–36.
Sprau, Ryan James. "The Commonweal in the Heartland: Charles T. Kelly and Iowa's

Bibliography

Industrial Army." Dissertations and Theses @ UNI. 653. https://scholarworks.uni.edu/etd/653.
Stead, W.T. "'Coxeyism': A Character Sketch." *Review of Reviews* 10 (July 1894): 47–59.
Steeples, Douglas W., and David O. Whitten. *Democracy in Desperation: The Depression of 1893.* Westport, CT: Greenwood Press, 1998.
Stimson, Grace Hillman. *Rise of the Labor Movement in Los Angeles.* Berkeley: University of California Press, 1955.
Thomas, John L. *Alternative America: Henry George, Edward Bellamy, Henry Demarest Lloyd and the Adversary Tradition.* Cambridge, MA: Belknap Press, 1983.
Tygiel, Jules. "Tramping Artisans: Carpenters in Industrial America, 1880–90," in Eric H. Monkkonen, ed., *Walking to Work: Tramps in America, 1790–1935.* Lincoln: University of Nebraska Press, 1984.
United States War Department. "Annual Report of the Secretary of War for the Year 1894." Vol. 1. Washington, D.C.: Government Printing Office, 1894.
Veblen, T.B. "The Army of the Commonweal." *Journal of Political Economy* 2 (June 1894): 456–61.
Vincent, Henry. *The Story of the Commonweal.* London: British Library, 1894, Historical Reprints ed. 2011.
Vinson, Edrie Lee. "General Jacob Sechler Coxey and His Relationship to the Industrial Armies of the Pacific Northwest." Thesis, Carroll College, 1973.
Voeltz, Herman C. "Coxey's Army in Oregon, 1894." *Oregon Historical Quarterly* 65 (September 1964): 263–95.
Wahl, K. Jane. "The Raiders from Sullivan's Gulch." *The Pacific Historian* 15 (Summer 1971): 12–19.
Walter, Dave. "Hogan's Army: A Petition with Boots On," in Harry W. Fritz, Mary Murphy, and Robert R. Swartout, Jr., eds., *Montana Legacy: Essays on History, People, and Place.* Helena: Montana Historical Society Press, 2002.
White, Thomas W. "Railroad Labor Protests, 1894–1917: From Community to Class in the Pacific Northwest." *Pacific Northwest Quarterly* 75 (January 1984): 13–21.
Whitten, David. "Depression of 1893." EH.Net Encyclopedia, edited by Robert Whaples. August 14, 2001. http://eh.net/encyclopedia/the-depression-of-1893/.
Wilma, David. "Northwestern Industrial Army Marches to Join Coxey's Army on April 25, 1894." HistoryLink.org Essay 2181. https://www.historylink.org/file/2181.

Newspapers

Anaconda (Montana) *Standard*
Austin (Texas) *Weekly Statesman*
Bismarck (North Dakota) *Daily Tribune*
Caldwell (Idaho) *Tribune*
Cheyenne Daily Leader
Cheyenne Daily Sun
Colorado Daily Chieftain (Pueblo)
Colorado Weekly Chieftain (Pueblo)
El Paso (Texas) *International Daily Times*
Emmet (Idaho) *Index*
Great Falls (Montana) *Weekly Tribune*
Helena (Montana) *Independent*
Idaho County Free Press (Grangeville, Idaho)
Laramie (Wyoming) *Republican*
Los Angeles Herald
Ogden (Utah) *Standard*
Omaha Daily Bee
Philipsburg Mail (Granite City, Montana)
River Press (Fort Benton, Montana)
Rocky Mountain News (Denver)
Sacramento Record-Union
Salt Lake (City) *Tribune*
San Bernardino (California) *Daily Courier*
San Francisco Call
Scott City (Kansas) *Republican*
Seattle Post-Intelligencer
Sidney (Nebraska) *Telegraph*
Topeka State Journal
Weiser (Idaho) *Signal*
Yakima (Washington) *Herald*

INDEX

Numbers in **_bold italics_** indicate pages with illustrations

act to regulate the use of the capitol grounds 29
Alexander, Benjamin 88
American Bimetallic League 16
American Federation of Labor 2–3
American Federationist 31
Anaconda Standard 98, 141
Anderson, Adj. Gen. Charles J. 52
Aylesworth, Barton O. 76–77

Baker, George 53, 72–73, 83
Baker, Ray Stannard 9, 25
Barber, Lucy 3
Beatty, Judge James H. 121, 153; finds Scheffler's Portland army guilty of contempt of court and imposes harsh prison sentences 121–24; issues injunction 116
Bellamy, Edward 13; plan for state-run workshops 15; popularizes term "industrial army" 14
Bellinger, Judge Charles B. 121, 123; issues injunction 110; orders release of arrested men 115
Bemis, Mayor George 62
Bennett, Henry 47, 148
Bierce, Ambrose 166
Billings Weekly Gazette 96
bimetallism 14, 16–17
Borah, William 117
Brands, H.W. 112
Brough, Mayor Charles M. 60
Brown, Arthur J. 107
Brown, Gov. Frank 144
Browne, Carl 1, 6, 16, 17, **_18_**, 21, 22, 24–25, 30, 33, 35, 51, 73; 128; arrested 30; background 17–19; dispute with "Great Unknown" 27–28; guilty of misconduct 31

Butte Bystander 96
Butte Home Guard 102, 141
Butte Miner 100
Butte Miners' Union 89, 91

Caldwell Tribune 117
Cantwell, Frank "Jumbo" 6, 52, 129, 132, 133, 139, 140,141, 144, 145; assumes leadership of Tacoma industrial army 128
Carlisle, Sec. Treasury John S. 126
Carter, Henry 47, 163; arrested for train hijacking 157; chosen to lead Salt Lake industrial army 155; leads South Platte River flotilla 161; rejects offer of work 156
Central Labor Union of Council Bluffs 72
Central Labor Council of Omaha 103
charities 7–8; assistance in Denver, Colorado 146–47; network in Portland, Oregon 106–07
Charlotte, Dora 128, 129, 141; assumes leadership of Tacoma industrial army 140
Chidester, Marshal W.C. 137
City Board of Charities (Portland, Ore.) 107
Clark, William 89, 90
Cleveland Plain Dealer 9
Cleveland, Pres. Grover 11, 59, 87, **_96_**, 97, 112, 114, 138, 153, 170, 171; philosophy of government 12
Clinch, Thomas 87
Cody, "Buffalo Bill" 62
Council Bluffs Nonpareil 67
Coxey, Jacob 1, **_17_**, 21, 24, 31, 45, 69, 77, 89, 134; army boatyard **_160_**; army demonstration **_154_**; army group **_91_**;

183

Index

army on the Chesapeake and Ohio Canal *29*; army on the march *24*; army scenes *158*; background 15; Coxeyism 2; Coxeyites at morning roll call *120*; found guilty of misconduct 31; prevented from reading speech 31; public works plan 8, 16–17; settles "Great Unknown" mutiny 27
Coxey, Jesse 21, 30, 51
Cunningham, William 93, 95
Curtin, Mayor John C. 98

Daggett, Marshal William 142
Dallas Times Herald 40
Daly, Marcus 88, 90
Davis, Mayor Webster 104
Denver Chamber of Commerce 147, 159
Denver Home Guard 153–54, 159, 163
Denver Trades and Labor Assembly 146
Des Moines Citizen's Committee 79
Des Moines Leader 76
Drake, Marshal James C. 131, 133
Dray, Philip 97
Dundy, Judge Elmer S. 124; orders arrest of Colorado industrial army 164

economic conditions 6–9, 88; in Colorado 146–47, 149; in Los Angeles 33; in Montana 87–88; in Utah 155; in Washington state 126–27
Edwards, John 103, 104; chosen to replace Hogan as leader of Montana industrial army 101
Eggert, Gerald 122
Ellert, Mayor L.R. 53
Emmett Index 117
Everett Times 166

Finn, Superintendent J.D. 89, 90, 91–92; tries to stop hijacked train 93–94, 97
Flower, Gov. Roswell P. 12
Fort Benton 98, 99, 100
Fort Leavenworth 153
Fourier, Charles 13
Fry, Lewis 33, *34*, 37, 38, 42, 51, 52, 53, 85, 145; appointed temporary commander of the Commonweal 50; army encampment *50*; arrested for vagrancy 37; background 34–35; refuses offer of work 45; statement of principles 35, 38
F.T. O'Connell barge carrying Fry's army 51

Galvin, Thomas 85, 145; leads breakaway group from Fry's industrial army 48–49, 51
Geary, U.S. Rep. Thomas 21
Gompers, Samuel 15
Grady, Marshal Henry C. 110, 111, 115–16; plots to trap Portland industrial army 113–14
Grayson, William 147
"Great Unknown" 6, 22, 23, 73; dispute with Carl Browne 27–28
greenbackism 14
Gresham, Sec. of State Walter Q. 170
guarding Coxey's army *136*
Gutman, Herbert 132

Haley, Deputy Marshal M.J. 92, 94
Hanford, Judge Cornelius 131; sentences marchers for violating court order 138
Harper, Edna 68, 69, 80, 83–84
Haywood, William "Big Bill" 56–57
Hazen, Sheriff John T. 64
Helena Relief Committee for Coxeyites 99
Hillis, Mayor Isaac 76
Hogan, William 6, 74, 95, 105, 130; background 89; found guilty of violating injunction 98
Hogg, Gov. Stephen 38, 39–*41*, 42, 171
"Hoosier" detachment 50
Hooten, Annie 68, 69, 80, 84
Hubbard, Judge Nat A. 64; issues inflammatory comments 65
Hunt, Chief of Police Charles H. 108, 113

Indianapolis Journal 164
Industrial Army March song lyrics *46*
Industrial Legion 89
injunction 3, 112, 171, 172

Jackson, Gov. Frank 64–65, 66
Jeffries, Edward J. 52, 139, 142; background 133; draws up platform for future action 144; promotes self-help program 145; quoted 143, 145; replaces Shepard as leader 132
Jennings, Allen 50, 145
Jones, Christopher Columbus 28, 30, 31
Jones, "Mother" Mary 148, 149

Kain, Charles E. 45, 107, 108, 109
Kearney, Denis 17, 18

Index

Kelly, Charles T. 55, 60, 62, 63, 69, 74, 145, 149; background 54; begins to lose popular support 84–85; decides to build boats 78–79; makes keynote speech in Omaha 55–56; reacts to Coxey's arrest 77; suffers challenges to his authority 72–73, 81
Kelly, Sheriff Penumbra 111
Knowles, Judge Hiram 90, 105; finds Hoganites guilty of violating injunction 98
Kruttschnitt, Julius 40–41

"laissez-faire" 2, 7, 12, 126, 168
Lamont, Sec. of War Daniel S. 112, 171
Lewelling, Gov. Lorenzo 151, 152, 171
London, Jack 6, *70*, 72, 75, 78, 83, 167; chases after Kelly's industrial army 70–71; gives account of river travel 80–81
Looking Backward 13

Mayhew, Anne 169
McAdoo, Asst. Sec. of the Navy William 52
McDermott, Marshal William 90, 96, 139
McGraw, Gov. John Hart 131–32
McKinley, Gov. William 48
McMurray, Donald 6, 8, 47, 54
Merritt, Judge S.A. 157
Miller, Colonel E.S. 142
Missouri Pacific Railroad 150–51
Montana division of Coxey's army *99*

The Nation 140
Nebraska Federation of Labor 72
Neely, Marshal S.T. 152
Northgern Pacific Railroad 129, 130, 131; works to stop Northwestern industrial army 131, 134
Northwestern industrial army at Yakima, WA *137*

Oakes Republican 142
O'Ferrall, Gov. Charles T. 144
Ogden Standard 157
Olney, Att. Gen. Richard 90, 96, 97, *111*, 113, 114, 120, 123, 164, 171; background 111; develops plan to curtail train hijackers 112–13; quoted 121, 167–68, 170, 172
Omaha Bee 62, 63
Osborne, Gov. John E. 61

Otis, Gen. Elwell S. 113, 114, 130, 138
Ottumwa Courier 82

Page, Lt. Col. John H. 97
Palmateer, Dmitri 108
Panic of 1873 14
Panic of 1893 1–12, 36, 87, 125–26, 149
Pardee, Mayor George 54, 55
Peffer, U.S. Sen. William 21, 145
Pennoyer, Gov. Sylvester 109, 111, 171
"Petition of the Unemployed" 145
Pinkham, Marshal Joseph 118–19; arrests Montpelier train hijackers 121
Pittsburg Press 25
political economy 12, 13
Portland Evening Telegram 107
Portland Oregonian 107, 109, 166
public protest 1–3
Pullman strike 3, 104, 142, 172

railroads 11–12, 36, 59–60, 112, 117, 171
Rankin, Marshal J.P. 119–20
receivership 11, 89–90, 112
Reno Detachment 56, 70, 71
Rickards, Gov. John E. 89, 97
Riner, Judge John A. 120, 121
Rock Island Railroad 74, 78; deputies harass Kelly's men 82
Rocky Mountain News 152, 161
RS 5298 112, 138, 171

St. Louis Post-Dispatch 83
Salt Lake Tribune 57–58, 59, 155, 156, 157
Sanders, John Sherman 6, 44, 45; found guilty of obstructing the U.S. Mail 153; leads Cripple Creek industrial army 149
Scheffler, Solomon L. 130; army at prison camp *123*; commands Portland industrial army 109–10; given jail sentence 122; Portland army members *122*
Schofield, Gen. J.M. 97, 113, 114, 171
Schwantes, Carlos 5–6, 22, 59–60, 86, 126, 170
Scott, Harvey W. 107
Seattle Post-Intelligencer 166
Shelby, Mayor Eugene 108
Shepard, Henry 127, 132
Sherman Silver Purchase Act of 1890 16, 87–88, 126, 146, 149
Short, Jack 109
Smith, Judge H.W. 157

Index

Smith, J.B. 109
Social Darwinism 12
Southern Pacific Railroad 36; defies territorial governor in Utah 57–58; sets trap for marchers in Texas 39
Sovereign Grand Consul of the Woodmen of the World 72
Speed, George 73, 83
Spokane Chronicle 117, 166
Sprague, William 98
Stampede Tunnel *135*
Stead, W.T. 20, 21, 25, 166, 168, 170
Steeples, Douglas W. 6, 11
The Story of the Commonweal 49
Strong, Thomas Nelson 107, 108

Tacoma Ledger 166
theosophy 19
Topeka State Journal 44, 149
Townsend Leader 166
"tramp menace" 13, 106–07, 170
Turner, Frederick Jackson 6

Union Pacific Railroad 61–62, 64, 110, 114, 115; actively resists train hijackers in Idaho 116–18, 120–21, 134; responds to train theft in Nebraska 164

Veblen, Thorstein 3, 169
Vincent, Henry 49
Vinette, Arthur 44, 45, 145; leads Fry's second regiment 42–43; quoted 169

Waite, Governor Davis 155, 159, 171
Washington News 28–29
Washington Post 141
Weaver, James B. 76, 77
West, Gov. Caleb 57–60, *58*
Western Federation of Miners 149
Whitten, David O. 6, 11
Williams, Dick 119, 121
Workingmen's Party of California 18

www.ingramcontent.com/pod-product-compliance
Lightning Source LLC
Chambersburg PA
CBHW032046300426
44117CB00009B/1212